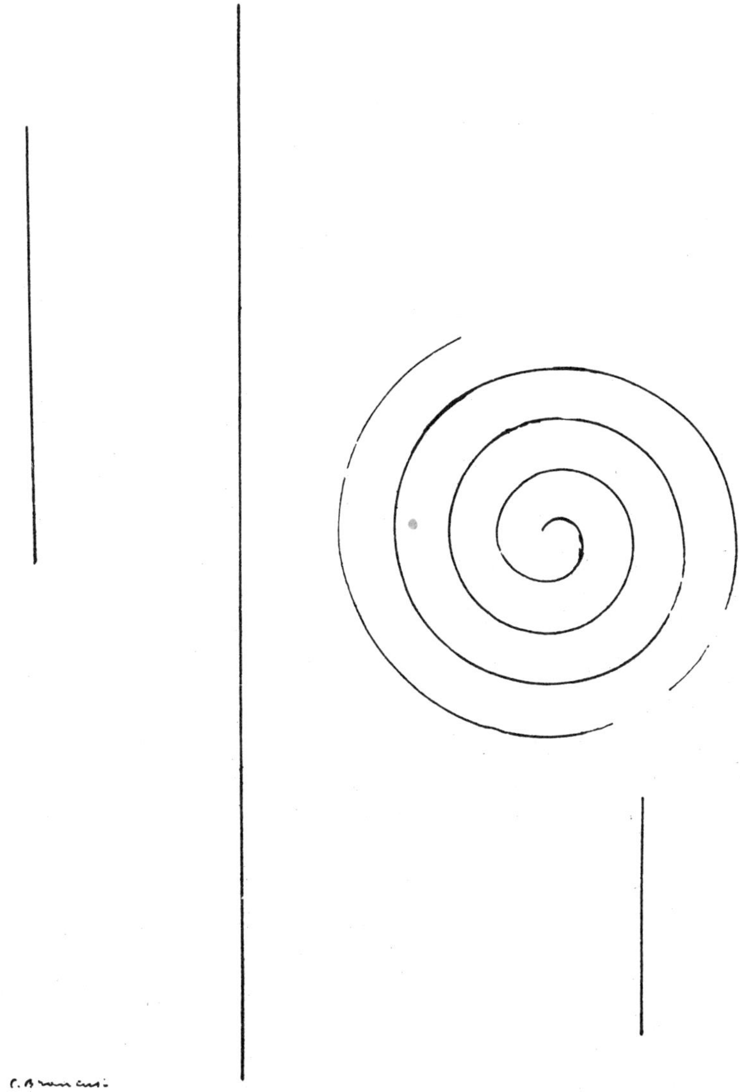
C. Brancusi

Postmodern Studies 15

Series
edited by
Theo D'haen
and
Hans Bertens

Postmodern Studies 15

Laurence Sterne in Modernism and Postmodernism

Edited by
David Pierce and
Peter de Voogd

Rodopi

Amsterdam - Atlanta, GA 1996

Essays based on a conference held at the University of York in April 1993 under the auspices of the Laurence Sterne Trust and the James Joyce Broadsheet.

This volume is dedicated to Pieter Bekker and Jacques Berthoud, fellow organisers of the York Conference.

∞ The paper on which this book is printed meets the requirements of "ISO 9706:1994, Information and documentation - Paper for documents - Requirements for permanence".

ISBN: 90-420-0011-2 (bound)
ISBN: 90-420-0002-3 (paper)
Editions Rodopi B.V., Amsterdam - Atlanta, GA 1996
Printed in The Netherlands

CONTENTS

ACKNOWLEDGEMENTS

The following essays arose from an international conference on Sterne in Modernism and Postmodernism, held at the University of York in April 1993. The initial starting-point for the conference was a concern felt by the Conference organisers to explore the territory that Sterne and Joyce occupy. This was then widened to the relevance of Sterne for modern critical theory and modern critical theory for an understanding of Sterne. Once the conference convened, it was clear that, although the four miles of Yorkshire countryside surrounding Shandy Hall was the object of attention, the scope of the papers and the nationality of the participants were anything but narrowly defined. Seemingly, Sterne's micro-world has become co-extensive with the world itself. Of the forty participants, four came from Spain, three from France, two from Italy, three from Germany, four from the Netherlands, three from the United States, one from Japan; and the other half from Britain. Each of the participants was asked to submit a synopsis of their paper, and these were then collated, and distributed ahead of the conference. The emphasis, then, from the outset was on ensuring an *exchange* of ideas.

The keynote addresses, not all of which have been included in the collection of essays which follow, were given by Carol Watts ('The Modernity of Sterne'), Melvyn New ('Sterne, Nietzsche, and Tartuffery'), Judith Hawley ('Sterne, Joyce and Midwifery'), and Peter de Voogd ('The Influence of Joyce on Sterne'). David Alexander presented a guest slide-lecture on 'Sterne and the Eighteenth-Century Print Market'. In attendance throughout the conference, we were privileged to have Kenneth Monkman, Curator of Shandy Hall. No conference in York on Sterne would be complete without taking in the environs. Bernard Barr, Sub-Librarian at the Minster Library in York, laid on an exhibition of Sterne material in the Minster Library and accompanied participants on a tour of the sites in York associated with

Sterne. An afternoon trip was arranged to Coxwold, where we were welcomed by Kenneth and Julia Monkman. The Reverend David Johnson kindly made available St Michael's Church, and it was there that Graham Parry delivered Sterne's sermon 'The House of Feasting and the House of Mourning Described'.[1] The conference banquet was held on the final evening at Beningborough Hall and was preceded by a concert of eighteenth-century music given by Barbara Parry (soprano), Edwina Smith (baroque flute), and John Bryan (harpsichord).

The conference organisers owe a debt to all those who made the conference a success, and these include: Francesca Wilde, Manon Burgher, Annelise de Klerk (Assistants), Gill Fox (Former Secretary, Department of English and Related Literature, University of York), Margaret Silcock (Deputy Conference Officer, University of York), Jennie Kilvington (Secretary, Leeds Metropolitan University), R.G. Barker (Administrator, Beningborough Hall). The conference was sponsored by the Department of English and Related Literature at the University of York, and especially indebted therefore to Professor Jacques Berthoud. The conference organisers were Pieter Bekker (Leeds Metropolitan University), Jacques Berthoud (University of York), David Pierce (University College of Ripon and York St John), and Peter de Voogd (Universiteit Utrecht). The editors wish to thank Nikki Truijens for her invaluable help in preparing the copy for the publisher.

[1] For reflections on this event, see Melvyn New, 'Sterne as Preacher: A Visit to St Michael's Church, Coxwold', *The Shandean* 5 (November 1993), 160-67.

ABBREVIATIONS

ASJ	Laurence Sterne, *A Sentimental Journey through France and Italy by Mr. Yorick*, ed. Gardner D. Stout, Jr. Berkeley: University of California Press, 1967.
FW	+ page and line number. James Joyce, *Finnegans Wake*. New York: Viking Press, 1939; London: Faber and Faber, 1939. These, and subsequent paperback editions, have identical pagination.
J-Letters	+ volume and page number. *Letters of James Joyce*. Vol. 1, ed. Stuart Gilbert. New York: Viking Press, 1957; reissued with corrections 1966. Vols. 2 and 3, ed. Richard Ellmann. New York: Viking Press, 1966; London: Faber and Faber, 1966.
S-Letters	*Letters of Laurence Sterne*, ed. Lewis Perry Curtis. Oxford: Clarendon Press, 1935, 1965, 1967.
TS	Laurence Sterne, *The Life and Opinions of Tristram Shandy, Gentleman*. The Florida Edition of the Works of Laurence Sterne, vols. 1-2, *The Text*, ed. Melvyn New and Joan New; vol. 3, *The Notes*, by Melvyn New, Richard A. Davies and W.G. Day. Gainesville: University Presses of Florida, 1978, 1984. References to the text of *Tristram Shandy* are to original volume and chapter, followed by page number in the Florida Edition; thus '*TS*: 2.2.98' means: volume 2, chapter 2, Florida Edition p. 98.
U	+ episode and line number. James Joyce, *Ulysses*, ed. H.W. Gabler, et al. New York and London: Garland Publishing, 1984, 1986. In paperback by Garland, Random House, Bodley Head.

INTRODUCTION

DAVID PIERCE

The Laurence Sterne Bicentenary Conference, held at the University of York in September 1968, resulted in *The Winged Skull* (1971). To compare that volume with the present one is to see at a glance both continuing preoccupations and the wholly new focus that has come into English studies with the advent of postmodern theory. The 1993 Conference deliberately sought a more direct exchange of views from younger scholars working in the fields of eighteenth- and twentieth-century literature, and hence the contrasts with the previous conference stand out more sharply. In the 1968 Conference (Cash, 1971: 41), a fleeting reference is made to Barthes's *Elements of Semiology* (1967), attached to which there is a footnote explaining Saussure's distinction between 'a thing' and a mental representation of 'a thing'. A quarter of a century later, critical assumptions have disturbed what were once thought ground-breaking distinctions. Claude Rawson in that earlier conference suggested that, 'outrageous as it may sound', Swift's *A Tale of a Tub* is really parodying Sterne in advance. Modern critical theory is less prone to outrage than perhaps it should be and has less difficulty therefore enlisting narrative techniques such as analepsis (or flashback), prolepsis (or anticipation), and other manipulations of time-schemes and combining them with Freudian concepts such as *Nachträglichkeit* (or retroactive post-effect) to shed light on Tristram's sense of identity and Sterne's place in European literature.

Equally noticeable in retrospect is the way the earlier conference handled the international dimension to Sterne. It was assumed that overseas contributors would report on the influence of Sterne in their own countries: Sterne and Japan, Sterne and Spain, Sterne and Italy, Sterne and Germany. The 1993 Conference made a different assumption: that all those working in the field were familiar with current theoretical debates and were participants in the same discussion. Through its internationalisation of ideas, modern critical theory has provided the basis for the articulation of what can now be discerned as a form of common culture. A British contributor such as Michael Bell is quite at home discussing Cervantes, Proust, or Márquez; in his essay 'Three Trapped Tigers in Shandy Hall', Luis Pegenaute, a Spanish contributor, moves effortlessly back-and-forth from Sterne's world to pre-revolutionary Havana in the work of the Cuban novelist Cabrera Infante; Carla Maria Laudando, at the time an Italian research student at the University of Manchester, settles to her task comparing Sterne's 'Fragment in the Manner of Rabelais' with Rabelais's *Gargantua and Pantagruel* and Beckett's 'Fizzles'.

As the essays which follow demonstrate, Sterne's work criss-crosses the whole field of the humanities. *Tristram Shandy* is the most wayward - and in some respects the most powerful - critique of Locke's theory of knowledge as articulated in his *Essay Concerning Human Understanding*. Sterne's interest in the gulf between biological and clock time makes him a contemporary of Proust and Bergson. In obscuring the fine line between autobiography and fiction, Sterne belongs to the generation of modern writers that includes Joyce and, as Madeleine Descargues argues, Vladimir Nabokov. In his deliberate refusal to construct a 'goahead plot',[1] the phrase Joyce used in referring to *Finnegans Wake*, Sterne belongs with the 'backwards or forwards' (*TS*: 3.9.197) march of the moderns, and thereby commends himself to students of Conrad and to contemporary narratologists alike. In his concern with personal identity, he anticipates the Heideggerian concept of being thrown into existence and the Derridean stress on 'trace'. In his recognition of the intimate relation between body and mind - 'rumple the one—you rumple the other' (*TS*: 3.4.189) - he anticipates Blake and the Romantic conception of the unity of life. In his promiscuous borrowings from past authors, he offers himself as a suitably perverse model for the school of postmodern theory. In his attention to matters of typography and to a

[1] 'One great part of every human existence is passed in a state which cannot be rendered sensible by the use of wideawake language, cutanddry grammar and goahead plot.' Joyce to Harriet Shaw Weaver, 24 November 1926 (*J-Letters*: 3.146).

visual language, he provides a running commentary on almost every aspect of the relationship between word and image.

Part of Sterne's attractiveness for today's reader is the suppleness of his prose, the unexpectedness of his thought, and his peculiar ability to step out of the pages of his writings. At the beginning of *Tristram Shandy*, he tells us to:

__________________Shut the door__________________

And, if we are serious about his call to intimacy, we do so. It may be a 'scurvy and disasterous world' (*TS*: 1.5.8), but 'as we jogg on' (1.6.10), you, the reader, 'must have a little patience' (1.6.9). Eventually - if that is ever an appropriate word in Sterne studies - Sterne, the consumptive who had 'bled the bed full' (*S-Letters*: 180) while an undergraduate at Cambridge, unloads the heart of his *Shan*deistic philosophy:

> True *Shandeism*, think what you will against it, opens the heart and lungs, and like all those affections which partake of its nature, it forces the blood and other vital fluids of the body to run freely thro' its channels, and makes the wheel of life run long and chearfully round. (*TS*: 4.32.401)

Sterne's chief fictional persona Yorick tells us he 'had an invincible dislike and opposition in his nature to gravity' (*TS*: 1.11.28). To sustain his spirits, Sterne wrote 'against the spleen' (*TS*: 4.22.360), and in doing so settled on forms that allowed for sudden turns of mood. The grim reaper is there at every point, but, as Michael Hart suggests in '"Many Planes of Narrative": A Comparative Perspective on Sterne and Joyce', the black page, while it does contain inky depths, also calls attention to itself in a way that drains it of much of its grave power. Yorick's end is known from the outset: he is 'buried in a corner of his church-yard, in the parish of —' (*TS*: 1.12.35). But as a character of fiction - and contrast this with the Gothic atmosphere that pervades Joyce's story 'The Dead' - he is rarely accompanied by the *danse macabre*, that motif which spread through Europe in the middle of the fifteenth century and which imagined death haunting all our actions on earth.

From 'shandymound' (*FW*: 323.2), from Sandymount, that is, the setting for 'Proteus' in *Ulysses*, to the 'shandy westerness' (*FW*: 21.21-

2) where the Prankquean 'rain, rain, rain', Joyce, too, felt an immediate rapport with Sterne. In fictional terms, as Hart reminds us, Joyce had learnt from Sterne how to 'build many planes of narrative with a single esthetic purpose' (Ellmann, 1982: 554). But the influence seems more personal. At the very beginning of *Finnegans Wake*, Joyce invokes an identity between his protagonist and Walter Shandy: 'And we put on your clock again, sir, for you. [...] The sternwheel's crawling strong' (*FW*: 27.34, 27.36). In Joyce's rewriting of his Irish tradition, Sterne is granted a prominent place, for Joyce fancifully imagines that the 'wildeshaweshowe moves swiftly sterneward' (*FW*: 256.13-4). Indeed, with his eye trained on puns, Joyce discerned that Swift was stern, and Sterne was swift. The only figure missing at this point from Joyce's list of self-conscious or self-reflexive Irish writers is the Victorian Gothic novelist Sheridan Le Fanu, the author of *The House by the Churchyard* (1863), but few readers get far into *Finnegans Wake* without discovering Joyce's profound debt to 'the old house by the churpelizod' (*FW*: 96.7-8).

Of course, the relationship between Joyce and Sterne can be given an entirely different slant or direction. Every writer in a sense creates his own predecessor(s). Equally, a writer such as Sterne creates his own successors. The influence of Joyce on Sterne is not, therefore, as impossible as it sounds, for, after Joyce, Sterne has the look of a precursor (see De Voogd, 1991). Indeed, the relationship can be even more closely defined, for in some respects, especially in his use of punctuation and in his ability to convey conversation, Sterne enjoys arguably a greater sense of freedom than Joyce:

> Writing, when properly managed, (as you may be sure I think mine is) is but a different name for conversation: As no one, who knows what he is about in good company, would venture to talk all;——so no author, who understands the just boundaries of decorum and good breeding, would presume to think all: The truest respect which you can pay to the reader's understanding, is to halve this matter amicably, and leave him something to imagine, in his turn, as well as yourself. (*TS*: 2.11:125)

Nowhere in Joyce is there such directness, such freedom, such a brilliant use of punctuation-as-speech-markers. Equally, nowhere in Sterne is there the range of voices and the struggle between ear and eye that we encounter in Joyce.

The history of Sterne criticism lends support to the theory that when it comes to Sterne each age sees itself or its opposite in the mirror. For Thackeray and the Victorians, Sterne was 'impure', 'a filthy Satyr'; for Woolf and the moderns, Sterne was their forerunner; for the morally earnest Leavis, Sterne was a nasty trifler. Today's critic, if the 1993 Conference is symptomatic, is inclined to cast Sterne and Joyce as bookends to the history of fiction. As Bell neatly suggests, the eighteenth-century move towards realism is retrodden backwards in the twentieth century. The leap from Sterne in the 1760s to Joyce in the 1920s is one we are now increasingly prepared to take. Once taken, however, the consequences cannot be ignored, only now the focus is less on the nineteenth-century omission and more on the theory that needs to be deployed to underpin such a yoking. In an inquiry into what is involved in 'making sense' of/in *Tristram Shandy*, Jean-Claude Dupas, in his essay '*A sun-dial in a grave*: the founding gesture', invokes Bakhtin's concept of the chronotope. According to a contemporary reviewer, as Carol Watts reminds us, *Tristram Shandy* was 'a *riddle* without an *object*'.[2] Today, we would want to investigate the theory that lies behind this insight. Sterne at once anticipates and challenges contemporary theory. Indeed, he invites such flexibility of argument and approach, for even basic conundrums, such as whether he says more than he reveals or reveals more than he says, remain to taunt us. Central to the collection of essays which follow is this many-layered difficult issue of continuity or discontinuity. Some essays, such as Laudando's and Antonio Ballesteros González's, seek to shed light on Sterne and his predecessors such as Nashe and Rabelais. Some, such as Laurent Milesi's, examine Sterne's relation with his contemporaries. Other essays consider Sterne and later writers such as Milan Kundera and Salman Rushdie. On display throughout there is a commendable ambitiousness to broaden the contexts for situating Sterne.

'Sterne in his own time' was not forgotten, or allowed to be forgotten at the 1993 Conference, for in his own time Sterne struck a different impression but he was no less a phenomenon. The two volumes of *Tristram Shandy*, which were placed in the window of Hinxman's Sign of the Bible Bookshop on Stonegate in York in late

[2] *London Chronicle*, 16 April 1765, 373.

1759, sold so quickly that R. and J. Dodsley the London booksellers immediately arranged for a London edition. As is evident from Cash's biography of Sterne, in those early months of 1760 Sterne took the literary world by storm and secured his fame for posterity. So wide was his reputation that in Paris in 1762, they were queueing up to meet him: the Duc d'Orleans, Denis Diderot, chief editor of the *Encyclopédie*, who was later to write *Jacques le fataliste* in imitation of *Tristram Shandy* , and Baron d'Holbach, with whom Sterne said he dined twice a week in winter and spring 1762. (Cash, 1992: 141) No-one reading history backwards can fail to be impressed by the series of grouped images in *A Sentimental Journey* of the starling in the cage, repeating its learnt catchphrase 'I can't get out - I can't get out', Yorick's meditation on the Bastille, and the coming French Revolution whose intellectual foundations had been laid by d'Holbach and others. In Germany, Sterne found an immediate champion in Goethe and Nietzsche. Goethe called Sterne 'the freest spirit of the century'; not to be outdone, Nietzsche in *Human All Too Human* (1879) described Sterne as 'the freest writer of all time'. Closer to our own times, it took a Russian Formalist Victor Shklovsky to recognise that in *Tristram Shandy* Sterne had written 'the most typical novel of world literature' (Shklovsky, 1965: 57).

For a conference set in York whose subject revelled in hobby-horses, it would be inexcusable not to digress at some convenient point and refer to York's Race Week. On 4 August 1749, if the Prebend of York had been present, which he usually was for the August Meeting, he would have seen Mr William Carr's grey colt 'Tom Jones' in action. Fielding's novel *Tom Jones* was entered in the Stationer's Register on 3 February 1749 (see Battestin, 1989: 451). Six months later, punters were placing bets at York Races on a horse which bore the name of Fielding's fictional character. If this were not enough to suggest the profoundly intertextual cultural milieu of mid-eighteenth-century England, we might be reminded of the other names from fiction that owners in 1749 gave to their horses: Pamela, Joseph Andrews, Sophia, Roderick Random. Tom Jones was obviously a winner, as was Joseph Andrews, for at least three owners that year decided to race under these names.[3] Given such a degree of homogeneity in the culture it would have been surprising if Sterne were not given to twisting and untwisting the same rope: 'Tell me, ye learned, shall we for ever be adding so much to the *bulk*——so little to the *stock*?' (*TS*: 5.1.408).

'The Modernity of Sterne' by Carol Watts provided a position paper for the Conference. In what sense is *Tristram Shandy* 'a thoroughly modern work in every respect except the period in which it is written'?[4] What is the relationship between an aesthetic practice which has much in common with modernist and postmodernist texts and the specific historical moment in the mid-eighteenth century that furnishes the context for Sterne's novel? Following Foucault, one suggestion Watts alights on is to figure modernity in terms of an attitude to contemporary circumstance, a relation of belonging, a sign of a world that looks to the future for its meaning. Eschewing a more inward interpretation, she stresses that Sterne's narrative looks to create the conditions where the alienated modern consciousness might find itself, in dialogue, with others. In her discussion of intertextuality and parody, Watts cautions against formalist abstraction, for the real question remains: why did such a complex narrative form arise at the mid-eighteenth century?

Other contributors tackle this issue of historicity in different ways. Hart suggests that *Tristram Shandy* belongs to an 'anti-tradition of unclassifiable books' that also includes *The Anatomy of Melancholy*, *A Tale of a Tub*, and *Ulysses*. Bell invokes Spengler's idea of the contemporary, as someone not just living at the same time but as living at an equivalent historical moment: twentieth-century fiction looks not to the nineteenth but to the eighteenth century for its significant contemporaries. Pegenaute cites Northrop Frye on Menippean satire, how writers from different periods can be classified according to their shared attack on erudition and intellectual pretension. Debts, influences, parallels - all these aspects have a part to play in the essays

[3] See Joseph Cheny, *An Historical List of Horse-Matches Run, And of Places and Prizes, Run for in Great Britain in 1749* (London, 1749). In the 1760s Sterne was similarly honoured when a horse was named after Tristram Shandy.

[4] Watts takes her phrase from McCaffery (1986: xv).

which follow, though such features constitute more a point of departure than the goal of inquiry. In a detailed consideration of *Tristram Shandy* and Rushdie's *Midnight's Children*, Walter Göbel and Damian Grant contrast Sterne's essentially dramatic mode with Rushdie's epic vision. But the authors quickly add that if the terms are changed, so too are the alignments. Thus Sterne's narrative, the future already used up, retreats and contracts, whereas Rushdie's narrative, its eye on the future, advances and expands. Jörg Rademacher examines the similarity between Shakespeare, Sterne, and Joyce in their fondness for fictional (auto)biography. The presence of *Hamlet* in Sterne and Joyce needs little insisting upon, but Rademacher goes on to suggest that Sterne and Joyce conceal their identities through their Shakespearean persona. Sterne brings out the narrative potential hidden in Shakespeare's Yorick; Joyce refuses to call his protagonist by a Shakespearean name in order to underline the unobtrusiveness of his own commitment to Prince Hamlet.

The postmodern interest in the free play of language, in the gaps and fissures in a text, in a concern with fragments, in what is involved in Derridean deferral or Sternean delay, in the impossibility of full presence, in the open work - all these have their place in the essays which follow. At the end of the eighteenth century, John Ferriar in his *Illustrations of Sterne* (1798) excoriated Sterne for being a literary thief; today, we are delighted when we find evidence of Sterne's use of past writers and we are frequently amused when he misquotes his sources. Sterne the plagiarist has become Sterne the parodist. As with Shakespeare and Joyce, nothing is lost by seeing his sources displayed. The issue of originality is central to Milesi's essay comparing *Tristram Shandy* and Diderot's *Jacques le fataliste*. Jacques's Captain was given to saying that 'tout ce qui nous arrive de bien et de mal ici-bas était écrit là-haut', that everything good or bad that befalls us here below was written up above. In a series of tantalising moves, and taking his cue from Freud and Lyotard, Milesi shows how *Tristram Shandy* not only occupies a primal scene of writing but, paradoxically, stands in a postmodern relationship to Diderot's novel. The relationship between the two texts can be characterised in Freudian terms as anticipation, trauma, and reparation-as-originary-repetition. Milesi then appeals to Lyotard: 'A work can become modern only if it is first postmodern'. Postmodernism is therefore, in Milesi's words, 'a foresight that will have anticipated the oversights of modernism'. It is also 'an ahistorical process which subverts the temporal linearity of past-present-future by attempting to reinscribe modernity before it has taken place'. If this sounds impossibly erudite, we should perhaps remember Henri Fluchère's aphoristic comment that *Tristram Shandy* 'is a book that begins before the beginning and ends before the end' (Fluchère, 1965: 101). Sterne's erudition can be coped with, as can his obscurity: it is his 'laid-bare' techniques that still present the most problems for the critic.

At the beginning of *A Sentimental Journey*, the English Protestant parson Yorick is 'predetermined' (*ASJ*: 70) not to give the Continental Catholic Franscican monk anything of his charity. In a thought-provoking essay on *Tristram Shandy* and the dilemma of postmodern physics, Stuart Sim shows how 'coping with the metaphysics of catastrophe is the main business of Sterne's world'. Tristram's task is to discover an enduring self and thus resolve the issue of personal identity. Confronted by a world of chance and determinism, Tristram resorts to sentiment, a sign of his powerlessness in the face of a hostile causality. In this way, Sims argues, Sterne 'strikingly prefigures the world of postmodern physics'. In 'Identity Reclaimed: The Art of Being Tristram', the issue of Tristram's identity is explored from a different angle by Herbert Klein, who strikes a more optimistic note. Tristram writes 'to experience himself living': in creating his world, Tristram creates himself. Tristram's first task is to deconstruct the identity imposed on him by others. By insisting on difference at the level of consciousness, Tristram betrays his postmodern character.

Clearly, such opposite conclusions, which can be allowed to stand here, should be expected in Sterne studies. Indeed, they are consonant with Epictetus' distinction, which Sterne cites in his epigraph to Volume 1, between *pragmata* or deeds and *dogmata* or opinions: 'Not things, but opinions about things, trouble men'. Running through the Conference was a debate between those who claimed Sterne as a precursor of existentialism (a view that repeatedly surfaces in *The Winged Skull*), and those who insisted that Sterne's scepticism issued from the confidence of his Anglican beliefs. In a challenging essay comparing Sterne and Kundera, Tim Parnell argues that Sterne's scepticism is underpinned by a thoroughgoing Anglican fideism and consistent, therefore, with a conservative tradition of apologetics dating from Erasmus and the Reformation. The existentialist viewpoint tends to focus on the scene in *A Sentimental Journey* where Yorick is discussing his name with Monsieur Le Count de B****: 'There is not a more perplexing affair in life to me, than to set about telling any one who I am.' Fortunately, on this occasion, a copy of Shakespeare lying on the Count's table comes to his aid and Yorick lays his finger upon YORICK: 'with my finger all the way over the name -- *Me, Voici*! said I' (*ASJ*: 221). Yorick, who is associated with death, here returns to haunt the living in a language not his own. His finger runs all the way over the name, insisting on his identity even as he assumes it.

Part of the difficulty in regard to an existentialist view of Sterne lies in determining if 'off-centeredness' is dependent on his acceptance of a centre. In a parallel way, the question can be posed about the dependence of *A Sentimental Journey* on Smollett's *Travels Through France and Italy*: parody, too, can only work if there is an original to burlesque. Perhaps Sterne deliberately plays with the idea of a fixed identity precisely because he is confident of his position vis-a-vis his Maker. From his mid-nineteenth-century, post-Hegelian, collapsed vantage-point, Kierkegaard argued that at a point of impasse, associated with the concept of *angst*, the subject makes a leap of faith: there is no other path from reason to faith, from man to God. From this perspective, Sterne belongs to a century that sought to prove the existence of God by recourse to natural religion. This is especially apparent in *A Sentimental Journey* in Yorick's reading of Nature, in his witnessing '*Religion*' in the dance in the illiterate peasant's house, and in the theme of charity which receives perhaps its most powerful expression in the hymn to SENSIBILITY after his encounter with Maria: 'I feel some generous joys and generous cares beyond myself' (*ASJ*: 278). Yorick's argument for the existence of God is essentially moral: 'I am positive I have a soul; nor can all the books with which materialists have pester'd the world ever convince me of the contrary' (*ASJ*: 271). For Yorick, in a move that shifts the Enlightenment's argument away from Reason and the image of God as Watchmaker, the generous impulse is a divine impulse: 'this is thy divinity which stirs within me' (*ASJ*: 277). On the other hand - always a useful recourse when discussing Sterne - it could be argued that his emphasis on the moral dimension might be further evidence of Sterne's links with existentialism, how it is in action and in taking ethical decisions than the subject defines his or her existence.

If to digress is to progress, then to conclude is, by cutting short the argument, to exclude. Some early editions of *A Sentimental Journey* carried an advertisement in which the

> Author begs leave to acknowledge to his Subscribers, that they have a further claim upon him for Two Volumes more than these delivered to them now, and which nothing but ill health could have prevented him from having ready along with these.
>
> The Work will be compleated and delivered to the Subscribers early the next Winter.

For some readers, Sterne is a huge disappointment: they are, as it were, for ever awaiting the final two volumes. What the following essays encourage us to do is to rediscover the text in the class, in the certain knowledge that certainty is a chimera.

THE MODERNITY OF STERNE

CAROL WATTS

A bibliographer of postmodern literature claimed in 1986 that Sterne's *Tristram Shandy* is 'a thoroughly postmodern work in every respect but the period in which it is written' (McCaffery, 1986: xv). This rather curious formulation rehearses one of the central critical problems in approaching the novel: the relationship between the narrative's experimental form and the mid-eighteenth-century moment at which it was written. That is, it directly poses the question of how we are to establish the historical status of a novel which appeared an aesthetic anachronism even to Sterne's contemporaries: 'a *riddle* without an *object*'.[1] Is it possible for us to read *Tristram Shandy* without underlining the disjunction marked in the bibliographer's statement between a certain aesthetic practice - a formal auto-representation - and its historical contextualization? What does it mean to appropriate this particular eighteenth-century text in these terms - as a modernist or postmodernist text *avant la lettre*?

'What a conjuncture was here lost!'

Tristram Shandy has always proved difficult to pin down, classify or encompass in any definitive manner - a source of frustration to category-conscious eighteenth-century critics. One William Mudford

[1] From a review of a French account in the *Gazette Littéraire* of the last two volumes of *Tristram Shandy*, as translated in the *London Chronicle* (16 April 1765), p. 373. Quoted in Howes, 1974: 168.

noted 'incoherency', 'fantastic irregularity' and 'deviation from all established rules of composition', asserting that 'to analyse his volumes may be pronounced impossible: to ascertain, with certainty, their object is, perhaps, no less impossible, and to establish a connection between them would defy the highest ingenuity of man' (Mudford, 1811: Vol. 3, i). Horace Walpole was rather more sanguine in 1760, viewing the strategy of humour as 'the whole narration always going backwards'. 'I can conceive of a man saying that it would be droll to write a book in that manner', he wrote, 'but have no notion of his persevering in executing it' (Howes, 1974: 55). Sterne himself wrote that '*Tristram Shandy* was made to baffle all criticism - and I will venture to rest the book on this ground - that it is either above the power or beneath the attention of any critic or hyper-critic whatsoever' (*S-Letters*: 411). We have been warned.

How then are we to confront the seeming divorce of the formal dimensions of Sterne's narrative from a historical context which is, after all, by no means overtly detailed in the text? How do we recover the novel's aesthetic distance, its formal play, as a condition produced *by* and in response *to*, such a context? Unlike Fielding's *Tom Jones*, with its broad sweep across the English social panorama, or Smollett's novels with their endless detailing of professions, trades and social accents, *Tristram Shandy*'s referential purchase on contemporary life seems so eccentrically local in its four miles' diameter as to be unimportant, so fragmentary as to be incoherent. If the novel is to be positioned in relation to history at all, then as now, it has usually been to what we call the background of the 'history of ideas': to that 'history-book [...] of what passes in a man's own mind' (*TS*: 2.2.98), Locke's *Essay Concerning Human Understanding*. *Tristram Shandy* is thus seen as a quasi-philosophic, rather irreverent treatment of Locke's theories of duration and association, informed perhaps by the radical empiricism of Hume. Its status in the history of ideas is provisional, by way of its parodic strategy - not a serious work, but a narrative game, play, in which anything more substantial is seen to be out of place. As Eve Sedgwick (1985: 79) has suggested, explications of Sterne's whimsical, ironic novels always run the risk of sounding 'plonking, churlish, literal-minded'.

There are of course other 'histories', other traditions, in which *Tristram Shandy* is again little more than a comic guest. Its *sui generis* placing within such histories can be illuminating in critical terms. In Ian Watt's seminal work, *The Rise of the Novel*, for example, the deviation of Sterne's 'anti-novel' from the standards of prose composition at the mid-century is used to underline the process by which the novel as a genre achieved canonic status. *Tristram Shandy* is here the parodic exception that proves the normative - realist - rule.

For Watt, as for Victor Shklovsky - who celebrated the 'revolutionary' formal reflexivity of *Tristram Shandy* and its defamiliarizing strategies of narration - Sterne's novel can be read in such a way as to demonstrate and confirm the critical method brought to the text. For both critics, despite the evident differences in their respective valorizations of modernist and realist narrative, Sterne's novel is understood as a text that lays bare the laws of novelistic form - laws which they proceed to claim. In its techniques of discursive estrangement and undermining of convention, *Tristram Shandy* is a novel whose *atypicality* confers upon it a representative status as a text that explores the fictional ordering of the real - limits discovered in the doxastic processes of everyday life. To the extent that it foregrounds the process of writing itself, the very impossibility of mimesis, it is a novel that appears to encourage the critic to wrest the narrative from its historical determinants, to engage in the pleasures of its formal play. It is thus a text that lends itself to critical appropriation.

It was a comic tradition, which D. W. Jefferson (1968) has famously called 'the tradition of learned wit', that was most often invoked by eighteenth-century critics in order to classify the seemingly dangerous innovations of Sternean parody. For some, Sterne's parody was of serious social consequence, for how should one receive a preacher 'who should mount the pulpit in a harlequin's coat'?[2] A barrage of names, precursors and influences flew out in reviews - Cervantes, Rabelais, Burton, Swift, Rochester, Scarron, Marivaux, Macaronic Latin, Menippean satire - to stun and affix the novel within a recognisable tradition. Occupying a space somewhere between the 'dirtiness' of Swift and the 'looseness' of Rabelais,[3] not quite as finely drawn as Cervantes and having almost 'outrochestered

[2] *Monthly Review* 22 (1760), 422.

[3] From an anonymous letter dated 15 April 1760, 'discovered' and reproduced in the *European Magazine*, 21 (1792), 169.

Rochester himself' (Howes, 1974: 95-99), the identity of Sterne's novel was cobbled together from the fragments of other comic writers, and laid accusingly at his door: Sterne the plagiarising copyist.

For John Ferriar in his *Illustrations of Sterne* (1798), Sterne's parodic use of quotations, compiled from numerous historical, scientific and literary texts, was a mark of his unoriginality. The method was no less than a deception, a theft of literary property. 'It was not the business of Sterne to undeceive those, who considered his Tristram as a work of unfathomable knowledge' (5) Ferriar noted, and piously set out to detail the passages that the author had lifted verbatim from other works. One of these excerpts, which opens Volume 5 of *Tristram Shandy*, is a consideration of the nature of plagiarism itself:

> Tell me, ye learned, shall we for ever be adding so much to the *bulk*———so little to the *stock*?
>
> Shall we for ever make new books, as apothecaries make new mixtures, by pouring only out of one vessel into another? (*TS*: 5.1.408)

The joke here, of course, is that Sterne has copied this passage from Robert Burton's *The Anatomy of Melancholy*, which in turn had been copied from more obscure sources. The chinese-box effect of the narrative would not be out of place in a novel by Salman Rushdie or Flann O'Brien, for whom Sterne is an important precursor. Yet what does it mean to make such a comparison? And how does Sterne's narrative employ such a fundamental parodic strategy?

History as Parody

For critics such as Linda Hutcheon who have attempted to theorize the heterogeneous set of twentieth-century artistic and cultural practices understood as postmodernism, parody is a cultural form that enables an interrogation of *historicity*. Parody, she suggests, is a 'challenge to a definition of subjectivity and creativity that has ignored the role of history in art and thought', working both 'to enshrine the past and to question it'. It is a moment of 'seemingly introverted formalism', but one which, by virtue of its reflexive introversion:

> paradoxically brings about a direct confrontation with the problem of the relation of the aesthetic to a world of significance external to itself, to a discursive world of socially defined meaning systems (past and present) - in other words, to the political and the historical. (Hutcheon, 1988: 22)

John Ferriar, in his diligent exposure of Sterne's literary borrowing, could hardly have known what an iconoclastic act he was undertaking, exploding as he does the assumptions of the Romantic aesthetic *avant la lettre*. By noting what Douglas Crimp (1983: 53) has observed in modern pop art as 'the frank confiscation, quotation, excerptation, accumulation and repetition of already existing images', Ferriar not only intentionally undermines notions of originality and depth of meaning in Sterne's novel, but inadvertently raises questions about a range of cultural concepts: the author-creator, the unity and authenticity of a work, the coherence of a designated literary period.

Yet Ferriar is no iconoclast. One critic's parody is here another's plagiary: to explore this semantic shift is to begin to recover the historical conditions of the novel's interaction with its context, and the difficult necessity of that confrontation between aesthetics and the wider social world.

In his dismay at Sterne's 'plagiarism', Ferriar echoes a wider late eighteenth-century concern at what Goethe and Schiller termed cultural 'dilettantism'. 'All dilettantes are plagiarizers', they wrote. 'They sap the life out of and destroy all that is original and beautiful in language and in thought by repeating it, imitating it, and filling up their void with it. Thus, more and more, language becomes filled up with pillaged phrases and forms that no longer say anything; one can read entire books that have a beautiful style but contain nothing at all' (Schulte-Sasse, 1984: ix). Goethe would not have included Sterne among the offenders, but *Tristram Shandy* is nevertheless, on one level, about such a phenomenon. Sterne's parodic pillaging of existing 'images' of discourse registers a certain scepticism about the authenticity of social language, one which Samuel Johnson also admits to in his grand lexicographic project. Literature had to come to terms with its structural dependence on the market, with the 'fugitive cant' of the new barbarians of literary commerce and the imitative logic of their production. Sterne's novel thus rehearses its status as a commodity within that market, while in the very act of parodic distancing managing to protest against it.

For Tristram Shandy to find himself 'in history' is thus to be constituted by textual traces, to conceptualize history as an object that has to be refigured, written. No longer a coherent, causal sequence of events, a 'background' against which the novel *Tristram Shandy* might, with some difficulty, be measured, history is rather understood as a *process* by which social meaning is contructed in language. As Linda Hutcheon (1988: 89) summarizes:

> What the postmodern writing of both history and literature has taught us is that both history and fiction are discourses, that both constitute systems of signification by which we make sense of the past. In other words, the meaning and shape are not in the events, but in the systems which make those past 'events' into present historical 'facts'.

To the extent that *Tristram Shandy* is 'about' the fictional - doxastic - refiguring of historical events, to the extent that it poses the central question of how a work of fiction 'belongs' to its historical moment, Sterne's novel might indeed be granted the title of 'the most typical novel of world literature', as Victor Shklovsky claimed (1965: 57). For it is not simply 'history', but historiography - the writing of history - which is the focus of Sterne's narrative.

The generic blurring of distinction between fictional discourse and written history was certainly not unusual in the eighteenth century, and was indeed crucial to the emergence of the novel, as Lennard Davis (1983) has shown. Eighteenth-century novels, at first designated 'true histories' to distinguish them from devalued romance forms, often included disquisitions on their historical method. Such an incorporation of 'theory' into the text was intended to alert the reader to the kind of contract offered by the text, to produce an awareness of the status of its truth-claim even as the narrative relied upon a suspension of disbelief. In Book 2, Chapter 1, of Fielding's *Tom Jones*, for example, the narrator describes his role as that of the 'selective historian' who has an eye to the attention span of his readership, comparing his presentation of the historical highlights with the exhaustive practice of a 'plodding historian', 'time's amanuensis', who claims to document every event in the historical continuum.

Tristram Shandy employs both historiographic strategies: the narrator is selective, 'as no one, who knows what he is about in good company, would venture to talk all; - so no author [...] would presume to think all', and exhaustive, since the 'transactions and opinions' of his life take up so much description. Indeed, he has a moral duty to the reader to consider what is involved when 'a man sits down to write a history':

> Could a historiographer drive on his history, as a muleteer drives on his mule——straight forward [...] he might venture to foretell you to an hour when he should get to his journey's end;-----but the thing is, morally speaking, impossible: For, if he is a man of the least spirit, he will have fifty deviations from a straight line to make with this or that party as he goes along, which he can no ways avoid. He will have views and prospects to himself perpetually solliciting his eye, which he can no more help standing still to look at than he can fly; he will moreover have various
>
> Accounts to reconcile:
> Anecdotes to pick up:
> Inscriptions to make out:
> Stories to weave in:
> Traditions to sift:
> Personages to call upon:
> Panygericks to paste up at this door:
> Pasquinades at that:————All which both the man and his mule are
>
> quite exempt from. To sum up all; there are archives at every stage to be look'd into, and rolls, records, documents, and endless genealogies, which justice ever and anon calls him back to stay the reading of (*TS*: 1.14.41-2)

Tristram's access to the past is mediated by texts - archives, 'rolls and records', inscriptions, traditions, stories. His very origin, the unrepresentable primal scene, is constructed by means of avuncular anecdote and an account from the paternal diary. He produces knowledge of his identity through the act of writing, producing multiple selves and perspectives, staving off the death that seems to lurk at the end of every sentence, like Scheherezade, through the loquaciousness of his narrative. If the historical subject who is Tristram Shandy is finally to confront the limit of the black page, he will nevertheless achieve a graphic perpetuity by means of his textual progeny, his written self. Where nature fails the patriarchal desires of Walter Shandy, culture, in the form of the act of writing itself, offers uncertain duration to his son. As the gentleman writes in Sterne's *A Sentimental Journey*, 'I have nothing to bequeath which will pay the expence of bequeathing, except the history of myself, which, I could not die in peace unless I left it as a legacy to the world' (*ASJ*: 255).

Sterne's 'legacy', then, appears to demonstrate many of the formal characteristics associated with postmodernist fiction: its use of parody and pastiche, its problematization of representation, its absurdist exposure of the limits of referential theories of language, its complex treatment of identity in time and history, its stress on the local rather than the universal, and the consequent provisionality of the 'I' subject, and so on. Yet the claiming of Sterne's novel as a postmodern text (sketched here admittedly as a litany of familiar critical moves) can do little, if it remains at the level of formalist abstraction, to reveal why such a complex narrative form should have arisen at the mid-eighteenth century. Nor, indeed, why in formal terms Sterne's narrative should appear so 'modern' in the late twentieth century.

If we return for a moment to the bibliographer's statement with which I began - that *Tristram Shandy* is 'a thoroughly postmodern work in every sense except the period in which it was written' - we can begin to set out the problem of determining the historical status of Sterne's 'experimental' narrative. Such a statement prescribes not only the novel's but also our own critical relation to history. In asserting that the novel is postmodern in every sense, the critic claims *Tristram Shandy* as the product of his or her interpretative labour, an offspring of the contemporary moment, just as for postmodernist critics the historical past is to be reworked in what Ihab Hassan (quoted in Hutcheon, 1988: 20) has awkwardly termed 'present-ification'. This is more than an acknowledgement of the truism that critical practice is always, in some sense, an act of possession or self-understanding. It is a statement of a relation between critic and text that is not necessarily one of reciprocity: one that can also be a form of narcissistic misrecognition. Tristram Shandy is postmodernist in every sense except the moment in which it was written: the 'except' is testimony to an act of denial or forgetting. What does it matter, if history is to be understood as a fabrication of the now, a mere textual play? What does it matter if, in Linda Hutcheon's 'dialogue with the past in the light of the present' (19), we hear only one voice, our own, see only our own intentions - terroristic, ironic, partisan, playful, provisional - endlessly circulating? Isn't this condition, this dialogue with the past, one which the narrative of *Tristram Shandy* is itself demonstrating - one that the novel is *about*? By entering into this set of specular relations, a hermeneutical circle in which *Tristram Shandy* becomes a superlative reflection of (post)modernist method, the bibliographer continues a twentieth-century critical tradition. One only has to recall Virginia Woolf's observation that 'the order of the ideas, their suddenness and irrelevancy, is more true to life than to literature [...] Under the influence of this extraordinary style the book becomes semi-transparent [...] We are as close to life as we can be' (Woolf, 1932: 79), where the very categories of her aesthetic are discovered exemplified in Sterne's narrative style. As Max Byrd (1985: 11) has written, 'if Sterne did not exist, Virginia Woolf would have had to invent him', the irony being that she already, in some sense, has. If Woolf finds in Sterne's narrative the processes of a contemporary consciousness - 'as close to life as we can be' - the significance of a denial of its eighteenth-century moment of origin becomes clear: an amnesic reaction to the birth and development, the very pre-history, of the modern. There is an inability, then, to face up to an imaginary realm, the primal scene: modernism's 'nightmare of history' itself. If we are to describe Laurence Sterne 'in modernism and postmodernism', then we have to place *Tristram Shandy*'s specific relation to the modern itself.

'Looking forward into futurity'

In his essay 'Modernity: An Incomplete Project', Jürgen Habermas defines the historical status of those texts that he describes as modern in a 'classical' sense:

> While that which is merely 'stylish' will soon become outmoded, that which is modern preserves a secret tie to the classical. Of course, whatever can survive time has always been considered to be a classic. But the emphatically modern document no longer borrows this power of being a classic from the authority of a past epoch; instead, a modern work becomes a classic because it has once been authentically modern. Our sense of modernity creates its own self-enclosed canons of being classic [...] The relation between 'modern' and 'classical' has definitely lost a fixed historical reference. (Habermas, 1985: 4)

Tristram Shandy, I argue, can be read as an 'emphatically modern document' in this Habermasian sense: its novelty not simply reducible to the vagaries of fashionable (commercial) taste in the mid-eighteenth century. In questioning the likelihood of the novel's ability to 'last', Samuel Johnson had inadvertently pointed to its modernity, its radical disjunction from the continuum of literary tradition.

The word 'modern' has been used since classical antiquity, according to Habermas, 'again and again to express the consciousness of an epoch that relates itself to the past of antiquity, in order to view itself as a result of the transition from the old to the new' (3). Past traditions are thus used as a form of historical orientation in the present, a means of understanding and controlling it, as a form of critique of the new, seemingly devalued, age. Jonathan Swift's *Battle of the Books* is perhaps the most familiar eighteenth-century example of the quarrel between the ancients and the moderns: the bee drawing on the honey of tradition representing the ancients, and the filthy spider suffering from historical amnesia, spinning his rapidly decomposing webs, denoting the moderns. Pope's *Dunciad* is of course another example of the debate. Yet in these cases, awareness of the past was always invoked as a classical supplement to a degenerate present, a model to emulate and thus recover. Sterne's narrative confirmation of the failure of this conservative project embraces a shift in the conception of what it was to be modern, and a new attitude to the temporal representation of it.

What Tristram Shandy discovers as his birthright is his inheritance as a citizen of the Enlightenment - an orientation towards the future rather than servile adherence to the forms of the past. The progressive and ameliorist model of history that underpins such a model is described in the first volume of Sterne's novel:

> Thus,---thus, my fellow labourers and associates in this great harvest of our learning, now ripening before our eyes; thus it is, by slow steps of casual increase, that our knowledge physical, metaphysical, physiological, polemical, nautical, mathematical, aenigmatical, technical, biographical, romantical, chemical, and obstetrical, with fifty other branches of it, (most of 'em ending, as these do, in *ical*) have, for these two last centuries and more, gradually been creeping upwards towards that Ακμη of their perfections, from which, if we may form a conjecture from the advances of these last seven years, we cannot possibly be far off. (*TS*: 1.21.71-2)

This version of cultural modernity sloughs off the past in its hurry to progress into the future, discovering its own laws, as we remember from Tristram's nod to his classical precursor: 'I should beg Mr. *Horace*'s pardon;——for in writing what I have set about, I shall confine myself neither to his rules, nor to any man's rules that ever lived' (*TS*: 1.4.5). In this era of Enlightenment, as Immanuel Kant described it aptly enough for *Tristram Shandy*, 'it is not easy to come of age': for 'there are few who have succeeded by their own exercise of mind and spirit both in freeing themselves from tutelage and in achieving a steady pace' (1984: 30). Sterne's protagonist may have shaken himself free of paternal control, but his path is consequently wayward, and his advance pursued at breakneck speed:

> What a rate have I gone on at, curvetting and frisking it away, two up and two down for four volumes together, without looking once behind, or even on one side of me, to see whom I trod upon! [...] Now ride at this rate with what good intention and resolution you may,——'tis a million to one you'll do some one a mischief, if not yourself——He's flung——he's off——he's lost his seat——he's down——he'll break his neck——see!——if he has not galloped full amongst the scaffolding of the undertaking criticks!—— he'll knock his brains out against some of their posts——he's bounced out!——look——he's now riding like a madcap full tilt through a whole crowd of painters, fiddlers, poets, biographers, physicians, lawyers, logicians, players, schoolmen, churchmen, statesmen, soldiers, casuists, connoisseurs, prelates, popes, and engineers——Don't fear, said I—— (*TS*: 4.20.356-7)

Caught up in the dynamism of 'modern' life, the mid-century subject is unable to find its bearings: writing the first sentence and 'trusting to Almighty God for the second' (*TS*: 8.2.656), living '364 times faster than I should write' (*TS*: 4.13.342); 'is a man to follow rules——or rules to follow him?', the narrator demands (*TS*: 4.10.337).

The effect of this rapid colonization of the future on the newly modern consciousness is contradictory. The mid-century subject seems enervated, bombarded with information and material in a manner reminiscent of Rousseau's Saint-Preux in *La Nouvelle Héloise*:

> I'm beginning to feel the drunkenness that this agitated, tumultuous life plunges you into. With such a multitude of objects passing before my eyes, I'm getting dizzy. Of all the things that strike me, there is none that holds my heart, yet all of them together disturb my feelings, so that I forget what I am and who I belong to. (Berman, 1983: 18)

Tristram Shandy, who has also experienced a crisis in belonging, responds to this spray of phenomena in a vain Johnsonian attempt to contain it by listing and naming, to totalize its diversifications into a manageable whole. Yet the more he tries, the more it eludes him. *Tristram Shandy* the novel begins to rehearse the limitations of a form of knowledge that has itself become another field of expertise ending in '*ical*': a specialized aesthetic domain increasingly divorced from a society it can no longer understand or coherently represent.

On the one hand, then, the mid-century subject exudes a dizzying euphoria and confidence. Yet on the other, such a liberation from the confines of tradition produces uncertainty, and at worse, a debilitating impotence and melancholy at the prospect of what Adam Smith described as 'a fatherless world' (Smith, 1976: 235). Certainties are under attack, the universe appears vicious and fragmented, and without the assurances of a patrilineal continuum - that Shandean bend sinister - the subject is faced with itself as a measure of the world: the mortal limits of its actions, its knowledge, its existence. It is perhaps not surprising that Sterne's narrator expresses the desire for a general amnesia and the return to the way that life once was, a condition perhaps to be recovered, in a Rousseauian sense, by the reconstruction of childhood. Contemplating the prospect of his culture reaching the summit of perfection in the near future, he suggests:

> When that happens, it is to be hoped, it will put an end to all kinds of writings whatsoever;——the want of all kind of writing will put an end to all kind of reading;---and that in time, *As war begets poverty, poverty peace*,———must, in course, put an end to all kind of knowledge,---and then———we shall have all to begin over again; or in other words, be exactly where we started. (*TS*: 1.21.72)

Yet this desire for amnesia is not indulged, despite its ironic undermining of the progressivist model of history that fuelled the Enlightenment *libido sciendi*. Tristram Shandy does not, ultimately, take up a mode of modernist forgetting that guarantees his status as a newly modern consciousness. Nor, as we have discussed, does he return to the past as a place of safe anchorage from which to measure and incorporate the transforming present. His childhood, with its sash windows, broken noses, and intimations of bastardy, is no secure haven. What the narrative brings about is more complex, involving a different form of historiographic modernity - a way of remembering, in the words of Rousseau's Saint-Preux, 'what I am and who I belong to'.

Allegory and the Mid-Century Subject

Tristram Shandy can be read as a complex allegory of the condition of civil society in the England of the mid-eighteenth century: one which enacts the relation between an emergent modern sensibility and its socio-historical environment. Such a reading is not wholly external to the way that the narrative presents itself. In the fourth chapter of the novel, the narrator expresses the hope that his book 'will take in all ranks, professions and denominations of men whatever' - that is, address itself to the contemporary social spectrum - and 'be no less read than the *Pilgrim's Progress* itself' (*TS*: 1.4.5).

The reference to Bunyan's narrative proves a fruitful point of comparison, not because Sterne's novel addresses itself to Christian exegesis and divine salvation, but because it indicates in what ways a reader might be expected to approach the narrative, and how its structural principles might be understood. In Bunyan's novel, the pilgrim's temptation to take the most straightforward route to the celestial city is also that offered to the reader who believes that a literal interpretation will provide the surest path to the meaning of the narrative. Both reader and pilgrim learn to find the way by their mistakes. Moreover, Bunyan's novel operates according to a complex temporality characteristic of allegorical works: the simultaneous relation between a 'horizontal', chronological time, and a transcendent spatial dimension, which the reader must negotiate. In *Pilgrim's Progress* this is clearly used to explain the literal narrative of human daily life according to the overarching pattern of Christian spirituality. The allegory works to draw human agency into contact with the possibility of grace and redemption, and thus bring about a transcendence of historical time.

In an excellent chapter on Bunyan in his *Origins of the English Novel*, Michael McKeon has shown how this temporal structure can also be read against the grain (mis-read) as a process of secularization. The transcendent dimension of allegory and the spiritual values it represents are thus incorporated, literalized, in order to validate the life of an upwardly mobile 'new Christian': 'a model of how the average, earnest, modern Protestant may pursue his calling somewhere within the antithetical extremes of utter selfishness and utter selflessness' (McKeon, 1987: 311-12). It is a model, then, of worldly conduct, and an apology for materialistic enterprise.

What interests me about McKeon's 'misreading' is its stress on *literal* interpretation as a strategy, not just on the part of the critic, but one depended upon for specific ends by the narrative form itself. The process of secularization that McKeon discovers in Bunyan's *Pilgrim's Progress* - the material application of the spiritual in the conduct of a common life - in fact hinges upon a form of narrative identification characteristic of texts that are less evidently allegorical in nature: that in the novel the 'progress' of a protagonist is to be understood as a 'literal' exemplar. The literal reading of a narrative is thus one method of observing its 'rules of propriety': in other words, a way of making a text one's own. The relation between exegetical methods of reading and the eighteenth-century reader's approach to the novelistic text is pertinent here. As an author of sermons Sterne was well aware of such methods and their didactic uses. What is interesting is the way that they are introduced into *Tristram Shandy*.

The invitation to 'read, read, read, read' Sterne's narrative appears to dissuade the reader from seeking a literal meaning to the text. The narrator notes the 'vicious taste' of 'reading straight forwards, more in quest of the adventures, than of the deep erudition and knowledge which a book of this cast, if read over as it should be, would infallibly impart with them.———The mind should be accustomed to make wise reflections, and draw curious conclusions as it goes along' (*TS*: 1.20.65). Yet the habit of 'reading straight forwards', the Archimedean 'shortest line [...] from one given point to another' (*TS*: 6.40.572), is of course precisely what the narrative relies on to ensnare the reader in its games and traps - the euphemisms, the reversed chapters, the dual text Latin and English of the excommunication and so on. All of these techniques force the reader into an awareness of his or her reading practice, bringing about a critical reflexivity.

A literalization of *Tristram Shandy* is thus essential to the comprehension of its formal method. It is also integral to the temporality of the narrative. The spatial form of the novel has often been interpreted as an escape from the tyranny of historical time: a flight represented in literal terms in Volume 7, when Death pursues Tristram in person across France. It is my view that the narrative does not *escape* from historical time, but rather interrogates it in a complex way. On the level of the literal reading the 'horizontal' axis is the world of the 'hypercritic' for whom action of 'two minutes, thirteen seconds, and three fifths' duration should take exactly the same amount of time to relate: the world of impossible mimesis, bounded by the black page. On the 'vertical' axis is a complex time of consciousness that transcends the black page, which attempts to engage with the 'riddles and mysteries' of the universe, by simultaneously drawing on the temporalities of past, present and future. By continual interruption of the horizontal progression of the narrative, the reader is forced to draw 'curious conclusions': is brought, in a sense, to a healthy awareness of his or her limitations as a physical being in the grand scheme of things, just as Walter Shandy contemplates his own boundaries as he stares into the fishpond.

Yet if we operate that process of *misreading*, which Michael McKeon uses to expose the socio-historical dimensions of Bunyan's narrative, the strategies of *Tristram Shandy* are revealed to be 'about' the inscription of history itself. The reader, made to negotiate a number of temporal levels at once, begins to comprehend him- or herself in terms of a constellation of past, present and future norms, meanings and intentions - as a subject in history. The search for literal meaning - for a coherent 'story', relations of cause and effect, for the straightforward relevance of the text to its mid-century moment - fails. Yet in its failure history is revealed as a construct, but one that, for all its fictionality and 'cock-and-bull' absurdity, is nonetheless historically *lived*.

If the specific moment, then, is one of disorientating change in an emergent modern world that defies description or categorization, the effect of this historicity is twofold. On the one hand, despite its disengagement from the security of tradition, the modern sensibility is reassured of certain limits and boundaries, its horizon established. Despite the fact that the narrator is progressing at a precipitate speed, bombarded with 'views and prospects to himself perpetually solliciting his eye' (*TS*: 1.14.41), there are certainties: that the 'world' upon which he is focusing is four or five miles in diameter, that the black page is a finitude, that a degree of ignorance is only to be expected when 'the most obvious things, which come in our way, have dark sides, which the quickest sight cannot penetrate into' (*TS*: 4.17.350). On the other hand, the 'allegorical' dimension of the narrative provides a strategy by which the modern sensibility can move beyond this quiescence, to *remember* its pre-modern history and orientate itself towards the future. If allegory can be understood as a complex reassembly of disparate elements and fragments, drawn from the socio-historical formation - in addition to a form of temporal 'mapping' - it becomes in *Tristram Shandy* a mode of historical *cognition*. It does not promise to represent the world as a coherent unity, but offers historical transcendence of the literal boundaries of identity, by means of which, in the words of Jürgen Habermas (1987: 6.29), 'one's own standpoint was brought to reflective awareness within the horizon of history as a whole'. It is a way, then, of moving beyond alienated subjectivity and the disabling deracination - the amnesic loss of roots and tradition - which are facets of the experience of modernity itself. The inheritance of the mid-century subject becomes, therefore, a right of historical self-authorship.

Youth and Maturity

What I have been arguing for here is an understanding of modernity less in terms of its location as a specific historical period in which Tristram Shandy discovers himself than as what Michel Foucault calls an 'attitude' to contemporary circumstance:

> A mode of relating to contemporary reality; a voluntary choice made by certain people; in the end, a way of thinking and feeling; a way too of acting and behaving that at one and the same time marks a relation of belonging and presents itself as a task. A bit, no doubt, like what the Greeks called an ethos. (Foucault, 1984: 39)

A 'relation of belonging' that at once 'presents itself as a task': the plotting of bastardy in Sterne's *Tristram Shandy* is a register of modernity to the extent that it throws a notion of 'belonging' into consternation, forcing a nascent modern consciousness to negotiate its historical identity. Freed from paternal tutelage, what emerges from the break-up of the generational continuum is a concept of 'youth'. No longer to be absorbed into a continuity of familial and communal values, 'youth' begins to operate as a contradictory sign of society's sense of itself as modern. A sign, then, which expresses the dynamism and instability of a modern culture, and yet, by virtue of its youthful apprenticeship to modern life, is also the hopeful sign of a world, as Franco Moretti (1987: 5) has written, 'that seeks its meaning in the *future* rather than in the past'.

The Shandean child that emerges uncertainly into the mid-eighteenth century, 'circumscribed by rights', is a tentative expression of a wider cultural impatience for liberty which begins to manifest itself in the 1760s, in a trend towards the critique of authority in numerous journals, in electioneering debacles such as that surrounding the figure of John Wilkes, in calls for American independence which Laurence Sterne was never to witness. The child becomes what Peter Sloterdijk (1988: 55) terms 'the living security deposit of enlightenment', but not because it guarantees a parent's stake or claim on the future in the manner of the vain desires of Walter Shandy. As Immanuel Kant stated in his essay *Was ist Aufklärung*?, 'an age cannot bind itself and ordain to put the succeeding one into such a condition that it cannot extend its (at best very occasional) knowledge, purify itself of errors, and progress in general enlightenment. That would be a crime against human nature' (32). Walter Shandy's parental love is thwarted because it attempts to hold on to its own traditional ambitions. Tristram Shandy is a child that learns to love itself, to begin to recognize its 'daring hope', as Richard Savage's poem 'The Bastard' suggests, even as its task appears impossible. And that task in *Tristram Shandy* does not bring about a reconciliation with the social order, though such an incorporation is sealed by the time of Sterne's later novel, *A Sentimental Journey*, as we will discover.

Yet what is the 'task' set such a modern consciousness? Perhaps paradoxically, it is, as Foucault describes in his reading of Kant's *Was ist Aufklärung*?, to establish an attitude of *maturity*. Set loose from its dependency upon traditional structures by what Foucault (35) terms 'an act of courage', daring to face a form of historical illegitimacy, the modern subject answers an Enlightenment imperative: *sapere aude*, 'have the courage to exercise your own understanding' (Kant, 1984:

30). Confronted with a world in which, as Samuel Johnson had stated, 'every variation of time and place makes different from itself' ('Preface' to the *Dictionary*, 1755: 2), however, the modern subject which we have discovered in *Tristram Shandy* does not simply embrace such contingency, or celebrate its continual mutation. Rather, in Foucault's words, 'this deliberate, difficult attitude consists in recapturing something eternal that is not beyond the present instant, nor behind it, but within it' (39). As he continues:

> For the attitude of modernity, the high value of the present is indissociable from a desparate eagerness to imagine it otherwise than it is, and to transform it not by destroying it but by grasping it in what it is. (41)

The refiguring - re-imagining - of the present forges a new, abstract form of temporality, which is a measure of a historical contradiction. It is an index of the problem of an age whose self-diagnosis suggests both a radical break from the past, and yet, as Hans Blumenberg (quoted in Habermas, 1987: 7) puts it, 'the incongruity of this claim with the reality of history, which is never capable of starting anew from the ground up'. Modernity must provide from within itself its own means of orientation, yet what such an attitude demands is an acute *historical* self-reflexivity, and one, moreover, which has the strength to constitute its break from the past as a process of potentially endless renewal. It is this seizing of a rigorous responsibility for self-authorship that stands for maturity, and it is a condition that Sterne's novel aspires to: one characterized, perhaps paradoxically, by its critique of traditional seriousness.

This process of continual - historical - refiguring thus manifests itself in Sterne's novel in several ways. On one level the protagonist-narrator takes on the task of producing himself, learning, in the words of Richard Savage's poem, 'to glory in the Bastard's glowing name' (1984: 214). Both disengaged observer and the historical object of his own observation, this ironic self-construction is informed less by a Humean formulation of identity as a bundle of habitual associations than by a radical form of Lockean *cognition*. Functioning as his own *tabula rasa*, Tristram Shandy inscribes himself into history by reconstruing his origins as a complex constellation of memories, textual accounts and associated ideas: a self-construction only made possible by a degree of distanciation from the course of common life and its 'Opiniatry', as Locke called it.

Yet if Tristram Shandy, the modern subject, does practise the 'radical reflexivity' that Charles Taylor (1989: 163) regards as central to Locke's philosophy, in attempting to understand who he is and who he belongs to, his distanciation from common experience does not take the form of a Lockean attempt at rational control. It is rather produced by comic means: a wise laughter that seeks parodically, on the one hand, to question the 'gravity' that stands for knowledge, and the forms of social power underpinned by such seriousness, without, on the other, succumbing to a bland frivolity and the logic of the trivial. As the epigraph to Volume 3 suggests, 'I do not fear the opinions of the ignorant crowd; yet I ask them to spare this little work, in which it has always been my purpose to pass from the gay to the serious and from the serious to the gay'. The 'dialectic' between wit and judgement offered us in the 'Author's preface' in Volume 3 thus provides the method for the mode of historical cognition which Sterne's novel pursues. The focus on incongruity central to its comic strategy can be understood as part of a wider cultural attempt to manage and understand the nature of social contradiction: between discursive claims to truth, between competing accounts of history, between definitions of the nature of social identity.

Tristram Shandy's collective aim - 'that all mankind should write as well as myself' (*TS*: 9.12.762) - is therefore to be understood as a statement of the *ethical* position that Foucault regarded as the 'attitude' of modernity. Sterne's narrative presents its readers with a historical investigation into the constitution of the mid-century subject, his 'life and opinions', an investigation into civil society itself. The novel's purpose, as a mode of 'conversation', is to inculcate in the reader a form of responsibility, a recognition of 'ourselves as subjects of what we are doing, thinking, saying' (Foucault, 1984: 46). Sterne's narrative looks to create the conditions where the alienated modern conscious-ness might find itself, in dialogue, with others.

Yet 'True Shandeism' - an anticipated resolution of incongruity in 'the body politic as body natural' - sets out the individual and psychological preconditions of the construction of an ideal society, appropriately enough, perhaps, by means of a contradiction. On the one hand the mid-century subject is encouraged to locate him or herself in the historical moment in a deliberate act of distanciation, and thus to work to comprehend it, to imagine it against the grain of tradition: in other words, to use a formalist term, to defamiliarize it. On the other hand, the potential for critique that such an attitude might provide - that taken up in the novel by the figure of Yorick, who offers a protest against unmediated authority and the inequalities at work in the construction of history, and is punished for his pains - is largely disarmed. For the novel's anticipation of social harmony as psychic harmony - represented as a form of *aesthetic* pleasure for both the reader and Tristram - begins to develop into a mere cerebral compensation for the shortcomings of society: a compensation known as sentimentalism. In Sterne's later *A Sentimental Journey*, familial relations are re-established as a means of smoothing over inequalities that the incoherent, incongruous form of *Tristram Shandy* had in its wayward, abstract way managed to acknowledge. The child in the sentimental novel becomes interchangeable with all those social innocents (servants, unfortunates, the poor, the mad) who are to be brought under paternalist care. In *Tristram Shandy* by contrast, the child is an irrepressible modern, insisting on telling his story in his own way, on making his new, historical claim.

LAURENCE STERNE AND THE TWENTIETH CENTURY

MICHAEL BELL

We may initially distinguish three possible kinds of relevance of Sterne to twentieth-century literature. The first is to see him as a modernist and postmodernist *avant la lettre*. This seems to me historically misguided and likely to cause a darkening of counsel. More fruitfully, he can be seen to have provided a usable past for writers throughout the century. This is widely recognised although doubtless there are fresh angles to be seen. My present interest is different again: it is to suggest Sterne rather as a relevant benchmark within the development of European fiction and of sensibility generally. In other words, modern writers making no conscious recourse to Sterne rework his themes and devices in historically revealing ways.

One can express this by playing a variation on Oswald Spengler's notion of a 'contemporary'. He defines this not just as one living at the same time but as one living at an equivalent historical moment. Twentieth-century fiction has repeatedly recognised its significant contemporaries in the eighteenth rather than the nineteenth century. But this is a similarity by inversion. Where modern novelists have frequently problematised the totalising ambition of nineteenth-century fiction, their eighteenth-century 'contemporaries', such as Sterne and Diderot, were not escaping from this model. Therefore, although these writers can be seen in retrospect as moving towards a practice of realism which mirrors the modern writer's move away from it, their sense of what was at issue was quite different. I suggest that such an inverse contemporaneity with Sterne can profitably be seen in the modernism of Proust and in the postmodernism of García Márquez but it is necessary first to pause on the moment of sensibility, and the corresponding fictional vehicle, of Sterne himself.

'The Story of Le Fever': Sentiment and Fiction

I have discussed at length elsewhere (Bell, 1983) the complex interaction between the ethics of sentiment and the practice of fiction in the eighteenth century. Briefly, there is a significant homology between the philosophical belief in the goodness of feeling and the novelist's desire to arouse the feelings of the reader. But although the attempt to base the moral life on feeling had an important and enduring truth at its core, it was highly unstable in the literalistic, and rhetorically effusive, form in which it was typically conceived. Furthermore, the corresponding conception of fictional meaning was similarly literalistic, whether overtly so as in Richardson or implicitly as in Sterne. Yet the resulting instability of the fiction of sentiment was in itself to prove a creative growing point: it led by the next century to a more subtle understanding of fiction and feeling as distinct, yet mutually necessary, realms.

Sterne's brief career takes us from Rabelaisian satiric humour to the ethics of sentiment and the shift can be seen over the course of *Tristram Shandy* itself. A moment that especially focuses the historically pregnant interplay of sensibility and fiction is the comically sentimental 'Story of Le Fever' in Volume 6 of *Tristram Shandy*. This is a sentimental occasion which Sterne has chosen, quite unnecessarily in narrative terms, to tell not just through Tristram but through Corporal Trim and he reinforces this secondary narrative frame by our constant awareness of Toby as the immediate listener to the tale. The secondary narrative frame has a subtle impact on the sentimental material. By an apparently innocent, non-analytic means, it achieves a complex discrimination which an analytic account, such as this, must come limping after.

A central ambivalence of the ethics of sentiment lay in the moral significance of benevolent feeling. If, as Shaftesbury argued, such feeling is natural and pleasurable, does it not then become an end in itself and lose the very ethical value it claims? One may have benevolent feeling without necessarily acting upon it. And indeed the feeling may be a self-regarding substitute for action as R.F. Brissenden (1974: 4) has pointed out in the amusing instance of Vernes' Sentimental Traveller who replaces his money in his purse to give a deserving beggar something better, a tear of sympathy. Diderot, speaking in praise of Richardson, remarks without irony that after reading him you feel as if you had spent the day in charitable actions (Diderot, 1965: 30-31). In the literalistic terms of the novel of sentiment there is a constant danger, for both characters and readers, of drowning an important psychological truth in a quagmire of insincerity. Such a satisfaction of benevolence without action turns the benevolence into a kind of pure fiction; and hence the intimate mutual relevance of sentiment and fiction.

In the present instance, Sterne's multiple narrative frame is a device for discriminating the layers of sincerity and insincerity within this dilemma of ethical sentiment. As readers, we listen to the pathos of Le Fever's situation over Uncle Toby's shoulder so that we respond half separably to the event and to the manner of its narration. Now in so far as the episode is a classic in the literature of sentiment, is in other words an exemplary arousing of benevolent feeling, this double frame has in the first instance an intensifying effect. The framed narrative concentrates the pathos by separating it in some measure from the centrifugal energies of the main narrative. We are invited to be moved by the narration as well as by the event and if we find Trim's manner in some measure comic this partly serves to reinforce the pathos. Dickens was to understand very well from his eighteenth-century masters, including Sterne, the necessary obliqueness and comedy of sentiment. In the economy of the imagination, a joke pays for a tear.

But where Dickens would normally combine the comic and the sentimental in one voice, in the present instance the two tones help to reinforce the felt separation of narrative levels. The pathos of the event contrasts with the comedy of its telling; an effect which is highlighted typographically by the subtitle 'The Story of Le Fever'. This latter device points to Sterne's forebear, Cervantes, who had an interest in the narrative act not fully appreciated even by Cervantistas. His 'Novela del curioso impertinente' from *Don Quixote* Part I is a richly characteristic example. The characters from the main action pause to read, out of curiosity, the story of a fatally mischievous curiosity. Over and above the thematic links this suggests between the subnarrative and the main one, Cervantes is exploring the effect of placing such material within a separate narrative frame (see also Bell, 1990: 172-98). And Sterne does something comparable in his different cultural context as he seeks not only to exercise but to scrutinise the ethics of sentiment. For the separate narrative frame serves to detach as well as intensify.

As we 'listen' to Trim's tale we can afford detachedly to enjoy the humour of its telling and our pleasure is not alloyed by the urgent needs of Le Fever. For us, after all, the events are set in a distant past and their object is purely fictional. Toby by contrast is hearing of a charitable necessity in his dramatic present and far from finding the tale amusing he wishes he could be asleep to avoid the pain it causes him. Although he serves *for us* to frame Trim's narrative, he himself is not outside its world. Le Fever therefore constitutes a demand upon his benevolence, and his purse, which we as readers do not face.

By this simple but subtle means Sterne has negotiated a central dilemma of the sentimentalist ethic. His double narrative frame distinguishes the different orders of emotional truth which are properly involved. Whereas Toby responds to the event with benevolent action, we respond to the 'same' pathos as a specifically fictional exercise in fellow feeling. Listening over Toby's shoulder, we quite properly enjoy an aesthetic object while part of the very object we enjoy is the connection of feeling to action which Toby represents. Sterne thereby legitimates the purely aesthetic exercise of feeling while insisting on the necessary relation of feeling to action in the ethical sphere.

This is a pregnant moment both for the afterlife of the sentimentalist ethic and for European fiction. We can see a potential watershed here between different views of sentiment enshrined in different kinds of fiction. The great writers of Victorian England, and pre-eminently Dickens, kept faith with the sentimentalist impulse partly by recognising its affinity with fiction. Their commitment to imagination, in both the ethical and the narrative realms, allowed them to express as one, more implicit, complex the double truth which Sterne has delicately discriminated. But the other possibility lurking in the doubleness of the Le Fever story is that feeling may indeed be enjoyed for its own sake rather than for its ethical application. Or in other words, it is possible for feeling to find an aesthetic home. This latter possibility is particularly important in the French tradition. The condemned cell of Julien Sorel, the antechamber to eternity in which he can finally recognise his true love, is a step towards the aesthetic mode of Flaubert. The aesthetic perfectionism of *Madame Bovary* makes the novel itself such a condemned cell since the romantic longings of the reader and author have ultimately no more home in the real world than do Emma's. This is Flaubert's sardonic adaptation of the cult of sentiment. Sterne does not point towards such an aesthetic emphasis; he rather recognises the possibility in order to discount it. But further down the line Proust was to inflect the powerful aesthetic vision of Flaubert back towards more overtly ethical concerns and at that point intriguing parallels with Sterne begin to emerge.

Sterne and Proust: Inverse Contemporaries

Of the trio of great modern European novelists who made time their central theme, Joyce and Mann are known to have had direct recourse to Sterne. In Proust's case, however, there seems to be no evidence of his having read Sterne although it is Proust's subject and method which most deeply and fully rework the Sternean example. Parallels have, of course, been noted between the two authors but these have usually involved either the general theme of time or specific images and themes. Melvyn New (1988) has commented on the similarities between the starling episode in *A Sentimental Journey* and Proust's *The Captive*. He goes on to express scepticism, which I share, about alleged similarities such as the 'stream of consciousness' which collapses enormous differences in the models of the psyche involved. But for this very reason it becomes illuminating to perceive the inverse contemporaneity of the two writers. The closeness of narrative strategy between *Tristram Shandy* and *A la Recherche* has not, to my knowledge, been remarked. If this has occurred unwittingly on Proust's part, impelled simply by the inner logic of his theme, then the parallel becomes so much the more revealing.

Sterne is an eighteenth-century Proust, or Proust a twentieth-century Sterne, in that each wrote a *roman fleuve* attempting to transcend time and mortality. In each case the sustained bravura of the narrative act becomes in itself the central thematic device although each uses a model of fiction, and of human psychology, available in his day. While Sterne continually subverts Lockean values, his very doing so remains within the terms of Locke's psychology. His satiric play with Locke only reinforces the fundamental model. Likewise, Proust should not be seen as simply a Freudian yet he is a significant contemporary of Freud in that his model of the psyche gives a crucial significance to a realm beyond consciousness and, to that extent, beyond time. What is remarkable is that both authors use similar narrative strategies within their radically different psychological premises.

Both narrators present themselves, ironically, as incompetent, or at least as following the drift of private association at the expense of narrative progress. Both thereby communicate their participation in a process larger than could be consciously controlled. Thus the incompetence of Marcel proves to be not so much personal as the generic incapacity of consciousness by itself to bring him to the paradisal intuition he is seeking. His conscious quest in time traces a huge, unwitting circle at the centre of which, as he finally recognises, the paradisal transcendence of mortality is always equidistant from any point in time. It is always and never present. Sterne has no such deep, timeless region of the psyche available for this purpose and he seeks rather a collapsing of time. Instead of creating the nostalgic depth of memory, he disrupts linear time so that the most distant moments, even those before the narrator's birth, are experienced simply as a continuing narrative present. The constant digressions treat the events of the past like a pack of cards which can be endlessly reshuffled with the top facing card of the narrative present always the same distance from the onlooker. Tristram makes this explicit during his continental travels:

> I am this moment walking across the market-place of Auxerre wih my father and my uncle Toby, in our way back to dinner———and I am this moment also entering Lyons with my post-chaise broke into a thousand pieces——and I am moreover this moment in a handsome pavilion built by Pringello, upon the banks of the Garonne, which Mons. Sligniac has lent me, and where I now sit rhapsodizing all these affairs.
>
> ———Let me collect myself, and pursue my journey. (*TS*: 7.28.622)

The strategic importance of this collapsing of past time is that it disorients our sense of the future. For such a narrative has no teleological purpose beyond the continuance of the narrative consciousness in its own ever-moving present. And hence the gradual shift by which the action has become, by the time of this quotation, a narrative flight from death. The narrative act becomes a defiance of mortality: a humorous rejection of gravity and of the 'grave'. Of course, both authors are ultimately dealing in metaphors. Sterne and Proust, like God and Nietzsche, are all dead. The true enemy is not death but the fear of it and what is ultimately at stake is an emotional disposition.

Sterne and Proust are humorous writers and much of their humour circles around the same topics. It particularly arises from the comic collisions and the mechanistic self-parody caused by emotional self-enclosure. The Proustian obsession, in effect, is an avatar of the Sternean hobbyhorse: both are highly linguistic in focus and usually somatic in origin. Bodily gestures are frequently more expressive, or revealing, than language so that language itself becomes gestural in meaning. Charlus gives a startled doubletake when introduced by M. Verdurin as 'one of us' since he assumes the phrase to be a reference to his homosexuality rather than to inclusion in their snobbish circle which is the Verdurins' obsessive preoccupation (Proust, 1988: 332, 359). The confusion arising from a wrong association of ideas here is pure Sterne yet it equally reflects the central themes and structure of *A la Recherche*.

The Sternean hobbyhorse is itself highly ambivalent. It extends from the destructive manias of Walter, through the benign pleasures of Uncle Toby, and on to the genial creativity of Tristram's narrative. While from a Lockean point of view the hobbyhorse represents a breakdown in the communication of ideas, from an anti-Lockean standpoint it is a unique mode of emotional communication. It objectifies the inner life of the individual and makes it expressively available to sympathetic onlookers. As a blend of humour, feeling, subjectivity and creation it anticipates the principal elements by which romantic thought would eventually dissolve the Lockean world view. At its crudely comic level, the hobbyhorse performs something of the function of a work of art. Proust's narrator likewise observes the obsessions of other characters while eventually transforming his own into a transcendent and paradisal vision. Hence, in both cases the obsessive states of other characters help to define the significance of the narrative itself. Where minor characters seem often bound within their hobbyhorsical obsessions, the narrators bring out by contrast the transcendent and expressive aspect of their own obsession, the narrative we are reading. This points ultimately to the mysteriously inward-facing quality of a work of art which strangely frees it from subjectivity and self-preoccupation. In Proust, the work of art, like the paradisal experience, is a freedom from self.

This intimate bearing of other characters' obsessions on the narrator's arises also from the mutual porousness of characters and narrator throughout. Tristram describes his own 'life and opinions' through anecdotes concerning Walter, Toby, Trim and Yorick. He can appropriately do so not just because these characters have formed his personality and provided much of the substance of his memories, but because they are all aspects, or possible aspects, of himself. This is why Sterne's characters never seem mere caricatures and another reason is that, in so far as Toby, Walter and Trim *are* independent beings, they are still presented as creatures of Tristram's emotional memory. By the same principle which D. W. Harding defined in Jane Austen as 'regulated hatred', the element of caricature is a function of Tristram's feeling rather than of Sterne's creation. The Walter we actually meet is not the appalling husband and father he might be in reality but an entertaining figure who makes the 'real' Walter emotionally acceptable to Tristram and to us.

This element of implicit psychomachia is evidently at work in Proust too. The whole story of Swann's love for Odette would be a grotesquely swollen digression if we did not understand that it traces the inner structure of Marcel's own experience. At the same time, the very fact that Marcel is able to enter so imaginatively into an experience not literally his own reflects his capacity, by the time of the narration, to transcend the kind of emotional enclosure Swann exemplifies. The porousness of the characters to the narrators, therefore, has both aesthetic and ethical implications. Swann confuses the aesthetic and the non-aesthetic in a way that Marcel, in his own life, comes to understand. Despite the differences, we may relevantly recall how Tristram, listening to the Story of le Fever through Uncle Toby, is at once identified with, and detached from, Toby's response.

Indeed, Proust's thematising of such confusion of the ethical and the aesthetic often has a distinctly late eighteenth-century ring. Lionel Trilling in *Sincerity and Authenticity* has noted the gradual shift in pre-occupation from sincerity in the eighteenth century to authenticity in the twentieth. As the original cult of sensibility sought to replace traditional ethical principle with feeling, there was an inevitable mismatch between principle and feeling and a corresponding anxiety about sincerity. Taking Nietzsche as a watershed, we can see a more pervasive modern willingness to subordinate general principle to psychological wholeness. There is a shift from a problem of sincerity in ethics to an ethics of authenticity. This means that most modern writers have broken with the earlier concern with sincerity which was often thematised by the image of acting as in Diderot's *Paradox on the Actor*.

In this general context, Proust is unusual in retaining a continuity with the earlier terms. The incident of Vinteuil's daughter and her lesbian lover is highly theatrical. The two girls watch themselves watched by the dead father's picture while the whole episode is watched by the young Marcel. The older Marcel who narrates has a lucid understanding of Mlle Vinteuil's essentially innocent sadism in needing to defile her father's image. Her actual love for him is the condition of her imaginary, performed evil. The reference to Sade in the episode does not suggest its modern use as a psychological term but rather acts as a reminder that Sade was a development of the eighteeenth-century literature of sensibility in which evil and innocence are frequently idealised projections and susceptible to inversion. Mlle Vinteuil's 'evil' is an aesthetic device parallel to Swann's aesthetically induced love of Odette. Both arise from a blurring of categories.

But Proust's frequent closeness to the older literature of sensibility does not make him simply at one with it. He rather constitutes a complex summary of the whole tradition from a later, post-realist and post-aestheticist standpoint. Ironically perhaps, this can be seen in a further point of parallel with Sterne. For when it comes to making the necessary discrimination between the ethical and the aesthetic, Proust's narrative has a further strategic similarity with *Tristram Shandy*. The narrators in both works are porous not just to other characters but to their real authors and thus to the world of the reader. Tristram and Marcel are clearly authorial personae and this reflects in each case a significant blurring of aesthetic closure. I have already remarked how, in the 'Story of Le Fever', Sterne implicitly recognises the value of an imaginative arousal of benevolent feeling while refusing any purely aestheticist inflection of it by simultaneously insisting on the need for charitable action. Proust, by contrast, follows Flaubert and a whole generation of aestheticism so that his strongly ethical implication comes through an implicit commitment to artistic self-transcendence. In the modernist generation generally, the *symboliste* inheritance is both continued and inverted. If Schopenhauer's privileging of the aesthetic is the metaphysical correlative of *symbolisme*, then Nietzsche's inversion of Schopenhauer is the essential metaphysic of modernism. While retaining the special category of the aesthetic Nietzsche now affirmed it as a form of life. There is something comparable in the overall experience of Proust's Marcel. His aesthetic ambitions fail to produce the paradisal intuition. Instead, that blessed state finally wells up quite unexpectedly outside the artistic forms upon which he has so assiduously meditated. Yet, of course, the paradisal moment is still contained within the larger narrative which we then recognise to have been subtly preparing for this moment all along. The experience is itself the result of a meticulously aesthetic creation. The conditions of the experience, in other words, are importantly aesthetic and non-aesthetic at the same time.

This doubleness is a hallmark of high modernism in its method and in its implicit metaphysic but it precisely echoes the doubleness seen in Sterne's 'Story of Le Fever'. Sterne's jokey manipulation of the literalistic conceptions of fiction and of ethical feeling prevalent in his day produced a complex emotional truth which finds an ironic equivalent in Proust's high modernist, post-aestheticist synthesis.

The Little Worlds of Sterne and García Márquez

> ——by which word *world*, need I in this place inform your worship, that I would be understood to mean no more of it, than a small circle described upon the circle of the great world, of four *English* miles diameter (*TS*: 1.7.10)

One of the central geo-political problems at the end of the millenium is how to share the planet without losing local identity and difference.

The point here perhaps is not to seek answers so much as to modify consciousness and that may be part of the import of books like *Midnight's Children* and *One Hundred Years of Solitude* which are at once global and intensely local. If *Midnight's Children* has an evident debt to *The Tin Drum* it also registers a difference. The non-German reader of *The Tin Drum* reads it over the German reader's shoulder. It has a very specifically national concern. But with *Midnight's Children* one might rather say that the Indian reader has to read its densely local concerns with an outsider's eye. This interplay of insider's and outsider's perspectives is vital to *One Hundred Years of Solitude* and is thematised within it. To focus this it is helpful to note that the late twentieth-century phase of culture which Márquez reflects has its inverse parallel in Sterne. *Tristram Shandy* creates precisely such a small world as Márquez is seeking to problematise.

Having raised the question explicitly in Volume 1, Chapter 7, Sterne returns to play further variations on the word 'world':

> It is so long since the reader of this rhapsodical work has been parted from the midwife, that it is high time to mention her again to him, merely to put him in mind that there is such a body still in the world [...] I think I told you this good woman was a person of no small note and consequence throughout our whole village and township; - that her fame had spread itself to the very out-edge and circumference of that circle of importance, of which kind every soul living, whether he has a shirt to his back or no, - has one surrounding him; - which said circle, by the way, whenever 'tis said that such a one is of great weight and importance in the *world*; -- I desire may be enlarged or contracted in your worship's fancy, in a compound-ratio of the station, profession, knowledge, abilities, height and depth (measuring both ways) of the personage brought before you. [...] In the present case, if I remember, I fixed it at about four or five miles, which not only comprehended the whole parish, but extended itself to two or three of the adjacent hamlets in the skirts of the next parish;

And he goes on to prepare the reader for

> such passages, incidents, or inuendos as shall be thought to be either of private interpretation, or of dark or doubtful meaning after my life and my opinions shall have been read over, (now don't forget the meaning of the word) by all the *world*;--which, betwixt you and me [...] I am determined shall be the case.———I need not tell your worship, that all this is spoke in confidence. (*TS*: 1.13.40)

Tristram refers here to a double shrinkage of purview. The world of the novel is local and many of its meanings are likely to be private. And this indeed points to a central feature of the work: it takes the great public, military events of earlier in the century and reduces them both to the harmless pleasures of the bowling green and to the hobbyhorsical obsessions of the characters. Toby is an old soldier who literally will not hurt a fly. And the public scale of history is most radically privatised when Tristram defines his book as a 'history-book, Sir, (which may possibly recommend it to the world) of what passes in a man's own mind' (*TS*: 2.2.98).

On the face of it this comic transposition of public life into the key of domesticity might seem to entail a critique of, or an escape from, the heroic values of a militaristic nationalism. And to a degree it does so. But the reduction of Malborough's campaigns to a game still allows for some vicarious identification with their values. Indeed, the nationalistic spirit is protected by becoming harmlessly lovable. Toby's anti-papistry, while amiably quaint, touches a deep and permanent chord in English national culture; so deep that only people of Catholic upbringing seem to be aware of it. As a supposed alternative to the spirit of controversy, Toby whistles the anti-papist song Lillibulero and there is a deeply unwitting appropriateness in the fact that the BBC, the national symbol of moral neutrality, should have chosen this as its signature tune for the 'World' Service.

What is partly at stake here is the meaning of the English eccentric and Sterne recognises his own contribution to a tradition. Tristram remarks that the inconstancy of the climate 'has furnished us with such a variety of odd and whimsical characters' and goes on to note that 'the great *Addison* began to patronize the notion, and more fully explained it to the world in one or two of his Spectators;——but the discovery was not his' (*TS*: 1.21.71). The prizing of eccentricity is a characteristic English way of accommodating potential social disruption. And such humorous licence is enjoyed not just by Toby but by the more problematical Walter. Walter is an eighteenth-century Basil Fawlty, a quintessentially English type unknown to the rest of the world. But the late twentieth-century figure of Basil Fawlty, like the much earlier generation of Don Quixote, Falstaff and Jonson's humorous figures, is ultimately a satiric object. He reflects an historical moment when the elaborated alibis of repression embodied in his type no longer seem worthy of even humorous identification. And, of course, to highlight the satire the appropriate location is a tourist hotel. This is also the historical moment of García Márquez' comparable reversal of the Sternean spirit in the creation of his little world of the Buendías.

Márquez had carried around the project of *Hundred Years* since his earliest days as a writer. The recognition of how to write it, which came upon him, as he recounts, with the force of sudden inspiration, was bound up with his seeing that he must write it in the manner of his small town grandmother who spoke of marvels as if they were everyday events. But the preparation for this recognition includes his long and varied career as a journalist in which he had worked in turn for a local paper, a national paper, as a European correspondent, and then for Prensa Latina in various locations in the Americas. The constant dilation and contraction of the reporter's eye, as he explained the world to a local readership or local events to a continental public, clearly created a subtle consciousness of mixed scales.

Indeed, it is striking that one of his stylistic tics in his journalism is a play precisely on the word 'world'. He plays endless variations on the expression 'Most x in the world' as in 'the most beautiful girl in the world.' The use of the clichéd phrase reflects Márquez' populism while the variations he plays on it gently ironise the populism from within. For whereas the formula 'most beautiful girl in the world' is a hallowed piece of emotional rhetoric almost devoid of objective sense, Márquez jostles it with related phrases invoking a literally global reference as when he remarks in a film review that the Italians are the second greatest consumers of film in the world (Márquez, 1982: 174). Or he can play comic variations on the formula as, for example, in the title of his review article on the year 1956: 'The Most Famous Year in the World' (527). His constant play on the word 'world' reflects a pervasive consciousness of the question Octavio Paz had discussed in *The Labyrinth of Solitude*: that national history was now to be lived in a global context and *vice versa* (Paz, 1985: 161).

Much of the charm and the power of *One Hundred Years of Solitude* lies in the way its local life is at once quaint and yet not condescended to. The tragic resumé of regional history is modified but not anulled by this affectionately humorous consciousness. The novel also plays repeatedly on the word 'world' and the spirit of this can be seen in the remark of the founder of Macondo, José Arcadio, when he is first drawn into the spell of scientific knowledge: 'The earth is round like an orange' (Márquez, 1987: 75). This quaint recognition of the earth's roundness takes us back to the moment of Columbus as the book starts its condensed history of Latin America. If the remark also recalls Paul Eluard's 'La terre est bleu / Comme un orange', it is only to remind us how the surrealist inheritance in Latin American 'magic realism' is no longer an oppositional anti-rationalism so much as a popular expression of wonder. Furthermore, the roundness of the orange here shrinks the great globe to a familiar scale; only as such a complete image can the counter-intuitive roundness of the earth be taken in. Yet this same reduction also anticipates the book's many constricted circles of emotional solipsism; the ultimately destructive trait of the Buendías. Indeed, José Arcadio's scientific obsession is already a crucial example of such enclosure.

The problem of inhabiting different orders, and scales, of 'world' simultaneously is not 'answered' in the book. In true postmodernist style its narrative and thematic structures revolve endlessly on themselves like a Moebius strip. But the effect of this continuous circling is to embody a constant, half-consciousness of the competing scales. The figure who focuses this particularly is Melquíades. Having travelled the globe, he retires to the absolute privacy of the magically timeless room and a dead language to chronicle the future of the Buendías. When Aureliano Segundo seeks to learn from him

> Melquíades told him of the world, and sought to instill in him his ancient wisdom, but refused to translate the manuscripts: 'No one must know the meaning for a hundred years' he explained. Aureliano kept forever the secret of these interviews. On one occasion he felt his private world was being destroyed when Ursula came into the room while Melquíades was there. (262)

The ambivalence of solitude in *Hundred Years* is caught here in the two contrasting uses of the word 'world'. Melquíades speaks of the global 'world' but his knowledge is private to the point of being hermetic and it is experienced by Aureliano Segundo as a 'private world'. At this point, the incestuous solipsism of the Buendías acquires a more positive echo in the solitude of Melquíades, a figure perhaps of the writer himself, through whom the whole narrative is related. The little world of Macondo is chronicled by an outsider by birth, Melquíades, who helps an outsider by culture, Márquez, to bid it a protracted and nostalgic farewell. Melquíades' concentration of a vast and tragic regional history into a comically affectionate chronicle is a mode of emotional liberation.

An attitude of nostalgic farewell, as opposed to satire or celebration, is what Borges saw as Cervantes' view of the romances in *Don Quixote* and it may be significant that Márquez has borrowed Cervantes' figure of the fictitious foreign historian as his central device in *Hundred Years*. (Borges, 1970: 229). When Thomas Mann had just embarked on the Joseph tetralogy he reread and meditated on Cervantes. Being himself in exile from Nazi Germany, and voyaging to America with Jewish emigrés, he focused on the incident of Ricote, the expelled Moor, in *Don Quixote* (Mann, 1947: 429-64). He commented on the way Cervantes exposes, without overtly attacking, the exclusivist spirit behind the 1609 expulsion of the Moors from Spain. The Joseph tetralogy is among other things an extended meditation on exclusiveness, openness and exile in Joseph's life and in the whole Jewish tradition he represents.

Mann's focus on anti-semitism links him to his modernist contemporaries Joyce and Proust and he declared that while composing the tetralogy he frequently reread *Tristram Shandy*. But such a conjunction of Sterne and Cervantes in this late, incipiently postmodern, work of Thomas Mann suggests a further possible function of Sterne in the twentieth century.[1] In the latter part of the century, as sophisticated postmodern fiction is produced around the world, the humane relativity of Cervantes is more pertinent than the genial but enclosed world of Sterne. From that point of view, Sterne is rather a stepping stone back to his great forebear, Cervantes. Carlos Fuentes has remarked (1987: 137) that '*Don Quixote* should not be alien to an Anglo-American reader. There is this barrier and yet we are talking about a text which is the founding novel of modern

[1] I have discussed Thomas Mann's conscious glimpse of postmodernism in the Joseph tetralology in 'Novel, Story and the Foreign: Cervantes, Thomas Mann and Primo Levi'. This lecture was for a conference on 'Cervantes and the Twentieth Century' at the University of Edinburgh, November, 1991, the proceedings of which are to be published.

Europe, it is the novel with the most illustrious descendants, *Tristram Shandy*, Diderot, a good part of Dickens, Dostoyevsky and even Jane Austen'. Fuentes is only one of several Latin-American writers who have made Cervantes our contemporary. If the eighteenth-century move towards realism is indeed retrodden backwards in the twentieth, it makes sense that Sterne should be a significant 'contemporary' of the great modernists and Cervantes of recent writers in Latin America.

DIGRESSION AND INTERTEXTUAL PARODY IN THOMAS NASHE, LAURENCE STERNE AND JAMES JOYCE

ANTONIO BALLESTEROS GONZÁLEZ

'Non enim excursus hic eius,
sed opus ipsum est' (Pliny, V, Ep. vi)

Books are always related to other books; this is a kind of axiomatic truth which no literary critic would dare to ignore. Julia Kristeva's fortunate coinage of the term *intertextuality* has precisely emphasized the fact that literature is based on the referential capacity that literary works have of being influenced by other literary works, no matter how the so fashionable theory of chaos may affect the assertion.

But intertextuality, in spite of its relatively recent consideration as such, had consciously and subconsciously worked as a successful notion even before it was given a denomination. Books, from the remote beginning of literature, maintain a certain organic link among one another. In this context, Homer - if such a poet ever existed and if he was the author of *The Iliad* and *The Odyssey* - would be the original point of departure for all the books that the literary tradition has defined as literary, as far as - and there is still hope - an older work is not discovered.

We know from the many instances one can come across when studying literary history that any literary tradition or convention necessarily contains in itself the seed of its own parody. Taking the example of Homer, the written origin of epic poetry is not only in his well-known poems quoted above, but also in the so-called *Batracomyomachia* (literally, 'The Fight between the Frogs and the Mice'), a composition attributed to him. Were this work or were it not the result of Homer's authorship, there is certainty that each literary genre always entails a parody of itself.

In this respect, the origin of the novel - if we accept that *Don Quixote* is the first modern exponent of the genre - is parodic in its essence, for one of the intentions of Miguel de Cervantes was to make a parody of some popular narratives of his own time, mainly chivalry books. Obviously, his attempt became something more and more complex as far as he was progressing in the writing of both parts of the novel (1605 and 1615, respectively). However, parody is one of the richer aspects of the book, and some of the most significant features in this respect convey the use of digression together with literary - sometimes metafictional - parody. The novel, which is in the end one of the possible metamorphoses of the epic genre, collects from its first examples - *Don Quixote*, *Gargantua and Pantagruel*, the Spanish picaresque, etc. - the fruitful parodic tradition.

Linda Hutcheon has seen in the origin of the novel: 'An already existing narcissistic trend [...] as it began parodically and was handed on through eighteenth-century self-awareness to nineteenth-century self mirroring' (Hutcheon, 1984: 153). Thus, the novel carries within itself its own reflection. Postmodernist narratives, with the experiments of Jorge Luis Borges, Julio Cortázar, Italo Calvino, the French *nouveau roman*, John Barth and so on, underline the development of what Linda Hutcheon calls 'narcissistic narrative', that is, that kind of novel which is self-referential and metafictional. Digression and intertextual parody are some of the most important factors helping this narrative type to reach the shocking effects they can create in the mind of the reader.

But metafictional parody is not a feature of postmodernist narrative alone. There is an obssession for self-reflection throughout the history of fiction from the very beginning. One of the ultimate consequences of intertextuality is self-referentiality, now that a novel is always related to another, but is also related to itself. Some narratives - most postmodernist fiction - make this explicit, some do not. However, there has been parody along the history of the novel, no matter whether this parody can be applied in an intertextual or an 'intratextual' or narcissistic way.

The rich development and rapid evolution of the novel in England in the eighteenth century seems to confirm our arguments. Jonathan

Swift, Henry Fielding and Laurence Sterne are the worthy inheritors of Cervantes, following - for different reasons - the parodic pattern which structures *Don Quixote*. Moreover, Fielding bases some of his most famous novels - *Shamela*, *Tom Jones* and *Joseph Andrews* - on a parodic criticism of Samuel Richardson's *Pamela*. Horace Walpole could be located at the top of the process from a thematic perspective, for *The Castle of Otranto*, considered the first 'Gothick' novel, stands for a hyperbolic parody of contemporary realist models, fantasy being a distorted mirror facing reality.

On the other hand, there is in eighteenth-century England a powerful realist tradition in the novel, a point of departure for the bourgeois narratives of the second half of the nineteenth century. The realist Victorian novel has many more things to share with *Pamela*, Daniel Defoe's or Fanny Burney's novels than with the formerly parodic examples mentioned above. The narratives of Richardson and Defoe epitomize the role of the novel as a pre-capitalistic genre serving the reading habits of the bourgeoisie.

However, apart from the exceptions provided by 'purely realist' novels, the parodic tradition in English fiction prior to postmodernism shows several peaks which establish a cohesive, integrative and fruitful pattern, with a quantitative and qualitative use of digression together with intertextual parody. Our discussion is going to be centred upon Thomas Nashe's *The Unfortunate Traveller* (1594), Laurence Sterne's *Tristram Shandy* (1759-1768) and James Joyce's *Ulysses* (1922). The three of them are, no doubt, different works in many respects, but, on the other hand, they share interesting narrative coincidences coming from their display of digressive and parodic elements.

The Unfortunate Traveller cannot be called 'a novel', if the term means anything. But it contains many narrative features which later on would be successfully turned into basic factors in the fictional world. Nashe's book, working on medieval precedents, collects many influences, both classical and Elizabethan: historical facts (although disposed in an anachronical way), social satire, picaresque elements, travel book, anti-romance, Elizabethan pamphlet, Jest book and, above all, literary parody. Most of the genres and styles used by the classical writers and his contemporaries are represented in *The Unfortunate Traveller*, and all of them are parodied to a certain extent: artificial language, historical and epic writings, religious tracts, the Petrarchan conventions, Ciceronian rhetoric, the Italian *novella*, pastoral narratives, Elizabethan tragedy and comedy, Humanist books, travel books.

Many digressions in the three works come from the conventional motif of the journey. This subject in *The Unfortunate Traveller* (it should be noticed that the title of the book does not fulfil the expectations of the readers, the same as the titles of *Tristram Shandy* and *Ulysses*) turns itself into a pretext for Nashe to link together any argument that the narrator, a bawd called Jack Wilton, is capable of sustaining. Nashe's main concern, like that of Sterne and Joyce, is language, and many digressions are centred upon literary language. Jack Wilton, like Tristram and several characters in *Ulysses*, becomes a literary critic on many occasions. There is travelling in Volume 7 of *Tristram Shandy*, where Sterne contributes autobiographical experiences in France, and both the inner and outer aspects of the journey are implicit in *Ulysses*, where the great Homeric *epos* - ten years going to and fro in the mythical Mediterranean landscape - is overcome by the mock-heroic ramblings of Leopold Bloom and Stephen Dedalus throughout Dublin.

The journey is a structural leitmotiv in the three narratives we are commenting upon. Nashe introduces Jack Wilton as an Elizabethan Englishman who, after visiting France, Italy, The Netherlands, some parts of today's Germany, etc., reaches the conclusion that the best place for him to be in is England, and the best people are his countrymen. His position and attitudes are not those of the person who enjoys sharing new experiences abroad. Quite the contrary, his nationalistic feelings are overemphasized. The digressions on travelling through the different countries in Europe are significant enough. Here is Jack's general impression of Italy (it should not be forgotten that the narrator is an average representative of a common Elizabethan Englishman):

> Italy, the paradise of the earth and the epicure's heaven, how doth it form our young master? it makes him to kiss his hand like an ape, cringe his neck like a starveling, and play at 'hey pass repass come aloft' when he salutes a man. From thence he brings the art of atheism, the art of epicurizing, the art of whoring, the art of poisoning, the art of sodomitry. The only probable good thing they have to keep us from utterly condemning it is that it maketh a man an excellent courtier, a curious carpet knight - which is, by interpretation, a fine close lecher, a glorious

> hypocrite. It is now a privy note amongst the better sort of men when they would set a singular mark or brand on a notorious villain to say he hath been in Italy. (Nashe, 1987: 286)

Intertextuality is underlined by the fact that Nashe is reflecting here a former digression on travelling in Robert Ascham's *The Schoolmaster* (1570), filled with anti-Italian flavour.

Volume 7 of *Tristram Shandy* deals almost exclusively with the narrator's *tour de France*, and episodes like the description of Paris (Chapters 17 and 18) do not differ very much from Jack Wilton's impressions abroad. But what is explicit in Nashe is turned into masterly irony in Sterne:

> The French are certainly misunderstood:————but whether the fault is theirs, in not sufficiently explaining themselves; or speaking with that exact limitation and precision which one would expect on a point of such importance, and which moreover, is so likely to be contested by us————or whether the fault may not be altogether on our side, in not understanding their language always so critically as to know 'what they would be at'—— I shall not decide; but 'tis evident to me, when they affirm, '*That they who have seen Paris, have seen every thing,*' they must mean to speak of those who have seen it by day-light. (*TS*: 7.18.601)

The travel motif is inherent to *Ulysses*, where the intertextual link with *The Odyssey* should provide a context for the hero's journey through the perils of the Mediterranean - moreover, it is extremely ironical that Joyce uses for his 'novel' the first referent in the history of world literature and, therefore, the origin of intertextuality. However, as the 'Wandering Rocks' (or Symplegades) episode shows, the pretext has been turned into a more complex element. The journey is now a petty physical wandering through Dublin and an inner journey of the mind, a series of streams of consciousness. The effect, for anyone searching for straightforward references between Joyce and Homer's works, is at first sight one of ironical and satirical counterpoint. Homer's *epos* is reflected in *Ulysses* in a chiastic way: the more grotesque, the more universally human.

According to Harry Levin (1941), Joyce avoids the heroic, and the same can be applied to Nashe and Sterne. They prefer the satirical perspectives of the mock-heroic style, adopting hyperbole as the main rhetorical constituent. The three authors are masters of a common technique in Roman rhetoric, extremely widespread in the Renaissance and consubstantial to digression: the *amplificatio*, an ornamental expansive way of showing off. In the hands of Sterne and Joyce this technique reaches the complex mastery of perfection, Nashe being a succesful forerunner.

The use of hyperbolic satire is connected in many cases with love for obscenity and the grotesque. Nashe is very fond of describing bloodthirsty episodes, very much in the vein of the Elizabethan period, as, for example, the passion for Seneca, bear-baiting and public executions seem to prove. This cruelty reaches a sensationalist climax in episodes like that of the tortures of the Jews Zadock and Zacharie, Cutwolf's public execution or the rape of Heraclide by Esdras of Granado. The parody of Elizabethan tragedy is here manifest, and Esdras's parliament on the effects of the plague before committing the horrible abomination - he rapes the lady using her husband's dead body as a pillow - would make an impressive dramatic scene, no matter how hyperbolically grotesque the context can be:

> What plague canst thou name worse than I have had? Whether diseases, imprisonment, poverty, banishment, I have passed through them all. My own mother gave I a box of the ear to and brake her neck down a pair of stairs, because she would not go in to a gentleman when I bade her. My sister I sold to an old leno to make his best of her. Any kinswoman that I have, knew I she were not a whore, myself would make her one. Thou art a whore, thou shalt be a whore in spite of religion or precise ceremony. (Nashe, 1987: 278)

What is Elizabethan cruelty and bloodthirstiness - or the swollen explicitness of Rabelais in *Gargantua and Pantagruel* - turns into delicately humorous obscenity in Laurence Sterne. The digressions on Uncle Toby's wound provide a magnificent example, but many of the dialectic games that the narrator plays with the reader - mostly the female reader - contain puns which stress the ambiguity of sexual - sometimes obscene - meanings. No wonder that the book scandalized the 'honest ears' of a part of the reading public, much more if attention is paid to the fact that *Tristram Shandy* had been written by a minister. The game is emphasized by Parson Yorick being an *alter ego* of Sterne himself.

The writer is attempting a parody of the excesive modesty and reserve which many literary authors feigned when writing. Sterne proves that every type of language - every semantic field, if vocabulary is concerned - is worth being used in the literary work, and in proving this he is increasing the potentialities of literary language in a high percentage. The limitations of the structural devices of the novel - emphasized by the explicitness of the skeleton of techniques that Sterne puts into practice - are contraposed by the immensely creative possibilities of language.

The parodic grotesque and the obscene form an intrinsic part of *Ulysses*. Scatological and excremental episodes are climatic in the book, as for instance the end of the 'Sirens' episode, where all the sublime and popular digressions about music find the counterpoint of Bloom's flatulences:

> Tip. An unseeing stripling stood in the door. He saw not bronze. He saw not gold. Nor Ben nor Bob nor Si nor George nor tanks nor Richie nor Pat. Hee hee hee hee. He did not see.
>
> Seabloom, greaseabloom viewed last words. Softly. *When my country takes her place among.*
>
> Prrprr.
>
> Must be the bur.
>
> Fff! Oo. Rrpr.
>
> *Nations of the earth.* No-one behind. She's passed. *Then and not till then.* Tram kran kran kran. Good oppor. Coming. Krandlkrankran. I'm sure it's the burgund. Yes. One, two. *Let my epitaph be.* Kraaaaaa. *Written. I have.*
>
> Pprrpffrrppffff.
>
> *Done.* (*U*: 11.1281-1294)

The burlesque is surpassed by the grotesque in fragments like that of the narrator and the discussion on Irish nationalism, where the citizen - a representation of the Cyclops - throws Bloom a biscuitbox. This twelfth episode in the narrative, together with the fourteenth ('Oxen of the Sun'), are the richest in intertextual parody throughout the book, although the amount of parodic quotations which can be found in *Ulysses* reaches an astounding number.

Playing with words - in Wittgenstein's and Austin's sense of the term - becomes an integral part of parody, as it is an integral part of literary works in general. Nashe, Sterne and Joyce give priority to this linguistic aspect in their works, and puns and *paronomasia*, together with other more or less identical rhetorical devices, receive an adequate emphasis. One important resource in this linguistic context is the use of foreign languages with a parodic intention. Our three authors are fond of this polyglot writing: intertextuality found a gold mine in the destruction of Babel.

Nashe appeals to Latin in order to achieve new parodic perspectives. It should be taken into account that most of his readers would be familiar with at least the conscious pig Latin that the narrator puts into practice. Intertextual reference is got by means of those sentences being found in classical authors. What Nashe does is to change the context of the word or *sententia* and provide it with a parodic meaning, as in the following passage:

> There was a lord in the camp, let him be a lord of misrule if you will, for he kept a plain alehouse without welt or guard of any ivy bush, and sold cider and cheese by pint and by pound to all that came (at that very name of cider I can but sigh, there is so much of it in rhenish wine nowadays). Well, *tendit ad sidera virtus*, there's great virtue belongs (I can tell you) to a cup of cider, and very good men have sold it, and at sea it is *aqua celestis* (Nashe, 1987: 211)

The pun consists in the similar graphical configuration of cider and sidera, and thus 'virtue tends to heavens' is changed for 'virtue tends to cider'. There is also parodic paradox in the fact that cider is *aqua celestis* (late Latin for *acqua caelestis*) at sea. In short, the example of this parodic use of Latin can be found all through the book.

Other languages appear in *The Unfortunate Traveller*, as for example Italian, French or even Spanish, but they abide by the same rules described for Latin.

Sterne continues with this parodic pattern, and his knowledge of different languages (mainly Latin, French and Italian; although there are some Greek quotations, he was a poor Hellenist) is made evident by the linguistic game he proposes to the reader. There are many examples in *Tristram Shandy* of the use of Latin in the same satirical and ironical way as Nashe's, but the book is more celebrated for experiments like Slawkenbergius's tale (Volume 7), in which the Latin text is faced by a 'translation' of the fable into English, or the 'Mémoire présente à Messieurs les Docteurs de SORBONNE' (Volume 1), a 'medical-ethical-legal document', as Sterne describes it. The supposedly erudite footnotes of some of these texts initiate that common practice in postmodernism of inventing intertextual references: Jorge Luis Borges would be a good example in this respect.

Chapter 11 in Volume 6 is another clear instance of Sterne's passion for playing with the sounds and meanings of foreign languages. In this case it is the use of musical terms - mostly Italian - the ones that are compared and applied to Yorick's funeral sermon. The paragraph which follows shows also Sterne's obsession to integrate literature with the other arts (music here), a purpose related to the studies of many literary critics nowadays:

> What *Yorick* could mean by the words *lentamente*,——*tenutè*, ——*grave*,—— and sometimes *adagio*,——as applied to theological compositions, and with which he has characterized some of these sermons, I dare not venture to guess.———I am more puzzled still upon finding *a l'octava alta!* upon one; ————*Con strepito* upon the back of another;———*Scicilliana* upon a third;———*Alla capella* upon a fourth;———*Con l'arco* upon this;———*Senza l'arco* upon that.———All I know is, that they are musical terms, and have a meaning;———and as he was a musical man, I will make no doubt, but that by some quaint application of such metaphors to the compositions in hand, they impressed very distinct ideas of their several characters upon his fancy,——whatever they may do upon that of others (*TS*: 6.11.515).

More complex, but derived from these patterns, are the many digressions in which Joyce uses languages other than English - a corresponding episode to that of *Tristram Shandy* quoted above is the 'Sirens' episode, where music is the most significant subject. The parodic use of Latin has two main sources: the Catholic Church and the distorted quotations of Roman writers, as is the case in the following excerpt:

> Mr Mulligan however made court to the scholarly by an apt quotation from the classics, which as it dwelt upon his memory, seemed to him a sound and tasteful support of his contention: *Talis ac tanta depravatio hujus seculi, O quirites, ut matresfamiliarum nostrae lascivas cujuslibet semiviri libici titillationes testibus ponderosis atque excelsis erectionibus centurionum Romanorum magnopere anteponunt*, while for those of ruder wit he drove home his point by analogies of the animal kingdom more suitable to their stomach, the buck and doe of the forest glade, the farmyard drake and duck. (*U*: 14.704-712)

Futhermore, the text belongs to the 'Oxen of the Sun' episode, a 'chapter' on parodies, for it attempts to compare the development of English prose from its origins to the birth of Mrs Purefoy's baby in the Maternity hospital. At the same time, the episode reminds the reader of the parallel chapter in *Tristram Shandy* (*TS*: 1.21) where Tristram's delivery gets under way, a fact which is going to be prolonged for a considerable part of the book.

Joyce reaches the climax of word play, and many languages are subjects of his experiments: German, Irish, Italian, Spanish, Hungarian, Greek, French. The semantic projection of the quotations deserves more detailed study, but what is certain is that a great number of them pertains to the context of parodic digression. Even former stages of English, and even registers, are parodied in *Ulysses*.

To summarize, Nashe's, Sterne's and Joyce's experiments with the generic indeterminacy of the novel form and language set up a coherent pattern of intertextual reference, at the same time that they adopt parody as one of the integral constituents of the genre from its very beginning. Other coincidences among their works, mainly thematic, are left out here (the Jewish topic, the use of the sermon form, the fragmentary composition of *The Unfortunate Traveller*, *Tristram Shandy* and *Ulysses* and their use of the techniques of pastiche and collage, etc.) However, the three of them accept the limits and the freedom - although both terms seem to be opposed in an 'oxymoronical' relation - of a flexible form, and, consciously (Sterne and Joyce) or unconsciously (Nashe) provide their link for the climatic chain to be complete. What remains is postmodernism, and this is another story.

'MANY PLANES OF NARRATIVE': A COMPARATIVE PERSPECTIVE ON STERNE AND JOYCE

MICHAEL HART

Readers of James Joyce's *Ulysses* began to compare it to Laurence Sterne's *Tristram Shandy* as early as 1922 when Joyce's novel was published by Shakespeare and Company in Paris. Ezra Pound and Valery Larbaud, picking up the thread of H. G. Wells' review of *A Portrait of the Artist as a Young Man*, made the comparison.[1] So did Wyndham Lewis in *Time and Western Man*, published five years later. Joyce himself encouraged the comparison. In his memoir, 'My Friend James Joyce', Eugene Jolas recounts a conversation he had with Joyce concerning *Work in Progress* in which Joyce, detailing the theme and structure of his most mysterious creation, referred somewhat cryptically to a parallel between his own methods and Sterne's. 'Did you ever read Laurence Sterne?' Joyce asked Jolas (Jolas, 1948: 3-18).

In making this comparison many critics enlist the names of Joyce and Sterne with a third writer, most often it is Rabelais. Burton, Erasmus, Cervantes, Swift, Byron, Carlyle, and Flaubert also appear frequently in the critical literature (e.g. Lampkin, 1984 and Hartley, 1970). Works such as *The Anatomy of Melancholy*, *A Tale of a Tub*, and *Sartor Resartus* provide a kind of anti-model for the novels of

[1] H. G. Wells is the first to compare Joyce and Sterne. In his review of *Portrait*, published in the *Nation* on February 24, 1917, he wrote of Joyce's handling of the Christmas dinner scene, 'that Sterne himself could not have done it better.' Ezra Pound's review of *Ulysses*, 'James Joyce et Pécuchet,' first appeared in the *Mercure de France* in June, 1922. Valery Larbaud's essay, 'James Joyce' was published in the *Nouvelle Revue Française* in April, 1922. All three are collected in Deming, 1970.

Joyce and Sterne, a literary category Harry Levin refers to as 'the class of unclassifiable books' (Levin, 1941: 165). Placed in the same context with these unclassifiable books, *Ulysses* and *Tristram Shandy* appear quite traditionally untraditional. 'What is James Joyce's *Ulysses*?' Pound asks in 'James Joyce et Pécuchet'. And he asserts that '[N]either *Gargantua*, nor *Don Quixote*, nor Sterne's *Tristram Shandy* had furnished the archetype'. In their place he puts Flaubert's *Bouvard et Pécuchet*, a work in the paradoxical category of an 'Encyclopedia in the form of farce'.

All of these attempts at finding literary archetypes for *Ulysses* and *Tristram Shandy* have one thing in common: they invert the logic of comparison. What is similar in these two works, they seem to say, is their radical difference from the conventional notion of genre. Unconventional, unclassifiable, and incomparable, these works incorporate in their structure the whole process through which literary types are made and passed on in the tradition. This is what Shklovsky meant when he said, '*Tristram Shandy* is the most typical novel of world literature' (Shklovsky, 1965: 57). As he lays bare the devices through which language becomes literature, Sterne typifies the literary process itself.

Alastair Fowler refers to this type of novel as the ''poioumenon' or work-in-progress novel' (Fowler, 1982: 123). This type of fiction incorporates a character or a narrator who is engaged in the act of writing the novel. As a variation of the play-within-a-play motif, made famous in Shakespeare's *Hamlet*, the 'poioumenon' is typically a novel concerned with its own poetics, a work, like *Tristram Shandy*, that refers again and again to its own making as often as it does to the fictional events it is describing. 'This is vile work', Tristram tells us, referring to the process of writing:

> For which reason, from the beginning of this, you see, I have constructed the main work and the adventitious parts of it with such intersections, and have so complicated and involved the digressive and progressive movements, one wheel within another, that the whole machine, in general, has been kept a-going (*TS*: 1.22.81-82)

As this passage illustrates, the machine is a metaphor for the narrative itself, a self-propelled mechanism that turns the reader around and around in its wheels within wheels. '————Endless is the Search of Truth!' (*TS*: 2.3.103).

From this perspective the comparison of *Tristram Shandy* to Rabelais and Cervantes makes sense. In the 'Author's Prologue' to *Gargantua* Rabelais draws an analogy between the meaning of his book and Plato's description of Socrates and the Sileni. The Sileni were painted boxes that had images of 'harpies, satyrs...and other such counterfeit pictures' painted on the outside, exciting those who saw them to laughter (Rabelais, 1927: xxxiii-xxxv). Inside were preserved rich drugs, jewels, and other priceless objects. To the author of *Gargantua* this image is an apt metaphor for the life of the Greek philosopher, Socrates, whose ugly appearance hid the jewel of his inner wisdom and knowledge. And both images taken together, the Sileni and the portrait of Socrates, can be construed as an analogy figuring the process of reading Rabelais' book. As the painted exterior of the Sileni is to Socrates' physical appearance, so is the comic perspective of *Gargantua*'s narrative to the surface meaning of the work. The truth contained within this comic perspective is hidden, like the jewels in the Sileni and Socrates' inner knowledge, within. In all three cases appearances can deceive and distract from the true reality. The narrative is doubled. Not in an allegorical sense, where one level of meaning points to another as the key to the hermeneutic code, but in the sense of creating an internal poetic structure that contains the surface level of meaning within it.

Cervantes takes the process one step further. As in *Gargantua*, the narrative of the adventures of *Don Quixote* is framed by the author's prologue. Employing the topos of the book-as-child, Cervantes develops the autobiographical nature of his fiction through the metaphor of procreation: the author, like a natural father, stamps his image on his creation. This is the 'law of nature' that 'like begets like' (Cervantes, 1981: 11). And yet, as we enter the hall of mirrors of the narrative itself, the relation of the author to his brainchild becomes bewilderingly complex.

The real author of the true history of the adventures of Don Quixote is, the narrator reveals to us, Cid Hamete Benengeli. However, the original manuscript, written in Arabic, has been translated by a third, nameless writer, whose notes, written on the margins of Benengeli's 'great history', are quoted at the beginning of ,

Part 2, Chapter 24. In those marginal glosses of Benengeli's text, the translator confesses his doubts concerning the truth of the narrative of Don Quixote's adventures, particularly the story of Don Quixote's vision in the Cave of Montesinos.

On one level the translator's scepticism concerning this incident makes perfect sense. The visionary nature of Don Quixote's experience in the Cave of Montesinos places it in a different category from the other adventures narrated in the book. On the other hand the distinction is based on a totally false premise. How can we distinguish between fictional and historical events when all the events narrated are fictional?

The false dichotomy, between romance and realism, upon which the narrative is based, is framed by a series of narrators whose relation to the events described is mediated by the author. The narrative of *Don Quixote*, addressed to the 'Idling reader', is the 'child of my brain', the author tells us in the 'Prologue'. As a fictional creation it cannot be true in the sense of a history. And yet the internalized poetics of the novel, a poetics based on simultaneous assertion of the narrative's truth and its falsehood, continually draws attention to the fact that the author is not a creator but a mediator of the truth as it is told through Cid Hamete Benengeli's adventures of Don Quixote.

Paradoxically, it is through the device of laying bare the fictional nature of the different planes of narrative running through the text that Cervantes is able to communicate the sad truth in the story: Don Quixote, the Knight of the Sorrowful Countenance, is ennobled by his heroic disregard of simplistic descriptions of reality. His story includes the layers of narrative doubling that create the ironic perspective of the novel and it is through this ironic perspective that we learn to understand the knight's curious fate.

A similar perspective underlies the narratives of *Tristram Shandy* and *Ulysses*. In Sterne's novel the narrator, who is also the author of the book, is Tristram Shandy. As a persona of the author he constantly breaks into apostrophe concerning the nature of writing:

> O ye POWERS! (for powers ye are, and great ones too)——which enable mortal man to tell a story worth the hearing,——that kindly shew him, where he is to begin it,——and where he is to end it,——what he is to put into it,——and what he is to leave out,——how much of it he is to

> cast into shade,——and whereabouts he is to throw his light!———Ye, who preside over this vast empire of biographical freebooters, and see how many scrapes and plunges your subjects hourly fall into;——will you do one thing? (*TS*: 3.23.244-45)

The 'one thing' Tristram requests is a 'guide-post', a map to show the author what direction to take when the narrative diverges at key points, such as when 'three several roads meet in one point'.

Tristram's metaphor, writing-as-journey, is central to the narrative structure of the novel. From the opening lines, 'I wish either my father or my mother,' right up to the ending, 'A COCK and a BULL, said Yorick --- And one of the best of its kind, I ever heard', the narrative is propelled forward by the force of Tristram's quest for self-understanding. Through the story of his conception, birth, education, and misfortunes Tristram writes his autobiography, the history of his 'Life and Opinions'. However, this 'history' includes the consciousness of the narrator/author within it. The journey toward self-identity is aligned with the act of writing. This is one of the qualities that makes *Tristram Shandy* appear so modern.

Max Byrd discusses this aspect of Sterne's novel in his book, *Tristram Shandy*. For Byrd the central question in the novel is the nature of subjectivity, or self-consciousness. How can a writer represent the fluid, multivalent flow of consciousness in the form of a narrative? This question, of course, recalls the work of Joyce, Proust, Woolf, and other modernist writers. Sterne anticipates the concerns of phenomenology, psychology, and twentieth-century art in general in this way. It also joins the theme of autobiography to the question of identity from the perspective of writing and self-creation. 'Scribo, ergo sum', Byrd writes, 'To be self-conscious therefore means to produce an image of the self, to contemplate an identity: "I think of *me*"' (Byrd, 1985: 55).

However, the act of self-creation through writing is never represented in *Tristram Shandy* as an act of pure self-reflection. Tristram's quest for self-identity, although clearly linked to the theme of writing, is not so much a question of self-representation as it is a question of the narrative projection of his life into the world around him. For this reason the problematic of narrative in *Tristram Shandy* places it in a tradition of self-conscious novels such as *Don Quixote* and *Ulysses* (Stonehill, 1988). The story of Tristram's life and opinions keeps dovetailing into the narratives of Walter Shandy, Uncle Toby, and Parson Yorick. It is in the dramatic and psychological circumstances of his conception, birth, education, and misfortunes that Tristram seeks self-knowledge, not in the interior circles of introspection. Like the young Stephen Dedalus in *Ulysses*, Tristram must encounter the reality of experience. The problem is that the world keeps receding behind an infinite regress of stories.

For Tristram, the best model he can find for the ebb and flow of stories woven around his life and opinions is in the art of conversation. In Chapter 11, Volume 1, he tells us:

> Writing, when properly managed, (as you may be sure I think mine is) is but a different name for conversation: As no one, who knows what he is about in good company, would venture to talk all;——so no author, who understands the just boundaries of decorum and good breeding, would presume to think all: The truest respect which you can pay to the reader's understanding, is to halve this matter amicably, and leave him to something to imagine, in his turn, as well as yourself. (*TS*: 2.11.125)

In both writing and conversation the whole story is never told. The writer, like the good conversationalist, 'halve[s] this matter' with the reader. This is not all. The writer also benefits from this process. By leaving 'something to imagine' the writer is led through the labyrinth of meaning without clear and distinct knowledge of what paths will take him back to his point of origin. Writing, like reading, implies an element of indeterminacy, a gap between sign and referent, to allow the free play of imagination.

As Peter Conrad points out, in *Shandyism, The Character of Romantic Irony*, this form of indeterminacy parallels the figure of romantic irony as it was developed by the German Romantics. In Conrad's analysis, romantic irony is characterized by its curious doubling effect. The 'ironic romantic intelligence' moves along a 'double plot' in which opposites are united. Great and small, tragic and comic, are united in an oscillating perspective that keeps the reader moving from one level of meaning to another. This is figured in Tristram's description of writing as a process of halving the meaning between the writer and the reader. Neither perspective, the author's or the reader's, renders the whole meaning. An ironic understanding requires both to be held in the mind simultaneously. 'Irony reconstitutes the double plot inside the paradoxical romantic mind', Conrad writes (1978: 23). The play-within-a-play that results from this paradoxical mind transforms the reader into the author, just as Tristram becomes the writer as reader.

Sterne uses this doubling effect as a device for creating unique characters. Tristram is both a participant and an observer, a writer and a reader, in his own life and opinions. He is also a palimpsest of other identities, some of whom live in Shandy Hall and others who have a more literary ancestry. As Tristram projects himself into the world around him, his identity is woven into the stories of others. Once again, the quest for identity is displaced by the pursuit of lines of narrative.

However, in Sterne the construction of narrative meaning does not originate in an oscillating movement between extremes, as it does in the figure of romantic irony. Rather, Sterne creates unique characters by playing with the multiple identities at the heart of self-identity. In the process of reading the stories of Parson Yorick and Uncle Toby we are prodded into contemplating the fate of other characters, such as Hamlet and Don Quixote, whom they resemble.

For example, in the first volume of *Tristram Shandy*, in the midst of a series of digressions on the subject of midwives, Tristram introduces us to the character of Parson Yorick. Even before the narrator identifies this character with King Hamlet's jester in act five of Shakespeare's *Hamlet*, the narrative of Parson Yorick's life is linked to the theme of fatality in the following passage:

> But there is a fatality attends the actions of some men: Order them as they will, they pass thro' a certain medium which so twists and refracts them from their true directions————that, with all the titles to praise which a rectitude of heart can give, the doers of them are nevertheless forced to live and die without it. (*TS*: 1.10.24)

In the context of the novel, this passage seems to refer to the 'moral of my story', that is, the story of Parson Yorick told in Chapter 11. And yet this could pass for a description of Hamlet, whose sense of fatality in act five of Shakespeare's tragedy, 'There is special providence in the fall of a sparrow', is echoed here. It could also refer to Don Quixote, 'The peerless knight of La Mancha', alluded to several times in this chapter. Indeed, the life of Parson Yorick is compared to the life of Cervantes' hero several times by

Tristram while Yorick's last words are uttered in a '*cervantick* tone' (*TS*: 1.12.34). Moreover, if we follow the metaphorical logic of substitution and literary metempsychosis, we have to admit that Parson Yorick, along with his Hamlet-like fatality and Quixotic refinements, also represents Tristram and Sterne himself (Lanham, 1973).

This palimpsest of characters overwritten in Sterne's portrait of Parson Yorick becomes linked to the theme of identity through a series of literary allusions to *Hamlet*. The first appears toward the end of Chapter 11. Yorick is described as a man 'unhackneyed and unpractised in the world':

> In a word, tho' he never sought, yet, at the same time, as he seldom shun'd occasions of saying what came uppermost, and without much ceremony; ----he had but too many temptations in life, of scattering his wit and his humour,——his gibes and his jests about him.----They were not lost for want of gathering. (*TS*: 1.11.29)

Tristram's allusion to Yorick's 'gibes and jests' recalls the graveyard scene in *Hamlet* in act five. We are invited by Sterne to compare Parson Yorick with the Yorick of Hamlet's imagination. This comparison is strengthened by the use of the phrase, 'Alas, poor YORICK!' as inscription, epitaph, and elegy for the grave of Parson Yorick at the end of Chapter 12.

In simple terms, Hamlet's Yorick, whose absence gives way to Hamlet's meditation on death, mortality, and the transience of life in Shakespeare's play, relives in Tristram's imagination as the quixotic parson. In this sense, Tristram plays the role of Hamlet, contemplating the mystery of fate through the narrative of Parson Yorick's life. However, Parson Yorick also plays at being Hamlet, meditating on a death's head, as the following passage illustrates:

> At different times he would give fifty humourous and opposite reasons for riding a meek-spirited jade of a broken-winded horse, preferably to one of mettle;——for on such a one he could sit mechanically, and meditate as delightfully *de vanitate mundi et fugâ saeculi*, as with the advantage of a death's head before him (*TS*: 1.10.20)

These literary parallels to *Hamlet*, although tantalizing, cannot be sustained. For, in the context of Sterne's novel, Parson Yorick is a figure closer to Cervantes' Knight of the Sorrowful Countenance than he is to the black prince or the jester in the Danish court. Yorick's death (of a broken heart according to Eugenius) and tragic fate is a tale of 'CRUELTY and COWARDICE, twin ruffians, hired and set on by MALICE in the dark' by Tristram's account. His foolishness is blindness to the flaws in human nature as John Stedmond (1959) has noted. These all strengthen the parallel with Cervantes' hero and undermine the allusions to *Hamlet*.

Ironically, Sterne himself calls attention to the arbitrary nature of the literary parallel he has gone to pains to establish with the black pages that close Chapter 12. The inky depths of the page are, quite literally, a sign of the grave, a sober reminder of Yorick's untimely end. And yet, as we ponder the mystery of death in its blackness, our attention is diverted to the surface of the text. The page becomes a black page. Just as Yorick is no more the jester in Hamlet's Elsinore, so the black page is not his grave. The text calls attention to itself as surface; the depths of meaning hidden behind it are illusory.

This play between surface and depth enables Sterne to manipulate the levels of narrative meaning as he creates a palimpsest of identities for the character of Yorick. Yorick is Hamlet, Don Quixote, and a persona for Sterne himself as well as a character in the comedy of Tristram's life. The roles that he plays represent phases in Tristram's quest for self-identity. As he projects himself into the world of Shandy Hall, Tristram finds images of multiple selves in the lives of those around him. As Parson Yorick plays at Don Quixote and Hamlet, Tristram finds himself contemplating the death of Hamlet's Yorick through the narrative of the quixotic parson's life. A double perspective is the result of these layers of characterization.

All of these elements (*Hamlet*, the quest for identity, and the presentation of character as palimpsest) go into Sterne's most complex use of narrative doubling in *A Sentimental Journey*.[2] In this novel the main protagonist and first person narrator is Sterne's alter ego, Mr. Yorick. As we shall see, this Mr. Yorick is another incarnation of Shakespeare's jester.

Toward the end of the novel Yorick's travels take him to Versailles to meet Le Count de B****, a lover of English books. A

[2] I am indebted to Tom Keymer for bringing this aspect of *A Sentimental Journey* to my attention.

bookseller at the Quai de Conti told Yorick about the Count's love of English literature and so he decides to visit him and appeal to him for help in obtaining a passport.

The most immediate difficulty Yorick encounters upon arriving at the count's estate concerns his identity. Like Tristram Shandy, Yorick finds it easier to tell the stories of other people's lives than to render an account of his own identity, 'There is not a more perplexing affair in life to me, than to set about telling anyone who I am——for there is scarce any body I cannot give a better account of than of myself' (*ASJ*: 221). While he ponders this problem, he discovers a copy of Shakespeare's works lying open on a table. He muses, 'for Shakespeare lying upon the table, and recollecting I was in his books' takes up the book and finds the gravedigger's scene in act five of *Hamlet,* and points to the name 'Yorick' saying to the Count, '*Me, Voici!*'

The Count immediately confuses the two Yoricks, Shakespeare's and Sterne's, an act attributed by Yorick to the French capacity to 'conceive better than they combine'. And, in a passage that seems to refer to Sterne himself, Yorick says, 'I wonder at nothing in this world, and the less at this; inasmuch as one of the first of our own church, for whose candour and paternal sentiments I have the highest veneration, fell into the same mistake in the very same case' (*ASJ*: 222). If this is true, and Yorick is referring to *Tristram Shandy*, then the levels of narrative attain a kind of fictional intertextuality.

Let's try to analyze these planes of meaning as they cut across the boundaries of autobiography, fiction, and parody. First, there is the narrative of events in the journeys of Yorick through France, the record of his sentimental education. As we know from Cash's biography, this is not a purely fictional account. It contains strong elements of autobiography. And, as many of Sterne's readers knew, the character of Mr. Yorick was a pseudonym of the author. This use of a comic persona caused some scandal when Sterne published his sermons under the name of Yorick. The first blurring of categories occurs in the mixing of fiction and autobiography.

Next, in addition to these autobiographical elements, there is the question of parody. Ian Jack notes, in his introduction to the Oxford edition of *A Sentimental Journey*, that the novel is a parody of other travel books of the time, including the *Nouveau Voyage de France* by

Piganiol de la Force and Smollett (Jack, 1984: ix-xx). At the same time, although Sterne took two trips to the continent, one in 1762-4 and the second in 1765-6, the actual biographical details are very fuzzy. Several incidents, such as the one with the dead ass and the fille de chambre episode, are unlikely to have a basis in fact. Sterne's use of parody elevates the autobiographical elements to the fictional level of farce.

With these contexts in mind, we can return to the problem of identity. From this perspective we have to ask, what is the importance of the scene at the Count de B****'s? Why does Sterne confuse the two Yoricks in the mind of the count? On one level the scene is another trope of self-begetting, a metaphor of the book's search for origins. Yorick, pointing to his name in the fifth scene of *Hamlet*, is Sterne drawing our attention to the fictional status of the narrator. The reader, aware of this deliberate confusion, attains an ironic distance from the count's befuddled state of mind. This is contrasted with Yorick's clear-minded knowledge of the difference between the living character he is and the dead one in Shakespeare's play. However, Yorick's knowledge of the truth is founded on an illusion: a blurring of the difference between fiction and reality. Sterne's Yorick, unless we identify him with the author (which is precisely what this passage calls attention to), is also a fiction. For this reason the argument he presents to the Count, that 'a period of seven or eight hundred years' separates the two Yoricks, is irrelevant - neither have reality outside their textual one.

In other words, the text calls attention to itself as a fiction, a made-up story. It is clear that this self-consciousness is also a source of irony and humour. The fact that the count is a great lover of English books (allowing for his ignorance of the historical status of Shakespeare's plays) makes it even funnier. ''Twas all one' he answers Yorick when he tries to debunk his illusion. And in the next section Sterne complicates the levels of narrative even further when he has Yorick read *Much Ado About Nothing*. Now we have one of Shakespeare's characters reading his text much in the way Sterne as Yorick is inscribed reading his own.

As this comedy of errors develops the mysterious departure of the count (Yorick muses on 'Mysteries which must explain themselves' while he leaves) is accounted for when he returns with a passport for

Yorick. It become clear, from the Count's comment, 'Had it been for any one but the king's jester [...] I could not have got it these two hours' (*ASJ*: 227), that he attained a passport for Shakespeare's Yorick and not Sterne's!

The episode ends when the count foils Yorick's attempts to clear up the confusion. Yorick tells him, 'I am not the king's jester'. The count replies, 'But you are Yorick? - Yes. - *Et vous plaisantez?*' To which Yorick concedes with the exception that his jests are always 'entirely at my own expence'. Yorick's self-deprecating stab leads into a sort of somber joke. He tells the count that he cannot jest at court because there is nothing to jest upon. The people are patriots and the ladies are chaste. To which the count answers, '*Voila un persiflage!*' (*ASJ*: 227).

As he dismisses Yorick's explanation, the Count's response crosses the barriers of translation. 'Un persiflage', an ill-natured banter, makes sense in French and in English. However, his response recrosses the boundaries of a multi-lingual pun when we consider the object of this epithet. Is he referring to the court or to Yorick's attempt to wriggle out of the dilemma of being mistaken for a character in a Shakespearean tragedy? Either way we take it, the exclamation, '*Voila un persiflage!*' makes sense. Here the narrative doubles not only the identities of the character of Mr. Yorick. It presents the reader with a real conflict of interpretation.

In many ways the narrative doubling and the problem of identity as it is represented in Sterne's novels is also present in *Ulysses*. The identities of Stephen Dedalus and Leopold Bloom, the main protagonists in the novel, correspond to other literary prototypes from Homer, Goethe, and Shakespeare much in the way that *Tristram Shandy* echoes *Gargantua*, *Don Quixote* and *Hamlet* (cf. particularly Brown, 1992: 75-81). Both Sterne and Joyce construct levels of narrative meaning through the use of allusion and parody.

Indeed, *Ulysses* 'contains' Sterne directly as the parody of *A Sentimental Journey* in the 'Oxen of the Sun' episode indicates. As an imitation of Sterne's style, it ranks quite low in Joyce's repertoire; the echoes of *A Sentimental Journey* are, at best, tenuous. And yet Joyce seems less intent on parodying Sterne's style as he does in giving us a sense of what he sees as Sterne's method of narrative development.

For this reason we can read this parody as Joyce's most sustained criticism of Sterne.

The narrator of this passage interrupts 'the narrative at a salient point' while he himself admits 'I wander from the point' (*U*: 14.770). The point, of course, remains elusive. As these textual markers indicate, Joyce is quite aware of Sterne's reputation for repetitive digression. While references to 'an equivalent but contrary balance' and 'an artless disorder' imply that Joyce understood the basic thrust of Sterne's art to be Coleridgean.[3]

The last three lines of the parody are the most consciously Sternean, in my opinion:

> The first, said she (and here my pretty philosopher, as I handed her to her tilbury, to fix my attention, gently tipped with her tongue the outer chamber of my ear), the first is a bath - But at this point a bell tinkling in the hall cut short a discourse which promised so bravely for the enrichment of our store of knowledge. (*U*: 14.794-98)

We don't have to recount the lengthy discussion of the medical students in the National Maternity Hospital on Holles Street in Dublin to appreciate the thrust of this parody. In this passage Joyce captures the conversational tone of much of Sterne's writing. He also points to the way Sterne's narrative follows a path of association, parodied nicely by the tinkling of the bell, which distracts the narrator from delivering his learned discourse.

We can infer from this passage that Joyce sensed the ironic structure of Sterne's fiction. Knowledge is promised but withheld as the threads of narrative are woven in and out of the story. This applies equally, if not more accurately, to *Tristram Shandy* as well as to *A Sentimental Journey*. Joyce's parody of this aspect of Sterne's fiction indicates that he judged Sterne's achievement by his ability to construct layers of narrative meaning. Stories are interrupted, narrators wander from the point because knowledge, at least of a narrative type, is endlessly deferred. The thrust of the narrative toward a unitary meaning is displaced by the aesthetic organization of

[3] Coleridge defined Sterne's humour in a famous passage: 'Hence in humour the little is made great, and the great little, in order to destroy both, because all is equal in contrast with the infinite' (Anderson, 1980: 485).

narrative into multiple layers or perspectives. We never actually reach the conclusion without an element of ambiguity and uncertainty. *Tristram Shandy* ends with the anecdote of the cock and bull; *Ulysses* in Molly Bloom's affirmative but ambiguous 'Yes!' Both narratives point back to themselves as aesthetic structures that defy critical reduction. They already contain within themselves a critique of their own poetics.

The structure of this internalized critique is exemplified in the notion of parody itself. As Linda Hutcheon has demonstrated in *A Theory of Parody*, the whole notion of multi-levels of meaning typical of parody involves a critical distance of one text from another (Hutcheon, 1985: 30-49). This distance, which is also a difference, sets into play the various narrative layers we have found so characteristic of novels in the tradition of *Tristram Shandy*.

In *Ulysses* these qualities - irony, parody, and narrative layering - appear anatomized in Joyce's encyclopedic farce. The Linati and Gorman-Gilbert Schemas, published in Ellmann's study *Ulysses on the Liffey*, have made Joyce's obsession with levels of meaning, literary parallels, and symbolic structure infamous. If we combine the schemas discussed by Ellmann with the annotations in Gifford's *Ulysses Annotated* and the Homeric and Shakespearean correspondences echoed in the text, we can get a sense of how Shandean Joyce's novel appears.

From this perspective we can say that *Ulysses* fits squarely in the anti-tradition that we have sketched here. *Gargantua*, *Tristram Shandy*, and *Ulysses* are 'unclassifiable' for the precise reason that they incorporate within their narrative structures the whole logical apparatus of classification, specifically as it operates on the level of narrative. To the extent that they follow a single line of narrative movement, novels represent a rational, empirical 'picture' of reality. When they begin to internalize this single vision, they become parodies of such simple reductions of reality.

Returning to the conversation between Jolas and Joyce alluded to earlier, perhaps we are now in a better position to understand Joyce's reference to Sterne. Here is the complete passage:

> 'There is really no coincidence in this book,' he said during one of our walks. 'I might easily have written this story in the traditional manner....Every novelist knows the recipe....It is not very difficult to

> follow a simple, chronological scheme which the critics will understand....But I, after all, am trying to tell the story of this Chapelizod family in a new way....Time and the river and the mountain are the real heroes of my book....Yet the elements are exactly what every novelist might use: man and woman, birth, childhood, night, sleep, marriage, prayer, death....There is nothing paradoxical about this....Only I am trying to build many planes of narrative with a single esthetic purpose....Did you ever read Laurence Sterne? (Jolas, 1948: 11-12)

Although Joyce is referring to the writing of *Finnegans Wake* in this conversation with Jolas, I believe it applies equally to *Ulysses*, especially the last part where he talks about 'many planes of narrative with a single esthetic purpose'. *Ulysses* also defies traditional methods of storytelling by its use of allusion, quotation, parody, and a variety of narrative techniques. The 'many planes of narrative' Joyce refers to can be found in the 'Sirens', 'Cyclops', 'Oxen of the Sun', and 'Circe' episodes of *Ulysses*.

However, we don't have to restrict the comparison between Joyce and Sterne to *Ulysses*. In *Finnegans Wake* Joyce took the anti-tradition of the self-conscious novel to Shandean extremes.[4] The important point is that Joyce's comments illuminate the whole question of finding a comparative perspective for discussing novels such as *Tristram Shandy* and *Ulysses*. In Joyce's description of 'many planes of narrative with a single esthetic purpose' we have an apt phrase for the kinds of fictional works we have been discussing in this essay. In *Gargantua*, *Don Quixote*, *Tristram Shandy* and *Ulysses* we find narratives that double the process of storytelling to include critical self-reflection on the act of fiction-making.

This, as we have seen, is the fundamental structure of parody, but it also reflects the unity-in-multeity characteristic of romantic irony. We can find it in Diderot's *Jacques le fataliste et son maître* and in Novalis' *Heinrich von Ofterdingen*. It is anticipated in the play-within-the-play in Shakespeare's *Hamlet*. And, despite the attempts on the

[4] I am grateful to Pieter Bekker for pointing out the importance of *Finnegans Wake* for the comparison between Sterne and Joyce. There is no full-length study of Joyce's use of Sterne in the *Wake*. James A. Atherton, 1959, documents some of Joyce's allusions to Sterne but I suspect there are many more than he discusses. Frank Budgen (1989) on Joyce's interest is illuminating on this literary relationship.

part of some critics to dismiss the similarities of literary structure that characterize this tradition and point in the direction of postmodernist fiction, the fact remains that these types of novels, so obviously different in form and structure from realistic novels of the Zola variety, point to a tradition of self-conscious fiction that goes back to the Renaissance.

It is the task of historical reflection and of cultural criticism to investigate the origins of such a pattern in literary history. However, the recontextualization of literature, so necessary for a concrete understanding of individual texts, should not blind us to the real affinities between writers that cross the centuries dividing them (see Warner, 1993). Such an affinity exists, I believe, between Sterne and Joyce. The anti-tradition of unclassifiable books is an intrinsic part of our literary heritage. Perhaps it reflects our self-conscious age. Nevertheless, as the earliest readers of *Ulysses* noticed first, one of the books that instantly springs to mind when we cast about for comparisons for Joyce's novel is Laurence Sterne's masterpiece, *Tristram Shandy*.

TOTALIZED (AUTO-)BIOGRAPHY AS FRAGMENTED INTERTEXTUALITY SHAKESPEARE - STERNE - JOYCE

JÖRG W. RADEMACHER

'The highest, as the lowest, form of criticism is
a mode of autobiography' (Oscar Wilde)

In this paper I want to explore Shakespeare, Sterne, and Joyce in terms both of Johann Wolfgang Goethe and of the critical faculties which they display in their works especially in their fondness for fictional (auto)biography. In his fiction as well as his autobiography *Dichtung und Wahrheit* and other similar confessions, Goethe presented full accounts of his spiritual and intellectual lives, his own image, so to speak. Shakespeare, Sterne, and Joyce preferred to insert fragments of their respective lives into what are generally considered to be fictional totalities, such as *Hamlet*, *The Life and Opinions of Tristram Shandy*, *Gentleman*, and *Ulysses*. They 'dress [their textual images] in borrow-ed robes' (*Macbeth*: I.iii.107-8). In this way, by means of a disguise, Shakespeare, Sterne, and Joyce inscribe real and fictional fragments into what are, as Wolfgang Iser (1991: 19-23) might argue, basically imaginary literary worlds.

While Shakespeare amply exploited source material, both historical and literary, our knowledge of his biography is scanty, but it is generally assumed that he introduced material from his personal life into his works, or, as A. C. Bradley (1981: 226-8) puts it, that he re-wrote his life in/as literature. Shakespeare in turn provided Goethe with a literary source, which he used for example in setting off Wilhelm Meister, one of his fictional alter egos, against Shakespeare's

Hamlet. The impulse behind *Wilhelm Meister* is critical rather than creative, selective rather than inventive. Joyce, too, conscious that critical and creative writing depends upon good authority, refers to Goethe's novel at the beginning of the 'Scylla and Charybdis' episode when 'the quaker librarian' describes it as a novel where '[a] great poet [writes] on a great brother poet' (*U*: 9.1-4). Sterne gives us Yorick, and even if we allow for Sterne's proverbial oddity, it is curious, but perhaps appropriate, that he should choose a character who occupies a small part in the gravedigger's scene (V.i.168-191). For it ties in neatly with Sterne's mode of associative and unreliable narration that not much is known about the 'King's jester' (V.i.176) in *Hamlet* and that Sterne was thus free to invent Yorick's life and opinions.

In assuming a configuration in *Tristram Shandy* similar to that in *Hamlet*, by a process of a 'retrospective kind of arrangement' (*U*: 16:1401) I place Tristram in Prince Hamlet's position and Parson Yorick in the position of Yorick, the jester. Yet apart from the identical name - 'what's in a name' (*U*: 9.986) - how differently have their lives and opinions been treated! There is no tragic hero in Shakespeare who speaks more and achieves less than Hamlet. And Yorick, who died when Hamlet was just seven years old, is remembered by Hamlet, the man, as the person to have stirred his fancy: 'and now, how abhorred my imagination is!' (V.i.182-3)

Conversely, Tristram is a mere five-year-old when Sterne stops or finishes writing *Tristram Shandy*, and as a result the reader learns little of Tristram's own life and opinions. On the other hand, our knowledge of Yorick's life and opinions and the part he occupied in Tristram's imagination are considerable. Sterne's procedure can now be described by saying that he extracts a minute detail from *Hamlet*, reverses the relationship between the two figures, inflates the one and deflates the other and finally tells a wholly new story. The reversal of the configuration is more radical: Hamlet's failure to act and deferring his revenge also imply that he is wary of attributing a real-life meaning to words. He hesitates and loses himself in words. Nonetheless, *The Tragedy of Hamlet, Prince of Denmark* proceeds as if there was something inevitable about the path of history or the course of (Aristotelian) drama. In a curious way, Hamlet tragically victimizes himself and others, but his personal failure is compensated for by the eventual success of history or by the satisfaction of watching the play yield up its fear and pity.

Tristram, however, tries to tell his tale (which he paradoxically likens to a machine with organic characteristics) in an equally 'digressive' and 'progressive' (*TS*: 1.22.81) manner. But, as Rainer Warning (1965: 49) suggests, while Hamlet fails as an actor to articulate a public history, Tristram, in looking for simultaneity, fails as an historian in his wish to represent a private world. Thus, Yorick's story as told by Tristram, which is also one of failure, becomes prominent for its very oddity and inconclusiveness, while the story of a novel as a whole, that is, a fictional totality (Aristotle's 'complete thing' with 'a beginning, a middle, and an end'), is in turn obscured.

While Yorick in Shakespeare occupies a marginal position as the court's jester, Parson Yorick stands in the very centre of *Tristram Shandy*. One might say that from Shakespeare to Sterne margin and centre have exchanged places inasmuch as historical and hobbyhorsical narrative has become either an impossible or a fully acceptable way of telling a story. In one respect, however, both Yoricks are similar to each other: neither of them is a physical presence when their stories are being told. In *Hamlet*, Yorick's skull is a physical reminder, there to evoke Prince Hamlet's memories. In *Tristram Shandy*, however, Yorick is a character taken from the treasure-house of memory. He is the result of a highly imaginative narrative exercise in mnemotechnic based upon the stories young Tristram listened to in his youth. Hamlet is troubled by the past because he cannot suppress feelings of guilt towards his father and mother. Neither can Stephen Dedalus in *A Portrait* and *Ulysses*. Whereas Hamlet and Stephen are fictional creations who fail to conceal their problems, Tristram in his own imaginary universe almost succeeds in presenting the oddity of humours as the alternative to life itself. As mixed modes of mainstream and subversive representations, *Hamlet*, *Tristram Shandy*, and *Ulysses* articulate aspects of their author's own images without becoming autobiographies. They are works of art because in them Shakespeare, Sterne, and Joyce expressly refuse to confess their own lives in order to be able to deal exclusively with themselves.[1]

[1] For a psychoanalytic approach to Joyce, cf. Loll (1992) and my review 'Who's Afraid of James Joyce's True Self' in *James Joyce Broadsheet* (February 1995).

But if *Hamlet* constitutes an (auto)biographical play, it has to be acknowledged that Shakespeare tells a story the basic facts of which do not coincide with his personal experience. Thus *Hamlet* from our belated point of view must be seen as a work whose supposedly (auto)biographical stance depends upon intertextual fragments. Or else it is a highly wrought version of a lost (auto)biographical sketch. To support any of these hypotheses, Shakespeare cannot be invoked as a witness. As Shakespeare's reader, Sterne too is reticent since he is primarily interested in re-creating Yorick. However, Sterne realized the narrative potential hidden in Shakespeare's Yorick because he had the critical insight to see such a potential before he obeyed his own creative impulse. In doing so, Sterne not only inscribes his narrative in a series of other narratives which are purportedly based upon (auto)biographical totalities, but he has also safely veiled his own (auto)biographical totalities by wearing a mask composed of intertextual fragments.

Shakespeare, Sterne, and Joyce - unlike Goethe - are not renowned for their work as literary critics. Yet they must be regarded as masters of revision who saw writing as a continuous process which, in the sense of Hans Walter Gabler's 'continuous manuscript text', can only be abandoned but never be finished.[2] In the course of manifold revisions of a given text the critical faculties come to the fore. Indeed, the history of a text 'digresses' and 'progresses' and will never be one unified whole. Having digressed from my topic in one direction I have progressed in another since I am now ready to turn to Joyce's *Ulysses*. Like its precursors, *Ulysses* forms part of the author's own image. In this, Joyce is utterly unlike Giacomo Casanova, Thomas de Quincey, Oscar Wilde or in recent times the East German dramatist Heiner Müller.[3] All these present their private lives in public even though Casanova published only a single novella in his lifetime in which he describes a duel as the turning-point of his life. While this narrative is in his native Italian, his monumental autobiography is written in

[2] Loll (1992: 106) maintains that Joyce simply collapsed after having finished *Ulysses* or parts of *Finnegans Wake* because he dreaded to face himself and his own personal involvement with life again.

[3] In the afterword 'Erinnerung an einen Staat' ('Memories of a State'), Müller (1992: 367) states that although he could revise he could not turn into literature the text of his autobiography.

French, that is, a tongue in disguise. It was published posthumously in 1798.[4] He obviously could not bear his life to be publicised. Yet he wanted it to be known. Therefore Casanova, like Joyce in *A Portrait* or Sterne in *The Journal to Eliza*, which he writes 'under the fictitious Names of Yorick & Draper' (*S-Letters*: 322), explicitly denies autobiography in order to write or revise a hidden or secret one all the time. Stephen Dedalus makes this point in 'Scylla and Charybdis' about Shakespeare and, more recently, Breyten Breytenbàch (1985: 149) says it about himself in *A Season in Paradise*. Many of these writers are exiles who live in a symbiosis with their textual image(s), and their imaginative writings often reveal fragments of (auto)biography which they so diligently strive to conceal.

In order to make his own commitment to Prince Hamlet appear as unobtrusive as possible, Joyce, unlike Sterne, decides to omit a character bearing a Shakespearean name. Nor does Stephen Dedalus refer to himself as Hamlet. Joyce, however, prefers to attribute such identifications by nickname to 'Buck' Mulligan or Haines. Reading David Pierce's (1992: 139) comments on 'Telemachus' reminded me that Stephen is both Hamlet and Yorick since Stephen has to identify with the role of a 'jester at the court of his master' (*U*: 2.43-4), that is, with someone like Yorick, before he can reject that role. And in 'Scylla and Charybdis' Stephen outlines his literary theory in which he states that Shakespeare:

> returns after a life of absence to that spot of earth where he was born, where he has always been, man and boy, a silent witness and there, his journey of life ended, he plants his mulberrytree in the earth. Then dies. The motion is ended. Gravediggers bury Hamlet *père* and Hamlet *fils*. (*U*: 9.1030-4)

Joyce's writings mirror a similar quest of absence as a higher form of presence, of exile as a peculiar form of being at home or of death as 'the highest form of life' (*U*: 15.2098). Like Shakespeare and Sterne, Joyce invariably goes back in life and history in order to move

[4] Casanova, 1988. In the last paragraph the narrator claims it is useless to commit the whole life (totality!) to paper because this (auto)biographical narrative would consist of 'outlines, reflections, digressions, the exact circumstances, critical observations, dialogues, monologues' (86). Ironically enough, Casanova's 'real' autobiography can be read like a linear narrative (132).

forward as an artist. He is a critic before he becomes a creative artist. Like Seamus Heaney, who, as Stefan Koch (1991: 1-3) suggests, unearths Irish history and pre-history to find his own voice, Joyce uncovers his own image as an artist by means of fieldwork as a literary archaeo-logist. And he does so from his point of view as writer in exile who cannot but return to what is his 'museyroom' (*FW*: 8.9) or his memorial storeroom. In a very personal way, however, Joyce has always proved incapable of re-membering his own version of his life. As Udo Loll (1992: 129-30) suggests, he just could not face his own image as a son and husband; he remained a failure in his father's eyes and his wife would have preferred him to be a sportsman or a tenor.

By way of conclusion, it is appropriate that somebody else's story and tradition - wo/man's collective memory - should provide Stephen with a whetstone for a new story in which he tries to imagine how Shakespeare wrote Hamlet by means of (auto)biographical projections. For the purposes of the discussion Stephen concocts an explanatory (auto)biographical totality which is composed of intertextual fragments taken from Shakespeare's works. Essentially, his version of Shakespeare's life is the critic's way of imagining the totality of a life as an intertextual mosaic. He reaches this goal by providing the missing links through creative extrapolations. Unlike Tristram, who does not care about his failure as an historian, Stephen must succeed in finishing the exposition of his theory for fear of being ridiculed. Yet he must also deny his belief in it, since belief in the theory would imply an absolute, and the sceptical Stephen knows there is no totality to grasp and no 'rite' which 'is the poet's rest' (*U*: 15.2088).

SALMAN RUSHDIE'S SILVER MEDAL

WALTER GÖBEL AND DAMIAN GRANT[1]

Talking about his novels during an (unexpected) appearance at a seminar in Cambridge in July 1992, Salman Rushdie remarked - with what some would call characteristic modesty - that although he would feel compelled to award the gold medal for narrative technique to Laurence Sterne, he would award the silver medal to himself. The object of this paper is to explore some of the ways in which Sterne's gold generates Rushdie's silver; to eavesdrop on the dialogue-of-one between these two writers, as Rushdie exploits Sterne's techniques to serve his own contemporary purposes.

And with these two novelists, both adepts at inception, we do really have to begin at the beginning, going back to where all stories start: which is not in 'the foul rag-and-bone shop of the heart' (the poet's sentimental version), but in the dynamics of the double helix - the transmission of our genetic inheritance. The macro-narrative of the human species is enacted by biology; and each individual human being lives his/her own micro-version of it. To adapt the structure of the Victorian three-decker novel, Volume 1 begins with our conception, and continues stereotypically with the evolutionary story that each of us recapitulates in the womb; Volume 2 opens with the adventure of birth, and is then preoccupied with the inevitably more miscellaneous circumstances of the life we actually lead, in history; while Volume 3

[1] Walter Göbel and Damian Grant each presented a paper on Sterne and Rushdie at the York conference. For the purposes of this publication they have agreed to 'halve the matter amicably', and so the present paper is a third version incorporating something of both originals.

brings death as closure (allowing always for a possible sequel, the unwritten and unwritable text of what may happen afterwards).

Given Rushdie's admission of Sterne's influence it is to be expected that we will find in his work many deliberate - even decorative - remembrances of the earlier writer.[2] But it is not the least intriguing aspect of the link between the two that it operates also at a fundamental (one might say, primordial) level. Rushdie in *Midnight's Children* reads off from Sterne at the very germination of narrative; Saleem Sinai's first-person narrative drawing its energy - and containing, one might say, its whole trajectory from the first nano-seconds of his life. Of course Sterne (the gold medallist) got there first; and his complex interweaving of social, biological and technological terms in the first chapter of *Tristram Shandy* sets up a system of interlocking metaphors that initiates the discourse of the novel in a truly exemplary way. Tristram is 'set a-going' (like a clock) in the very first paragraph: significantly, before the clock itself is actually mentioned. In that fatally interrupted moment he is conceived and delivered over to history, to the machinations (literally) of the clock whose mechanism he himself will never be able to understand.

Midnight's Children begins with a birth, rather than a conception: a bald announcement in the first-person that sounds for a moment more like Defoe than Sterne: 'I was born in the city of Bombay ... once upon a time'. Defoe would not have tolerated that 'once upon a time'. But he would have approved of the specificity (if not the rhetoric) of what follows:

> No, that won't do there's no getting away from the date: I was born in Doctor Narlikar's Nursing Home on August 15th, 1947. And the time? The time matters too. Well then: at night. No, it's important to be more ... On the stroke of midnight, as a matter of fact. Clock-hands joined palms in respectful greeting as I came. Oh, spell it out, spell it out: at the precise instant of India's arrival at independence, I tumbled forth into the world. (Rushdie, 1982: 11)

This we can confidently say is the subtle inflection of Sterne, not the patient registration of Defoe: and we note the crucial clock already

[2] Which has been acknowledged elsewhere: see for example Pattanayak (1983: 19-20, 22).

standing by, like some obstetric instrument. The bonding of micro with macro, the mechanical with the metaphysical, the trivial with the historical, is continued in the next sentence:

> A few seconds later, my father broke his big toe; but his accident was a mere trifle when set beside whaι had befallen me in that benighted moment, because thanks to the occult tyrannies of those blindly saluting clocks I had been mysteriously handcuffed to history, my destinies indissolubly chained to those of my country.

The birth is into history-as-life-lived; but it is also into history as narrative, the compulsion to record, to make sense of, to communicate. And the logic of the trajectory then has to include historiography, the theorizing of the attendant problems; the ultimate and intriguing story (for the curious novelist) of how stories get told at all.

The second paragraph of Rushdie's novel takes us straight to the anxious author - aged 31 - contending with time, resolving to work faster at his narrative in order to save from stalling and collapsing back into the void:

> Now, however, time (having no further use for me) is running out. I will soon be thirty-one years old [...] I have no hope of saving my life, nor can I count on having even a thousand nights and a night. I must work fast, faster than Scheherazade, if I am to end up meaning - yes, meaning - something. I admit it: above all things, I fear absurdity.

The reference here is to Scheherazade, and indeed the *Thousand and One Nights* is an important orientation point in *Midnight's Children*:[3] 100,1 being the equivalent of n+1,the number of infinity, of fiction, to set beside the statistician's literal thousand (or the computer operator's megabyte). But although the frame story of Scheherazade does imply some tension here, the terms of the narrative anxiety are distinctively Sterne's. Rushdie replicates the perplexity expressed by the narrator throughout *Tristram Shandy* whenever Tristram surrenders to an

[3] As it is throughout Rushdie's work. A more recent novel *Haroun and the Sea of Stories* (1990) is written very much as an Arabian Nights tale. One cannot but remark an irony here: Scheherazade saved her life by telling stories, Salman Rushdie has put his in peril by doing the same.

awareness of the onrush and the multiplicity of events he has somehow to set down; such as where he appeals to the 'POWERS! (for powers ye are, and great ones too)——which enable mortal man to tell a story worth the hearing', that 'where-ever, in any part of your dominions it so falls out, that three several roads meet in one point, as they have done just here,——that at least you set up a guide-post, in the center of them, in mere charity to direct an uncertain devil, which of the three he is to take' (*TS*: 3.23.244-45); or where before proceeding with the matter in hand he has 'fifty things more necessary to let you know first,——I have a hundred difficulties which I have promised to clear up, and a thousand distresses and domestic misadventures crouding in upon me thick and three-fold, one upon the neck of another [...] and all this in five minutes less, than no time at all' (*TS*: 3.38.278); or where he confronts philosophically the problem of living faster than you can write, coming to the conclusion that 'write as I will [...] I shall never overtake myself' (*TS*: 4.13.342).

It is consistent with Sterne's ironic parading of his perplexities that the third paragraph of *Midnight's Children* takes us further into Rushdie's authorial workshop, as Saleem first explains to the reader the problem he confronts with so much material to organize: 'There are so many stories to tell, too many, such an excess of intertwined lives events miracles places rumours, so dense a commingling of the improbable and the mundane!' The first chapter then introduces another important theme: that of the refracted identity of the narrator, as Saleem prepares us to inhabit a self in decomposition, fissured (as we learn later) 581 ways to accommodate the identities of the children of midnight surviving to their tenth year: 'I have been a swallower of lives; and to know me, just the one of me, you'll have to swallow the lot as well. Consumed multitudes are jostling and shoving inside me' (11).

The opening page of the novel also reveals that Rushdie has not forgotten the Sternean obligation of his narrator to record his own conception: or at least (the plot actually forbids this, since Saleem it turns out has been switched with another baby at the maternity home) to identify the rite of conception in the sexual act - in this case, his grandparents' conception of his father - as a central metaphor, generative of other meanings. The opening chapter is called 'The Perforated Sheet', and Saleem is guided, he tells us, 'by the memory of a large white bedsheet with a roughly circular hole some seven inches in diameter cut into the centre; and clutching this:

> clutching at the dream of that holey, mutilated square of linen, which is my talisman, my open-sesame, I must commence the business of remaking my life from the point at which it really began, some thirty-two years before anything as obvious, as *present,* as my clock-ridden, crime-stained birth. (11-12)

The sheet in question is one through which Saleem's grandfather was allowed first to touch (as her doctor) and eventually to see (as her fiancée) his future wife: the same sheet on which the wedding night is spent. The sheet, incidentally, is stained too, with three drops of old, faded redness. As the Quran tells us: '*Recite, in the name of the Lord thy Creator, who created Man from clots of blood*' (12). The sheet is a symbolic hymen, the 'open-sesame' that brings Saleem's parents and then Saleem himself to birth ... and, in due course, to his writing desk, where the aperture serves as a lens, a metaphoric point of view.

Tristram protests that he has told us when he was born but not how and confesses to a deepening frustration at not being able to bring himself on stage sooner (*TS*: 1.14); likewise, the complicated circumstances of Saleem's birth are not revealed until we're a hundred pages into *Midnight's Children*. This is in the chapter significantly called 'Tick, Tock', which marks the countdown to 15 August 1947 and the historic moment of Indian independence.

Meanwhile Padma Mangroli, Saleem's more-than-housekeeper as he writes his life story, expresses her own irritation at how long it's taking him to get himself born: 'To me it's a crazy way of telling your life story' she cries, 'if you can't even get to where your father met your mother [...] You'll die before you get yourself born' (38).

To return to a point made earlier: we should distinguish between the different levels of interaction between these two (following Shklovsky) typical fictions. There are many superficial parallels: the attention paid to doctors, and their mismanagement of obstetric procedure (like Tristram, Saleem's 'twin' Shiva is damaged at birth by forceps); the episode where Saleem has the top of his finger cut off by a closing door (shades of Tristram's misfortune with the descending sash-window); the invocation of Uncle Toby's idiom when Saleem's grandfather Aadam Aziz attempts to storm his young wife's 'ravelins and bastions' (41), which she has erected against the assaults of modern immodesty. These (and others like them) are as it were an explicit acknowledgement by Rushdie of the prior text, a conscious doffing of his cap to the master. But it is the thoroughgoing permeation of Rushdie's fiction by Sterne's example, at the level of conception, theme, metaphor, and narrative procedure - that is to say, in its basic writerly orientation towards experience - that the influence reveals itself to be most interesting. (It should also be noted that although Rushdie 'writes out' the influence of Sterne in this novel, by engaging it directly, there are continuing if less visible traces in his later works).

And as these remarks on the opening of *Midnight's Children* will have suggested, the treatment of time is one of the most obvious areas of genuine and general indebtedness to be identified. Rushdie's continuous counterpointing of biological time and clock time on the one hand against mental and imaginative time on the other is something which is closely modelled on Sterne's example. Sterne provides his lecture on 'duration and its simple modes' in Volume 2, Chapter 7, defending his narration against the 'true scholastic pendulum' of the literal critic who would have all unities, sequences and correspondences exactly observed. Of course, with such literalism there could be no narration: even Dr Johnson (no instinctive Sternean) remarks in his 'Preface to Shakespeare' that 'time is, of all modes of existence, most obsequious to the imagination' (Johnson, 1963: 502); and Sterne as we know exacts the fullest measure of temporal obsequiousness, providing Rushdie with the example to do likewise. Thus, at the very end of his story, Saleem Sinai sits at the apex of an isosceles triangle, imperiously processing the past (memory) and anticipating the future (prophecy); 'I shall have to write the future as I have written the past, to set it down with the absolute certainty of a prophet'.

But paradoxically, even while Sterne and Rushdie are asserting via their narrators their absolute dominion over imaginary time, - where it can intelligibly be said that 'a cow broke in (to-morrow morning) to my uncle *Toby*'s fortifications' (*TS*: 3.38.278) - their narrators are at the same time (one should say, in a *different,* narratorial time) presented as harassed by the unyielding pressure of the real time of narrating; real by analogy with the real time of reading. Tristram we noted earlier is assailed by the problem of living faster than he can write, while in Volume 7 he is pursued in his imagination by Death (complete with scythe and sandtimer), threatening to overtake him before his task is finished. Rushdie's Saleem Sinai is likewise hassled in his narration, not least by his interlocutor Padma, who is always urging him to get on with things:

> I am rushing ahead at breakneck speed; errors are possible, and overstatements, and jarring alterations in tone [...] as my decay accelerates (my writing speed is having difficulty keeping up), the risk of unreliability grows ...

Of course it is this very 'harassment' that provides both authors with some of their most brilliant effects. It is precisely at one of these moments, when he has 'fifty things more necessary to let you know first [...] a hundred difficulties which I have promised to clear up, and a thousand distresses and domestic misadventures crouding in upon me thick and three-fold' (*TS*: 3.38.278), that Sterne is able to transgress normal tense structure to accommodate the trespassing (and time-travelling) cow; and it is when Saleem feels threatened by the impatience of other characters to break into his narrative, that he keeps them most firmly in their place: 'Someone speaks anxiously, trying to force her way into my story ahead of time; but it won't work... someone, who founded this pickle factory and its ancillary bottling works... She nearly wormed it out of me then, but fortunately I've still got my wits about me' (209) - and his tenses too. Mary Pereira, the 'criminal of midnight' who switched the children, will have to wait until page 457 to be identified, and to take her due place as mistress of the 'chutnification of history' (459).

One special feature that Rushdie owes to Sterne is the management or conspicuous manipulation of several simultaneous present tenses. The classic example in *Tristram Shandy* is Tristram's vertiginous narration of two different journeys through the same city of Auxerre, which is further complicated by the third present tense of the narratorial moment itself:

> There is but a certain degree of perfection in every thing; and by pushing at something beyond that, I have brought myself into such a situation, as no traveller ever stood before me; for I am this moment walking across the market-place of Auxerre with my father and my uncle Toby, in our

> way back to dinner———and I am this moment also entering Lyons with my post-chaise broke into a thousand pieces——and I am moreover this moment in a handsome pavillion built by Pringello, upon the banks of the Garonne, which Mons. Sligniac has lent me, and where I now sit rhapsodizing all these affairs. (*TS*: 7.28.621-22)

To observe Rushdie's exploitation of this device, we have to look beyond *Midnight's Children* to *The Satanic Verses*, where the hero Gibreel Farishta is momentarily identified in no less than five simultaneous time-zones:

> he understands now something of what omnipresence must be like, because he is moving through several stories at once, there is a Gibreel who mourns his betrayal by Alleluia Cone, and a Gibreel hovering over the death-bed of a Prophet, and a Gibreel watching in secret over the progress of a pilgrimage to the sea, waiting for the moment when he will reveal himself, and a Gibreel who feels, more powerfully every day, the will of the adversary [...] And there is a Gibreel who walks down the streets of London, trying to understand the will of God. (Rushdie, 1988: 457)

Gibreel is not Rushdie's narrator in this novel, so one further plane is missing (as we might expect, of the silver medallist?). And indeed, Rushdie's intention is different here from Sterne's, to the extent that he is more interested in the degeneration of his central character - his decomposition into discontinuous selves - than he is in weaving a fictional web whose purpose is 'to keep all tight together in the reader's fancy' (*TS*: 6.33.557-58).

But to return to the novel with which we are primarily concerned: it will be instructive to notice other details in *Midnight's Children* itself where Rushdie has taken a hint from Sterne but developed the idea differently, as a way of introducing contrasts which are perhaps as fundamental as the similarities we have already dwelt upon. Sterne begins Volume 3, Chapter 14 with an observation concerning classical rhetoric:

> It is a singular stroke of eloquence (at least it was so, when eloquence flourished at *Athens* and *Rome*, and would be so now, did orators wear mantles) not to mention the name of a thing, when you had the thing about you, *in petto,* ready to produce, pop, in the place you want it. A scar, an axe, a sword, a pink'd-doublet, a rusty helmet, a pound and a half of pot-ashes in an urn, or a three-halfpenny pickle pot. (217-18)

Is it too fanciful to find here the fortuitous germ of Rushdie's famous pickle factory, elaborated through his novel as a metaphor for the fictional process - the fictional process being itself the key (not always admitted) to the 'chutnification of history'?[4] Sterne himself pursues the gastronomic metaphor, referring on one occasion to the 'thin juice of a man's understanding' (*TS*: 3.9.197), and we would like to believe that somewhere this stray idea might have provided one of the ingredients for what becomes a central, organizing trope in *Midnight's Children*. It is in the last chapter, Chapter 31 ('Abracadabra') that the metaphor is finally, fully articulated. It is his realization of the reality of death that sends Saleem in the end to Mary Pereira's pickle factory, and 'into the heart of a nostalgia which would keep me alive long enough to write these pages (and to create a corresponding number of pickles)' (450). As he writes this chapter, he can reflect that 'Thirty jars stand upon a shelf, ready to be unleashed upon the amnesiac nation' (460): it is more than the palate or the stomach, that may be upset by this confection.

Likewise, the metaphor of impotence is given a new and dangerous edge in Rushdie's novel. At one level it derives, clearly, from Tristram's parallel anxiety about his sexual and artistic powers - a metaphor which involves not only Tristram himself but also Uncle Toby, suffering as he does from the wound in his groin; and legitimately enough the widow Wadman, concerned as she is as to its gravity and effects. But whereas Tristram never suffers anything more traumatic (in the flesh) than circumcision by the sash-window, owing to Susannah's carelessness, Saleem Sinai actually becomes a fictional victim of Indira Gandhi's very historical compulsory sterilization programme, directed against a section of the Indian population in .... It is 'vasectomists and troops' (431) who clear out the artist's colony where Saleem has taken refuge with the magician Picture-Singh; it is in the 'Widow's Hostel' in Benares that Saleem is tortured to reveal the names of the other children, and where the operations are performed upon them: 'testicles were removed from sacs, and wombs

[4] Gérard Genette has commented on the scandalous fact that factual narrative has almost totally escaped the attention of critics, absorbed as they are in the narratives of fiction: 'les deux branches de la narratologie ont jusqu'a ici consacré une attention presque exclusive aux allures et aux objets du seul récit de fiction' (1991: 65).

vanished forever ... the children of midnight were denied the possibility of reproducing themselves ... gone forever, the possibility of flight and lycanthropy and the originally-one-thousand-and-one marvellous promises of a numinous midnight' (439). The fact that the Widow of Rushdie's imagination (partly derived, as he recalls, from the Wicked Witch in the Wizard of Oz) has 'drained' Saleem 'of past present future' as a man (402) does indeed empower him as an artist; but the fact that this widow is also Indira Gandhi also imbricates the fiction more provocatively with documentary record. Saleem is not only a fictional character; he becomes 'typical' in a sense closer to that of Lukács than Shklovsky, significantly singled out by the searchlight of history to play a representative role.

A similar process of contextualizing overtakes Rushdie's adoption of Sterne's metaphor of the nose. To begin with, Saleem's outsize nose (inherited from his grandfather) will be readily interpreted by the reader as a compensatory sexual appendage; much as the story of Slawkenbergius's nose in *Tristram Shandy* is the focus of an elaborate sexual fantasy (and also functions to concretize the system of *double-entendres*). But it soon becomes apparent that Rushdie's nose serves other - more choric and historical - purposes. Saleem's nose is an antenna which enables him to receive signals and to 'broadcast' to the other children of midnight, emphasizing his mythical ubiquity and representativeness (see the chapter 'All-India radio'). He loses the facility after an illness, but regains it after being bitten by a snake in the wilderness of the Sundarbans (364), where he has taken refuge after the Indo-Pakistani war of 1965. So what's in a nose? Rushdie has taken the idea from Sterne, but used it once again to bear a reference (like a buttress) that reaches outside the fictional frame.

This argument can even be applied to the awareness of the medium of language itself as it is deployed in both novels. As Sterne's own references to the Third Book ('Of Words') from Locke's *Essay Concerning Human Understanding* remind us, *Tristram Shandy* is to be read at one level as a demonstration of the impurity of language; an impurity which, while it may be the despair of philosophers, makes it for the very same reason readily available as a means of communication about ordinary matters between such imperfect creatures as ourselves. Uncle Toby is more threatened by linguistics than by ballistics: 'his life was put in jeopardy by words' (*TS*:

2.2.101). In order to hallmark his own alloy of fictional history, Rushdie needs to provide evidence - in the form of a local habitation - for Sterne's free-floating idea. And so the epistemological problem is promoted to a political problem, where words become not just the agents of innocent misunderstanding (as between Walter Shandy and Uncle Toby) but agents of ethnic division, ideological oppression and even weapons of war:

> the boundaries of these states were not formed by rivers, or mountains, or any natural features of the terrain; they were, instead, walls of words. Language divided us [...] in the city of Munbadevi, the language marches grew longer and noisier and finally metamorphosed into political parties. (189)

This retooling by Rushdie of Sterne's fictional workshop - this switch, with all it implies, from the rectory in Yorkshire to a pickle-factory in Bombay - underlines a shift in purpose and perspective that makes the differences between the two writers ultimately at least as fascinating as the similarities. And the underlying difference can perhaps best be expressed by identifying the dominant genre to which each writer implicitly subscribes. With Sterne it is the dramatic (or, the dramatic with a strong element of lyric): the characteristic field of the first person, or of multiple first persons, with polyphonic discourse as its typical mode. Whereas for Rushdie, in the end it is the epic vision that he is conjuring (like some divine ventriloquist) out of the personal voice, a voice which, while not restricted in range, is certainly recognizable as 'monologic' in terms of the distinction derived from Bakhtin.

But these descriptions are not offered as judgements of value. Change the terms, and the alignments also change their emphasis. For example: Sterne's narrative (for all its deviousness) retreats and contracts; the future is already all used up. Whereas Rushdie's narrative advances and expands, it addresses itself (indeed even sacrifices itself: as the epic voice will) to the future. 'Does India exist?' Rushdie recalls asking himself, as he worked on this novel (Rushdie, 1992: 32); and the novel sets out to provide an affirmative answer to the question. It is no 'mere' experimental fiction, but the epic of India that Rushdie has dared to try to write. It is the multitudes who have been 'jostling and shoving' within Saleem from the first page of *Midnight's Children* who are in the end its plural subjects, and it is they who lay claim to the meaning of the novel in its concluding paragraph: where the final dissolution of the hero is no postmodern device, but a surrender to larger and less containable significance:

> I am alone in the vastness of the numbers, the numbers marching one two three, I am being buffeted right and left while rip tear crunch reaches its climax, and my body is screaming, it cannot take this kind of treatment any more [...] they throng around me pushing shoving crushing, and the cracks are widening, pieces of my body are falling off [...] I am the bomb in Bombay, watch me explode, bones splitting breaking beneath the awful pressure of the crowd [...]
>
> Yes, they will trample me underfoot, the numbers marching one two three, four hundred million five hundred six, reducing me to specks of voiceless dust (462-3)

Rushdie has since written of this ending as 'if anything, too optimistic' (Rushdie, 1992: 32); in an essay which also seeks to play down the political (or at least, historical) pretensions of the novel. But this cannot detract from the epic scale of the novel itself, nor qualify the way it seeks to engage the reader's imagination on behalf of a continent. One reason for the writing of the novel (as presumably for reading it) is 'to understand the recent history of our times' (338); it is written against lies and amnesia, against all those intent on annulling the past - including the practitioners of 'Sperectomy' (a coinage we find on page 437) who would obliterate the future.

In conclusion, it may be interesting to recall that in an essay which addresses the question of political commitment in literature - claiming, one has to reflect ironically, that modern writers have no choice in the matter, living as they do 'in a world without hiding places' - Rushdie actually cites Sterne, lined up beside Lewis Carroll, as one of those writers who cannot be described as political but who are nevertheless 'as important to literature as Swift or Brecht' (Rushdie, 1992: 100). Well: we know that Sterne was familiar enough with the then-politics of Ulster, and it would not take great ingenuity to provide a political reading for the widow Wadman's anxieties over Toby's wound: a metaphor, if we are looking for one, of the epic antagonism between love and war. But we would prefer to leave our authors here, at this point of fertile bifurcation - leaving our readers something to reflect upon, as well as ourselves.

'A SUN-DIAL IN A GRAVE: THE FOUNDING GESTURE'

JEAN-CLAUDE DUPAS

'Five years with a bib under his chin;
Four years in travelling from Christ-cross-row to *Malachi*;
A year and a half in learning to write his own name;
Seven long years and more τυπτω-ing it, at Greek and Latin;
Four years at his *probations* and his *negations*——' (*TS*: 5.42.483)

Flaunting an aesthetics of dispersion, construing a 'dismemberment' of the self as first person narrator yet giving flesh both to the narrative and to the character, Sterne's *The Life and Opinions of Tristram Shandy, Gentleman*, 'digressive, and [...] progressive too,——and at the same time' (*TS*: 1.22.81), may be seen as an 'early' instance of the questioning of what I will call the ontological illusion in language theories whereby the self is viewed as an autonomous entity of 'reception'. Something would be and would occur to a self in a position of exteriority, ready to examine objectively the language act. The obverse (postmodern?) attitude, developed here, would argue that whenever a language act occurs, no actual self exists to receive it, except the self as it is already contained in the language performance. The issue then lies not in a talking to or a speaking with but in this that the self is one of the instances concurred with what occurs. In Jean-François Lyotard's words 'le «il y a» n'arrive pas à un sujet, ce qu'on appelle un sujet est lui même une des instances qui arrive *avec* ce qui arrive'. Or again, the self is invented <come into> with - and at the same time as - what occurs. Does this not provide a remarkable definition of the shandean self, unborn and yet present as the book begins, ceaselessly elaborated and commented upon, planned, engineered, yet tossed and maimed in the topsy-turvydom of hobby-horses, monomanias, incidental episodes and digressions?

Sterne's narrative strategy, characterized by its apparently constant button-holing of his reader, causes the analysis to go one step further. What is dramatised in the narration is a particular form of interlocution, I <as writer /narrator /character /persona> / you <gendered reader(s)>. Within the context of *Tristram Shandy*, this is shown to be an ironical quotation of the established autobiographical *topos*. It also stages the questioning of that essential pattern of re-cognition according to which the radical otherness of another self might be overcome through a process of identification, the other as same, 'brave new world'. The brilliant singularity of Sterne lies here in the insertion within the pragmatic minimalism of a conversation, or of a reading pact, of the impossibility of any *Mitsein*. In *Tristram Shandy*, the reader and the writer do not communicate, they do not create a 'we', an instance of the narration. On the contrary, Sterne is constantly announcing the *aphanisis* both of the writer and the reader as persons, as 'individualised selves', in favour of a presence to the text, of a 'there is' a writer/narrator, 'there is' a reader, as the text occurs; but no more; they are figurated, not meant or interlocuted.

Against this background, Sterne's text may be seen as calling both for a reflection on 'postmodernism' as a category of critical theory and an analysis of its narrative strategies in terms, not only of 'mock-autobiography' but as an occasion of the re-assessment of the founding enquiry: what narrative modalities of the self, what narrative instances of time and space are illustrated in Sterne's text? At the same time, the referential status of the title chosen for this paper means to stress the mimetic turn given it as a gesture posing analyses of *Tristram Shandy* as being themselves bound in/by the process of mimetic figuration originally involved in Sterne's mode of writing.

By 'figuration', I understand that process whereby the thing and the image of the thing are meant, to use well-known shandean parlance, 'too and at the same time'. Figuration then becomes the obverse side of representation and the issue less to ascertain whether an idea, person, notion or thing has been given to be seen than how this idea, person, notion or thing is introduced through the patterns which have construed its representation, through an invention of the occurrence. Such a pattern has to be considered as involving not only the written words but the printed page as a whole, as representation of black signs set on white paper, thereby including 'motley emblems' or what the reader might have written or drawn on the paper provided, but also the response of the reader, be it through his reading/decyphering/encoding activity or as the case may be as non-reader, or 'inattentive reader' ('How could you, Madam, be so inattentive', *TS*: 1.20.64). The act by which representation is figurated then implies the establishment of a 'rhapsodical partnership' between the writer and the reader. This process might be better viewed as one considers that Uncle Toby is characterised through his hobby-horse, not after the Jonsonian technique of the prevailing humour but, in a much more radical fashion, within the elaboration of that hobby-horse, as it invades, not only Uncle Toby as a character, but the whole narrative, thus, for instance, affecting Tristram as and because the weights have been taken out of the sash-windows. Representation, thus dis-jointed as figuration, is further moved by another turn of the rhetoric screw, this vertigo of learned wit experienced by the unwitting reader, in constant danger of being outwitted within the folds of a Zeuxian paradox as he/she will push aside the painted drapery - or is it a real curtain?

As is well-known, from the beginning of *Tristram Shandy*, the rhythm both of the figuration and of the narration is set by the winding of the clock, as an act, as an interrogation upon the actuality of the action and as, at least, *double entendre*. Time is essential. It also is within the present debate which might have appeared as a reading into *The Life and Opinions of Tristram Shandy* of potential philosophical or critical anachronisms, such as modernism or postmodernism, if it were not for this role of time and the issues it repeatedly raises. Is anything stationary? In *Physics*, Book 4, Aristotle contends that it is impossible to establish the difference between what was and what will be, without establishing a 'now'. Simultaneously, the flux of life, the flux of consciousness (flux rather than 'stream', to avoid obvious and sometimes illusory identifications), have it that no 'now' can be endowed with a satisfactory stability. One is thus left with an 'excess' as to a 'too late' or a 'too soon'. With the consciousness of this 'excess' Sterne fills the narrative space of his book as it deals with the constantly receding and evading 'now' of *Tristram Shandy*. A similar (parallel?) 'excess' is of course to be found in the use of the printed page, printed 'in excess'. Sterne's chronotope, as I am trying to trace it here, is made of and for the expression of the impossibility to say (write/print) the 'excess', and that other impossibility, not to say it, as it is the core of what is 'said' in the story.

In the potential pieces of learned witticisms regarding time, less as a concept than, literally, as a word, the chronotope is expressed. Indeed, etymology has it that time refers us back to the Latin *tempus* and with it to the idea of duration. Now tempus leads to the Greek [temno] and thus from circumstances (tempus) to the nicety of divisions ([temno]). Does not the word time contain, by which I mean figurate, the major shandean narrative plight inherent to what, for present purposes I shall call the 'hesitation' between duration and interruption, digression and progression, together with the necessity to fuse them in one moment, one narrative gesture, one word? If we follow up this point of view, the word time enters in iconic resonance with the very nature of Sterne's narrative and may itself be construed as a figuration of time. To phrase this differently, I am here trying to suggest that the basic chronotope established by Sterne consists precisely in that spacing out of time, which is one of the striking features of autobiography as fashioned in *The Life and Opinions of Tristram Shandy*.

Bakhtin, in the 1978 'observations' added to his writings on the chronotope, defines it as offering 'the foundation of artistic unity in its relations to reality'. He had first established the chronotope of the road, say from *Apuleius* and *The Golden Ass* to Fielding, that of the castle in the gothic novel and that of the drawing-room which might be estimated as extending from Jane Austen to Stendhal; Bakhtin then suggests the introduction of the chronotope of the threshold and the staircase, illustrated by Dostoyevsky, and exemplary of crises, of turning-points. To this characterization, I would like to contribute this idea that the narrative form developed in *Tristram Shandy* uses that same chronotope of the threshold and the staircase not in terms of individual psychological or metaphysical analysis but as a medium obversely figurating meta-fiction, or again as a means to express the essential relationship of time and space in the writing/reading of fiction, because it is the essence of time that it should be at the same time a necessary vehicle for circumstances and an unescapable source of divisions and suspensions. Mythical time is one where what was and what may be, where the beginning and the end of the story are made to coincide, in the novel, time begins with the first page, the first sentence, the clock is set to a new type of duration where a series of events are made to become meaningful and exemplary. 'Longtemps je me suis couché de bonne heure'. It is not so much the vastness of the events that counts than the fact that there can be no hesitation as to the clock having been duly wound up and its having started to tick from the moment the first letter has been written/read. Shandean time knows of neither sets of regulations and patterns and yet is neither a reduction to purely subjective, existential time, nor a desperately strained attempt at make-believe that time no longer exists or that it is not an apt category of perception. Time is so ever-present in *Tristram Shandy* that it often invades the whole page, the totality of the narrative space, as the when is often a condition of the how.

To illustrate the point I am trying to make, I will take into particular account the study of a specific instance of the Sternean use of the chronotope, selecting as my text *Tristram Shandy*, 5.16, Walter's writing of the *Tristrapaedia*; again an ironical quotation of a *topos*. This will be shown as particularly exemplary of (some of) the operations involved in 'making sense' of/in *Tristram Shandy*, of the particular mode(s) of *discordia concors* implied in saying 'too and at the same time' the cock (and bull) and the clock, that singular 'rhapsody' whereby the legitimacy of order is questioned and established in such a way that the disorder of the geniture brings about that of the nose, causing that of the name, calling for that of the education, of which none but the curves and lines of Volume 6 may eventually figurate a representation. It also so happens that this chain of figurations is connected with Walter, who, as Tristram's father and as a character in the book, even if it be in a parodical or paradoxical vein, stands for a representation of order.

Thus will 'making sense' appear as the construction / deconstruction / reconstruction of meaning it always is, yet with a vengeance, as the *Tristrapaedia* emblematizes the hesitations over creation and suspension, procreation and procrastination.

Ever-lagging behind the natural progress of life, the *Tristrapaedia* signals both Walter's desperate last hope to recapture his constantly receding control over his son, and the 'natural' discrepancy between living and writing about life. More particularly, it is the occasion of a meta-linguistic reflection on the notion of theory. Originally theory, /theorein/, means observation. What is at stake within the project underlying the *Tristrapaedia* is precisely the notion of 'observation'. As Walter fails to observe Tristram while engrossed in the act of writing the *Tristrapaedia*, the father, as he writes, occupies a portion of space distinct from that in which his son actually lives, the two time schemes then dramatically drift apart. I here mean 'dramatically' both as 'strikingly' and as 'in the form of drama'. The *Tristrapaedia* is not merely a satire or an internal characterization of Walter's idiosyncrasies, it belongs with the numerous *topoi* where writing is 'staged' by Laurence Sterne, with the 'web and flow' of life and opinions within *Tristram Shandy*. Walter Shandy has become a perfect figuration of the risks involved in the unobservation of the basic Sternean chronotope involved in writing, whereby time and space necessarily interact. The nature of such risks is here clearly underlined; what has been lost is not only contact with reality but the capacity to keep in touch with reality, as it changes. I am thus trying to claim that the establishment of what I call the sternean chronotope is an effort towards grasping, figurating, reality both as an image and as a movement.

In spite of differences in the approaches which cannot be discussed here but are, elsewhere, by Gilles Deleuze, this agonistic approach of time, as image and as movement, could benefit from the Bergsonian concept of 'the two recognitions' as illustrated in *Matière et mémoire* and which, together with the chronotope, may contribute a modelisation of Sterne's narrative posture expressed in the hobby-horsical mode of writing, in the constant warping of the crossing out of the narration. Bergson opposes, the first, immediate, recognition by which the cow identifies the grass, or 'I' identify my friend Peter, and the other, the *reconnaissance attentive*, whereby, in the same iconic space, various 'figurations' (Bergson writes '*plans*', planes) co-exist. The literary implication I would want to draw from this lies in the opposition between description, as it tries to give a faithful, perfect image, and this, other, presentation of reality where it is approximated through a succession, or a conflict, of ever-receding images. The, once, *nouveau roman* might be seen as an, easy although imperfect, illustration of this attitude. A further reflection could take as its base

Bergson's book *Durée et simultanéité*, which, from our point of view, is very aptly named, as I would argue that it takes for its title the very contradictory tension that Sterne is indeed grappling with. There, Bergson marks a radical break-away from the dominant tradition of philosophy for which conscience is a kind of projected light illuminating things, thereby bringing them to consciousness, for Bergson the luminosity is in the thing itself, it eventually 'meets' the consciousness. The thing and the perception of the thing are one and the same thing ('too and at the same time'?). Perceiving then is also a kind of estrangement to one's self, a form of *Unheimlichkeit*. Such an approach of perception would contribute a further commentary upon the dehiscence of the self. Taking this, once again, in sternean literary terms, it becomes blatantly clear that this is what is totally alien to Walter. He is figurating the exact opposite attitude. His conscience, his educational norm remain free from any contact with the child, with any reality, while the *Tristrapaedia* remains a perfect emblem of the projected light supposed to illuminate the child, with the grotesque inadequacy all readers have always smiled at. Unobserving theory, one which will not be informed by its object, is a damning oxymoron.

This very brief sketch may be considered as having further reaching consequences in terms of literary theory, particularly if it intersects with the questioning of the supremacy of the 'I as writer'. Writing would then not coincide with the delivery of a message, but offer a mode of communication, of which there are several. The text then ceases to depend on the arrogant pre-eminence of an encoder, or indeed a 'decoder', alternately the writer and the reader, whether it be, for example, in terms of moral reproof, psychological apprehension or reader-response theory, but will display the modalities of perception. I am of course not arguing this as a universal truth but as a means of coming to terms with Sterne's project, with the singularity of *Tristram Shandy*. 'Making sense' of/in *Tristram Shandy* now takes its full meaning. It indeed implies a form of fabrication (Claude Lévi-Strauss would call it 'bricolage') of a Bergsonian-like reconnaissance attentive, as opposed to natural perception in the same way that a Dickensian description or an Austenian characterization differ from the portrait of Uncle Toby or the account of Tristram's birth. Dr Slop's portrait, as near straight description as may be found in *Tristram Shandy*, has to be 'imagined' (*TS*: 2.9.121) while digressions are 'the sunshine' of reading (*TS*: 1.22.81).

All Sterne contends for, 'is the utter impossibility for some volumes, that you, or the most penetrating spirit upon earth, should know how this matter really stands' (*TS*: 1.18.56). This so provocative apparent disrespect paid the reader should also be seen in terms of time and space. It coincides with a narrative pattern of displacement to an often never existing moment/place where the information which has not/could not be given, will be offered. Basically is created what I will call a shimmering of the narrative, somehow the production of a halo around what has been written, both endowing it with greater credibility and making it somehow unreal. At the same time the apparent omniscience/omnipotence of the narrator is both figurated and questioned since, from within the context of autobiography, he shows himself as being over-ruled by some necessity of the narration, submitted to the laws of the chronotope.

Walter's *Tristrapaedia* is not only out of joint with its purpose, it is incapable of taking into account the tempus of Tristram's life, its circumstances. Two reasons are given to show that '*the chapter upon sash-windows*, with the bitter *Philippick* at the end of it, upon the forgetfulness of chamber-maids' (*TS*: 5.26.458) was not written by Walter in his *Tristrapaedia*. The first is that, had it been, the episode would not have taken place, the sash-sindow having been nailed up by attentive parents, the other consisting in Tristram's being the author of this chapter. Beyond the immediate opening of a humorous vein, particularly as Tristram as narrator defines this chapter as 'the most original and entertaining one in the whole book' (*TS*: 5.26.458), also beyond the obvious double-bind (either the chapter is present in the *Tristrapaedia* and absent in Tristram's life or present in Tristram's life and absent from the *Tristrapaedia*), this contributes to the establishment of the fictional implications of the Bergsonian *reconnaissance attentive*. Three 'levels' of recognition are given at the same time, what is (the untimely fall of the sash-window), what might have been (parental pre-knowledge of the potential danger), what should have been (this again on three distinct levels: fatherly concern for the actual child rather that with the child 'in his mind's eye', a critical distance towards the potential discrepancies between theory and experience, a sternean conception of the chronotope). This demultiplication of the levels is then presented as the only rendering of iconic reality as opposed to 'natural reality' which, in any case, the *Tristrapaedia* in particular, *Tristram Shandy* in general, amply prove to be remote from writing, be it only because the two time-schemes never can be made to coincide.

The sixteenth chapter of the fifth volume opens with the decision to write a *Tristrapaedia* and ends on the idea that 'every day a page or two became of no consequence', leaving Walter 'drawing a sun-dial, for no better purpose than to be buried under ground' (*TS*: 5.16.448-49). In between the sanguine beginning and the disenchanted final metaphor, lies a discussion of John de la Casse and of 'RESISTANCE' (the small capitals are Sterne's). My present purpose is not to discuss what little is known of Giovanni della Casa, archbishop of Benevento, or of his theories, at least those here attributed to him, or even the eventual bawdy overtones of the passage and of its references, but rather to stress this idea that the space which might have stood for what may have been written in the *Tristrapaedia* is 'reeled and cross-twisted [by] what other spinners and spinsters had spun before [Walter]' (*TS*: 5.16.445). This 'space' is thus shown as being occupied by a rehashing of past theories; Walter's chronotope offers the perfect image of the incapacity to approach reality or an image of it, the movement of life escapes him on account of his being 'so long in his acts of resistance'. This results from a conception of the life of the writer as 'not so much a state of *composition*, as a state of *warfare*' (*TS*: 5.16.447), in other words, one where no enduring self is held together because perception is the founding gesture of identity. Being is a matter of perceiving, not merely one of being perceived. Sterne's metaphor is particularly remarkable in that it furthers the figuration of the dichotomy between 'composition' as understood in the Bergsonian *reconnaissance attentive* and 'warfare', opposition, distinction inherent to 'natural perception' for which the conscience is the thing wherein the 'object of perception' would be caught.

The discrepancy between the two modes of duration, of life and of writing, is figurated by Sterne in two parallel narrative strategies. On the one hand, that Walter's ontological security should be established at the cost of his 'perceptive' in-security is well illustrated with the episode of the *Tristrapaedia*; on the other, the Sternean chronotope, which could be defined as the chronotope of the running commentary and the instrument of the *reconnaissance attentive*, I mean that process showing together the thing and the image of the thing, the perceived and the act of perception, a radical break-away then from any possibility of ontological illusion.

That Time and Place have, with this chapter, established and illustrated a singular presence as co-founders of the narrative, is given a further implication as the next chapter introduces one of the few precise dates in *Tristram Shandy*, which apparently does correspond to the moment of the writing of this seventeenth chapter of the fifth volume, '*August* the 10th, 1761'. At the same time, a legitimacy seems established for the constant running commentary offered by the nar-rator on his narrative, as the moment and place of the confrontation of reader and writer within the reconnaissance attentive.

If this should fail, the writer and reader will be outwitted by the very purpose they have set themselves. Both the perception and the expression of reality, not as a mirror-image but as a pattern under constant re-construction will prove an intemperate pursuit, one lacking in *temperatio*. An ultimate piece of learned wit is thus delivered, as 'the wisest of us all [...] forego our purposes in the intemperate act of pursuing them' (*TS*: 5.16.448). Intemperance meaning devoid of proportion, balance and regulation, it leads us back both to circumstances (tempus) and to the nicety of divisions ([temno]), while the Shandean 'firmness makes my circle just, / And makes me end, where I begunne', both with a mimetic mode of writing and the spatial progression (and digression) of suspended time, the founding gesture of the Sternean chronotope.

'ALL THAT EXIST ARE 'ISLANDS OF DETERMINISM'': SHANDEAN SENTIMENT AND THE DILEMMA OF POSTMODERN PHYSICS

STUART SIM

Theorists of the postmodern such as Jean-Francois Lyotard have been heavily influenced by both catastrophe theory and chaos theory - theories which posit a world where chance and determinism seem, paradoxically enough as well as bewilderingly enough, to operate simultaneously on causal processes. In the course of a discussion about these theories in *The Postmodern Condition: A Report on Knowledge*, Lyotard (1984: 59-60) comments that:

> All that exist are 'islands of determinism'. Catastrophic antagonism is literally the rule [...] Postmodern science - by concerning itself with such things as undecidables, the limits of precise control, conflicts characterized by incomplete information, 'fracta', catastrophes, and pragmatic paradoxes - is theorizing its own evolution as catastrophic, non-rectifiable, and paradoxical [...] It is producing not the known, but the unknown.

Not only does this capture one of the major dilemmas posed by post-modern physics - how to exist in a universe where catastrophic antagonism is literally the rule - but it also neatly conjures up the landscape of *Tristram Shandy*, a world where chaos is periodically punctuated by brief moments of respite in the form of remorselessly deterministic causal sequences: a world that is in its very essence discontinuous, catastrophic, non-rectifiable, and paradoxical. In each case determinacy exists *within* indeterminacy, certainty *within* uncertainty, in a manner calculated to call individual free agency into question. Those brief moments of respite are to be seen as moments of free will-destroying teleology occurring within an overall framework no less uncongenial to the notion of free agency.

I want to consider for the remainder of this essay Sterne's manner of grappling with a dilemma that postmodern physics has put firmly back on the individual's agenda. The site of the conflict in Sterne is personal identity (there are parallels with David Hume's project that I will consider later[1]) and the chosen method of defence will be seen to be sentiment.

'All that exist are 'islands of determinism''. Catastrophic antagonism is literally the rule. One can go on to ask whether being at the mercy of indeterminism or determinism is the preferable condition for the individual to find herself in - or indeed whether the individual's position differs all that much under either dispensation. As Lyotard also notes, with reference to the quantum physics which underpins both catastrophe and chaos theory, 'it is not true that uncertainty (lack of control) decreases as accuracy goes up; it goes up as well' (Lyotard, 1984: 59). That is, the more one organises a system the more likely it is to go catastrophically awry as if obeying some horrible anti-logic of its own. Sterne prefigures the postmodern in being only too aware of this effect - the so-called 'strange attractor' phenomenon of chaos theory.[2] Thus Tristram's christening inevitably

[1] While allusions to similarities in outlook between Sterne and Hume do get made on occasion they are rarely pursued in much detail. John Traugott has been one of the few critics to follow up this line of enquiry - 'the undermining skeptical arguments of Hume (which recommend his doctrine of sympathy) find almost a descriptive statement in Tristram' (1954: 19) - but his main concern is less to relate Sterne to Hume than to identify anti-Lockean tendencies in Sterne. James E. Swearingen also notes correspondences between Sterne and Hume, but his particular brief is to claim Sterne as a forerunner of modern phenomenological philosophy. The Sterne-Hume relationship is accordingly read through the work of Husserl: 'Sterne radicalizes the turn towards transcendental subjectivity in a way that neither Locke, Hume, nor Kant fully achieved' (1977: 34).

[2] Strange attractors are to be seen as hidden patterns to apparently random sequences in dynamical systems, 'the trajectory toward which all other trajectories converge' (Gleick, 1988: 150). Mapped by computer, strange attractors form inter-esting spiral structures whose loops never quite join or intersect; its exact shape as it unfolds is unpredictable and resists organisation: 'when scientists saw what computers had to show, it seemed like a face they had been seeing everywhere, in the music of turbulent flows or in clouds scattered like veils across the sky. Nature was *constrained*. Disorder was channeled, it seemed, into patterns with some common underlying theme' (152). The problem for humankind, however, is that these underlying patterns defy prediction: there *is* a logic involved, but not one that we can unravel enough to guarantee any of

endows him with the name that his father 'had the most unconquerable aversion for' (*TS*: 1.19.62-63) through what *appears* to be a series of chance events; thus Tristram is also fated to be present at a certain window at the precise moment that its sash chooses to come 'down like lightening upon us' (*TS*: 5.17.449), the climax to yet another series of randomly-connected events. Perhaps one should say 'random' and 'inevitable' simultaneously. The moral would seem to be that every *Tristrapaedia* will of necessity fail to impose a pattern on experience, and that stability is to be bought only at the expense of ever-increasing amounts of instability. '[W]hat a long chapter of chances do the events of this world lay open to us', as a bemused Walter Shandy observes (*TS*: 4.9.335). Chance and determinism, randomness and teleological inevitability, will vie with the hapless individual (an island of determinism in his own right given his genetic inheritance of well- or ill-disposed 'animal spirits') caught in the middle of what we might dub the 'metaphysics of catastrophe'. Coping with this 'metaphysics of catastrophe' is the main business of Sterne's world.

Sterne seems to have grasped a critical, and very postmodern, point about systems and their relationship to causality: the fact that *neither* chance *nor* determinism leave any effective scope for human agency, as Tristram's career so tellingly illustrates. The problem of grappling with processes beyond our control is experienced at individual level as a search for a fixed personal identity which will make sense of the stream of sense-impressions to which human consciousness, as Hume reminds us, is so remorselessly exposed:

> For my part, when I enter most intimately into what I call myself, I always stumble on some particular perception or other, of heat or cold, light or shade, love or hatred, pain or pleasure. I never can catch myself at any time without a perception, and never can observe anything but the perception [...] I may venture to affirm of the rest of mankind, that they are nothing but a bundle or collection of different perceptions, which succeed each other with an inconceivable rapidity, and are in a perpetual flux and movement. (Hume, 1962: 301-2)

In the absence of a fixed personal identity there is no realistic hope of structuring the apparent chaos of the world out there, hence the ten-

our efforts at organisation.

dency for Sterne's characters to take frequent refuge in sentiment, that intuitive, sub-verbal, sub-rational response to the plight of mankind in an irrational world. Sterne's complex attitude to the sentimentalism of his characters reveals sympathy on some occasions, irony on others, but little suggestion overall that sentiment is in any way an inappropriate reaction to mysterious forces that transcend human understanding. Faced with the effects of a strange attractor, or the 'retrograde planet' that Walter Shandy fears is 'hanging over this unfortunate house of mine, and turning every individual thing in it out of its place' (*TS*: 3.23.243), sub-rational responses seem only *too* appropriate.

What Sterne's characters are seeking is an 'enduring self', some form of stable entity amidst that never-ending stream of sense-impressions. This was of course also an objective of David Hume, who, like Sterne, has his roots in the epistemological theories of John Locke, particularly Locke's concept of 'association of ideas'.[3] In neither Sterne nor Hume can we find an enduring self held together by a notion of identity, and in Hume's despairing words:

> The whole of this doctrine leads to a conclusion, which is of great importance in the present affair, viz. that all the nice and subtile questions concerning personal identity can never be decided [...] Identity depends on the relations of ideas; and these relations produce identity, by means of that easy transition they occasion. But as the relations, and the easiness of the transition may diminish by insensible degrees, we have no just standard by which we can decide any dispute concerning the time when they acquire or lose a title to the name of identity. (311-12)

There is a consequent need to formulate some kind of strategy to cope with this psychologically very worrying state of affairs, a need that derives from an innate desire for a sense of purpose to our existence.

[3] 'Some of our ideas have a *natural* correspondence & connexion with one another; it is the office & excellency of our reason to trace these, & hold them together in that union & correspondence which is founded in their peculiar beings. Besides this, there is another connexion of ideas wholly owing to *chance or custom*. Ideas that in themselves are not at all of kin come to be so united in men's minds that it is very hard to separate them; they always keep in company, and the one no sooner at any time comes into the understanding but its associate appears with it; and if they are more than two which are thus united, the whole gang always inseparable, show themselves together' (Locke, 1964: 250-1).

The strategy that Hume offers us is 'custom'. We suspend our philosophical speculations about identity and causality (the fruitless search for a 'necessary connexion' between cause and effect), leave our study, and resume our everyday affairs, taking refuge in the custom and practice of daily existence and common belief: 'I dine, I play a game of backgammon, I converse and am merry with my friends' (318). In that daily round the existence of an enduring self is simply assumed, the 'constant conjunction' of cause and effect is simply interpreted as a 'necessary connexion'.[4] With Sterne on the other hand the chosen strategy will be sentiment, that 'True *Shandeism*' which 'opens the heart and lungs' to purportedly beneficial effect: 'it forces the blood and other vital fluids of the body to run freely thro' its channels, and makes the wheel of life run long and chearfully round' (*TS*: 4.32.401).

From the common Lockean starting point of associationism, therefore, Hume and Sterne eventually reach similar conclusions about the nature of personal identity, but Sterne's critique of the notion goes deeper than Hume's in its refusal to mask the psychological implications of the metaphysics of catastrophe. Sterne's is, ultimately, the less comforting solution in many ways. Custom may be a form of philosophical cheat (in effect, a turning of a blind eye to intractable metaphysical problems), but it does have the considerable virtue of providing some basis for renewed human endeavour; as Hume notes:

> Without the influence of custom, we should be entirely ignorant of every matter of fact beyond what is immediately present to the memory and the senses. We should never know how to adjust means to ends, or to employ our natural powers in the production of any effect. There would be an end at once of all action, as well as of the chief part of speculation. (8)

Sentiment on the other hand looks more like an admission of the essential powerlessness of human beings before the operations of

[4] 'We have no other notion of cause and effect but that of certain objects, which have been *always conjoined* together, and which in all past instances have been found inseparable [...] Now, as we call everything *custom* which proceeds from a past repetition, without any new reasoning or conclusion, we may establish it as a certain truth, that all the belief, which follows upon any present impression, is derived solely from that origin [...] necessity is something that exists in the mind, not in objects' (Hume, 1962: 140, 151, 217).

causality, strange attractors, retrograde planets and all. Sterne and Hume might be defined, in philosophical terms of reference, as reluctant antifoundationalists. Reluctant in the sense that both would clearly like there to be stable foundations to their belief systems, since both are dismayed by the antifoundationalist conclusions their researches yield. Both beat a retreat from stark antifoundationalism - Hume into custom, Sterne into sentiment - but in a very different psychological spirit. Whereas Hume's retreat marks a pragmatic compromise (if an uneasy one) with foundationalism, Sterne's represents an emotional reaction to the alienating impossibility of compromise: an impossibility that lies at the very heart of postmodern physics and its theorisation of catastrophic antagonism as the norm.

Personal identity is to be the site where the conflict between chance and determinism is to be felt most keenly. Tristram's dilemma is essentially that portrayed by Hume: how to structure in coherent form the stream of sense-impressions with which the individual is constantly being assailed. The problem becomes one of how to plot 'a tolerable straight line' (*TS*: 6.40.570), as Tristram puts it, through life's adventures such that a pattern discloses itself. Retrograde planets, however, militate against this wish for order (even given Tristram's elastic definition of 'tolerable'[5]) and reduce the individual to that state of ontological insecurity so vividly outlined in *A Sentimental Journey*: 'There is not a more perplexing affair in life, to me, than to set about telling anyone who I am' (*ASJ*: 221). The sense-impressions, whether randomly or teleologically directed, never *do* add up to a coherent pattern. This 'perplexing affair' is foregrounded as Tristram's narrative begins, when 'an unhappy association of ideas which have no connexion in nature' (his mother's linkage of sexual relations with the winding-up of the family clock) leaves him, as he sadly observes, 'the continual sport of what the world calls Fortune' (*TS*: 1.4.7; 1.5.8). It is characteristic of the problems that beset Tristram that even this effort to get back to origins (in a philosophical sense, foundations on which to construct a theory of identity, '*ab Ovo*' (*TS*: 1.4.5)) reveals merely further causal chains extending back to previous associations of ideas, and from there, one fears, back into infinity. Like Jacques Derrida's 'traces', which under investigation

[5] See the diagrams in *TS*: 6.40.570-71, for example.

always disclose further traces of traces, or the fractals of chaos theory, which keep yielding similar, if not quite identical patterns of structure when subjected to ever-increasing levels of magnification, Tristram's search can locate no originary or foundational moment, no moment of ontological certainty.[6]

There proves to be no basis from which to assume the existence of an enduring self, only the perpetual flux of the 'pitiful misadventures and cross accidents' which characterise Tristram's existence (*TS*: 1.5.9). Fate is obviously not very well disposed towards him, although it is not clear whether it is the chance of 'cross accidents' or the determinism of 'pitiful misadventures' that controls fate. Most likely it is some unholy alliance between the two, the alliance that we find described in chaos theory. Repeated attempts to locate some degree of organisation in Tristram's experience merely uncover (or should we say *create*?) larger and larger amounts of disorganisation - catastrophic antagonism is literally the rule. *Ab Ovo* onwards the narrative explodes in a variety of directions. Digression succeeds digression, and although these are held together in some sense by the consciousness of the self-conscious narrator, they conform to no perceivable pattern. Nor can we as individuals prevent the course of our digression-ridden destiny from being what it is determined to be:

> I defy the best cabbage planter that ever existed, whether he plants backwards or forwards, it makes little difference in the account [...] I

[6] For Derrida, 'a "text" [...] is henceforth no longer a finished corpus of writing, some content enclosed in a book or its margins, but a differential network, a fabric of traces referring endlessly to something other than itself, to other differential traces' (Jacques Derrida, 'Living On: Border Lines' translated by James Hulbert, in Bloom, 1979: 75-176 (84)). In consequence, much as Tristram finds, there is 'another story, always already begun, at the moment where it begins' (Derrida, 1984: 104). James Gleick has summed up the problems posed by fractal geometry and Mandelbrot sets (named after the mathematician Benoit Mandelbrot) as follows: 'But Mandelbrot found that as the scale of measurement becomes smaller, the measured length of the coastline rises without limit, bays and peninsulas revealing ever smaller subbays and peninsulas - at least down to atomic scales, where the process does finally come to an end. Perhaps [...] Mandelbrot likes to quote Jonathan Swift: "So, Nat'ralists observe, a Flea / Hath smaller Fleas that on him prey, / And these have smaller Fleas to bite 'em, / And so proceed ad infinitum"' (Gleick, 1988: 96, 103).

> defy him to go on cooly, critically, and canonically, planting his cabbages one by one, in straight lines, and stoical distances [...] without ever and anon straddling out, or sidling into some bastardly digression. (*TS*: 8.1.655)

Tristram's career is to be plotted through this sequence of bastardly digressions, whose unavoidable waywardness of line comes to symbolise the plight of the individual under the influence of the metaphysics of catastrophe. Indeed, fate's ultimate trick on the individual is to land him in a metaphysical stalemate where catastrophe relentlessly undoes the work of organisation. The theme is one of order-threatening dispersal (animal spirits, narrative digressions) alternating with the stultifying excess of order associated with determinism. An individual like Tristram is caught up in a seemingly endless conflict initiated by fate such that he can never impose a sense of unity on events, not even the events of his own past.

Eventually all that the self can do is to catalogue the countless digressions that form the pattern of its existence and pretend to make a virtue out of them:

> Digressions, incontestably, are the sun-shine;———they are the life, the soul of reading;---take them out of this book for instance,--you might as well take the book along with them;——one cold eternal winter would reign in every page of it; restore them to the writer;-----he steps forth like a bridegroom,——bids All hail; brings in variety, and forbids the appetite to fail (*TS*: 1.22.81)

This celebration of digression has its dark side, however, in that the recurrent intervention of digression prevents Tristram from ever managing to present his career in full to the reader to see what sense, if any, can be made of it. Remarking on the fact that it has taken a year's-worth of his writing time to set down the details of his first day of existence, Tristram is forced to admit that:

> 'tis demonstrative that I have three hundred and sixty-four days more life to write just now, than when I first set out; so that instead of advancing, as a common writer, in my work with what I have been doing at it——on the contrary, I am thrown so many volumes back [...] as at this rate I should just live 364 times faster than I should write——It must follow, an' please your worships, that the more I write, the more I shall have to write (*TS*: 4.13.341-42)

No complete retrospective of the self can be constructed, since in the present it is always being bombarded by new impressions ('I never can catch myself at any time without a perception', as Hume points out), and these continually deflect the work of introspection that is being undertaken.

Tristram's efforts to locate an enduring self and thus solve the problem of identity lead him ever more deeply into the tangled affairs of his family circle, only to become hopelessly enmeshed in complex causal chains that defy any attempt at rational analysis: his family may be a 'simple machine' consisting of 'a few wheels' only, but it is a machine set in motion by 'so many different springs' which act upon each other 'from such a variety of strange principles and impulses' that it has, as Tristram notes, 'all the honour and advantages of a complex' machine (*TS*: 5.6.427). All the disadvantages too we might add. Causality presents a complex phenomenon in *Tristram Shandy*, being a confusing blend of association of ideas ranging around freely in defiance of time's linearity ('whether he plants backwards or forwards, it makes little difference in the account'), and fatalistic determinism. Forces outside the individual's control conspire to use and abuse him according to their obscure purposes: ''Tis some misfortune, quoth my uncle *Toby*——That it is, cried my father,——to have so many jarring elements breaking loose, and riding triumph in every corner of a gentleman's house' (*TS*: 4.16.348). Pinpointing the origin, end, or logic of any given causal sequence is beyond the wit of any one individual, although he has no option but to engage with the problem somehow:

> But mark, madam, we live amongst riddles and mysteries——the most obvious things, which come in our way, have dark sides, which the quickest sight cannot penetrate into; and even the clearest and most exalted understandings amongst us find ourselves puzzled and at a loss in almost every cranny of nature's works; so that this, like a thousand other things, falls out for us in a way, which tho' we cannot reason upon it,——yet we find the good of it (*TS*: 4.17.350)

Finding the good of it when subjected to an endless series of disasters is no mean task, especially when the Shandy family is so consistently exposed to the riddles and mysteries of causality. When the dark side of chance or determinism overtakes any member of the Shandy entourage - as it does with Walter in the case of Tristram's naming -

the only course of action left is to set about eliciting the reader's sympathy:

> Will not the gentle reader pity my father from his soul?----to see an orderly and well-disposed gentleman, who tho' singular,——yet inoffensive in his notions,——so played upon in them by cross purposes;———to look down upon the stage, and see him baffled and overthrown in all his little systems and wishes; to behold a train of events perpetually falling out against him, and in so critical and cruel a way, as if they had purposedly been plann'd and pointed against him, merely to insult his speculations. ———In a word, to behold such a one, in his old age, ill-fitted for troubles, ten times in a day suffering sorrow;——ten times in a day calling the child of his prayers TRISTRAM!———Melancholy dissyllable of sound which, to his ears, was unison to *Nicompoop*, and every name vituperative under heaven——— (*TS*: 1.19.63-64)

The cross purposes of chance and determinism are the source of Tristram's identity crisis, and they are actively hostile to the construction of an enduring self. Tristram's researches into his own history disclose only a network of family and personal misfortunes, disasters, and catastrophes stretching back indefinitely like a fractal series. In Humean terms of reference a consciousness of unity to synthesise the individual's unstructured bundle of perceptions will remain frustratingly unattainable. Some one particular perception, plus its attendant associations, is all that will ever be found - never that magic moment when we 'acquire' identity. 'Who I am', other than the target of 'jarring elements' at 'cross purposes' is a question as undecidable in Tristram's case as it is in Hume's. 'Custom' is the psychological ploy we indulge in, according to Hume, to keep the fact of chaos at bay; custom being that 'easy transition to the idea of that object, which usually attends it', and which 'operates before we have time for reflection' (164, 152). Given the talent to move, pre-reflectively, from object to idea, we can go on initiating action and generally behaving as if necessary connexion did exist. The complications arise in Sterne's world when characters such as Tristram find themselves cursed with a talent for constant reflection - a not altogether unexpected affliction for one who is the son of 'a philosopher in grain' (*TS*: 1.21.76) only too well acquainted with the inflexible imperatives of the reflective temperament:

> Though my father was hugely tickled with the subtleties of these learned discourses——'twas still but like the anointing of a broken bone——The moment he got home, the weight of his afflictions returned upon him but so much the heavier, as is ever the case when the staff we lean on slips from under us—— (*TS*: 4.31.394)

Constant reflection reveals a world of catastrophic antagonism so hostile to human aspirations that a retreat into sentimentalism seems an eminently sensible response on the individual's part:

> Why could I not live and end my days thus! Just disposer of our joys and sorrows, cried I, why could not a man sit down in the lap of content here ——and dance, and sing, and say his prayers, and go to heaven with this nut brown maid? capriciously did she bend her head on one side, and dance up insidious———Then 'tis time to dance off, quoth I: so changing only partners and tunes, I danced it away from Lunel to Montpellier———from thence to Pesçnas, Beziers———I danced it along through Narbonne, Carcasson, and Castle Naudairy (*TS*: 7.43.651)

The display of sentiment is designed to capture a state of mind grown weary of constant striving to reconcile chance and determinism. The self is abandoned to a stream of sense-impressions (from Lunel to Montpellier, Pesçnas, Beziers, etc.) in what is a conspicuously anti-explanatory gesture. Emotion is allowed to dictate action as Tristram freely admits his inability to shape his life according to any rational plan. Behind this brave front, however, lies the discomforting knowledge that 'just disposers' ('unjust' too, presumably) will never be content to leave 'sports of fortune' at such a happy pass. Pre-reflective custom might be considered the inherently less disturbing strategy of the two given this realisation.

Sterne's recourse to sentiment as a method of coping with intractable problems is at its most marked in relation to Uncle Toby. The jarring elements of causality have indeed been most unkind to the latter's person, as his war-time injury amply testifies:

> he got it, Madam, by a blow.———A blow!---Yes, madam, it was owing to a blow from a stone, broke off by a ball from the parapet of a horn-work at the siege of *Namur*, which struck full upon my uncle *Toby*'s groin. (*TS*: 1.21.75)

The sequence outlined seems to sum up the Shandean quandary: a chapter of chances which just happens to end with Uncle Toby. Yet what else but a retrograde planet could have contrived to engineer such a maliciously Shandy-directed chapter of chances? Looked at in the context of Shandy family history such 'accidents' seem depressingly prone to occur. Organisation consistently breeds disorganisation: Toby's experience clearly illustrating this, with the highly organised activity of war irresistibly manufacturing the conditions for the disorganisation of personal injury. Like Tristram, Toby is concerned to return to origins - in this case the origins of his career-destroying injury - but with as little success. Toby's fate, and his stoical acceptance of it, inspires some of the text's most sentimental reflections:

> my heart stops me to pay to thee, my dear uncle *Toby*, once for all, the tribute I owe thy goodness.———Here let me thrust my chair aside, and kneel down upon the ground, whilst I am pouring forth the warmest sentiments of love for thee, and veneration for the excellency of thy character, that ever virtue and nature kindled in a nephew's bosom.———Peace and comfort rest for evermore upon thy head! (*TS*: 3.34.265)

Toby himself is easily aroused to sentiment by the misfortunes of others (most notably in the case of Le Fever and his son), and he is very much a 'true Shandean' in this regard, taking refuge in heart and lungs for the shortcomings of reason: 'Tears are no proof of cowardice, *Trim*.——I drop them oft-times myself, cried my uncle *Toby*' (*TS*: 4.4.329). John Traugott has tried to put an optimistic gloss on sentiment by arguing that, 'the core of Sterne's sentimentalism lies in his insistence that by certain public signs - conduct, reaction, and attitude - we can come to understand individuality' (Traugott, 1954: 19), but I would take issue with such a reading; 'understanding' seems altogether too strong a claim to make in this context. What we come to recognise, and to sympathise with, is the plight of others similarly at the mercy of the metaphysics of catastrophe. The powerlessness of individual human beings before a hostile causality forms an ever-present backdrop to the proceedings in Sterne.

Sentiment can only ameliorate, therefore, not change the human condition (the undertow of irony in the work keeps us uncomfortably aware of this fact), and the chapter of chances will continue. So too will the motions of retrograde planets. Individuals cannot escape the metaphysics of catastrophe and have nothing to protect themselves with but sentiment, which makes those easy transitions Hume sets so much store by all the harder to negotiate. From their common starting point in Lockean epistemology Sterne and Hume reach much the same conclusion about self and personal identity (no enduring quality to the former, no causal basis for the latter), and one that brings them both into the territory of the postmodern: but Sterne offers what is ultimately a more despairing view of the human condition overall, by giving us nothing more substantial than sentiment as a bargaining tactic against the combined influence of jarring elements and retrograde planets.

Sterne, therefore, rather strikingly prefigures the world of postmodern physics, where individuals are unable to find a basis for free will and some measure of control over their destinies, thanks to the unholy alliance of chance and determinism facing them. Lyotard considers such a condition highly desirable, arguing that it liberates him from servitude to traditional modes of thought and belief. 'We no longer have recourse to the grand narratives', he contends, 'we can resort neither to the dialectic of Spirit nor even to the emancipation of humanity as a validation for postmodern scientific discourse ... the little narrative [the individual] remains the quintessential form of imaginative invention' (Lyotard, 1984: 60). We may no longer be in thrall to tradition once postmodern physics asserts itself, but we are certainly still in thrall to the vagaries of causality. On that basis Sterne's sentimentalism can seem the psychologically more acute response.

IDENTITY RECLAIMED: THE ART OF BEING TRISTRAM

HERBERT KLEIN

On his travels in France, an official accosts Tristram with the demand to pay a royal tax for a service which he has no intention of using. The astonished Tristram tries to reason with him:

> ———My good friend, quoth I———as sure as I am I——and you are you——
> ———And who are you? said he.——Don't puzzle me; said I. (*TS*: 7.33.633)

Tristram's answer touches upon a question that had provoked the educated public since Locke (1975: Book 2, Chapter 27) added his chapter 'Of Identity and Diversity' to the second edition of *An Essay Concerning Human Understanding* in 1694 (cf. Fox, 1988: 38-68). In this chapter, Locke makes the revolutionary assertion that personal identity is not a substance, but is dependent on consciousness. The reverberations of this daring assertion, which has now become commonplace, can be traced through the first half of the eighteenth century and find their culmination in Hume's giving up the attempt to find a basis for identity (cf. Hume, 1978: 259).

It should not come as a surprise that Tristram makes an appearance in this debate, since from the very beginning of his narration he is concerned with the question of who he is. Ostensibly, this is explained once and for all by the circumstances of his conception and its consequences. A closer look, however, reveals that Tristram has a rather poor grasp of the theory of the animal spirits (which he has picked up from his father - cf. Myer, 1984a: 99-112) and that his source for the events of this allegedly all-determining night is his Uncle Toby - as unreliable a source in matters sexual as can be imagined (Stevenson, 1990: 80). Furthermore, a few pages on we learn that it is far from certain that this was really the decisive night, for despite Tristram's detective-like fixing the only possible date of his conception (*TS*: 1.4.6-7), it turns out that he was actually born just eight months later - not nine months, as he had earlier asserted (*TS*: 1.2.3) and as his father believed (*TS*: 1.3.4). So there is every reason to doubt that this episode really marks the beginning of Tristram's life and consequently that it had the effects that he pretends to attribute to it (*TS*: 1.5.8-9; cf. Klein, 1992: 415-427).

There are, however, even more events that should - at least according to his father's theories - determine Tristram's life and identity: at his birth, the precious nose that was to repair the fortunes of the Shandys is irreparably damaged; at his baptism, he is given the name that will inevitably bring misfortune upon him; and the fall of the sash-window has apparently such grave consequences that they can only be hinted at. And yet, although Tristram speaks frequently of his present miserable condition, the reader finds it hard to believe him. Quite to the contrary, the narration of these events seems to serve Tristram as an occasion to prove that his life is not determined by them.

Telling stories about oneself is an important means of manifesting one's identity both to oneself and to others (Gergen, 1988: 17-56). These stories ('self-narratives') are used 'to establish coherent connections among life events' (Gergen, 1988: 19 and Blasi, 1988: 226-242). This coherence is achieved through various devices, such as the selection of a meaningful end point and of events which lead towards it, their proper (i.e. causal) arrangement, and a clearly marked beginning and ending (Gergen, 1988: 20-22). As is evident from this catalogue, Tristram follows none of these conventions, but seems to take a special pleasure in turning them on their heads. His endeavours at composing his story never actually link up to a plausible picture of himself in the conventional sense. Without such a result, however, he either fails miserably in his stated attempt at giving us his 'life and opinions' or he sees his task as something quite different from what one would normally expect.

Although Tristram appears to carry to an extreme the conventions of autobiographical writing in beginning the story of his life with his very conception, he of course intends to do no such thing, as he makes clear from the start:

——for in writing what I have set about, I shall confine myself neither to his [Horace's] rules, nor to any man's rules that ever lived. (*TS*: 1.4.5)

Tristram is quite correct in stating his originality, since he does not write in the accepted autobiographical mode of the eighteenth-century novel, which looks back on the vagaries of a fulfilled (or misspent) life, gives it shape and draws a wholesome moral from it. Quite the contrary: he writes to experience himself living and to understand what this means (Harter, 1988: 44; Markova, 1987: 77). He is in the midst of it all, and this necessarily entails disruption, digression and equivocation without any attempt to force a coherent interpretation upon it. To pretend that any other procedure were possible would be dishonest, because nothing living ever is finished, and therefore Tristram's self-narrative will only come to an end with his death (*TS*: 1.22.82).

The events which Tristram maintains were so decisive for his future all occur during the first years of his life and are largely reconstructed from what has allegedly been told him by other people. Of his present circumstances and activities other than writing we hear very little, apart from his account of his trip to France in Volume 7. So the Tristram we actually come to know is the writer who reveals himself through what he writes about and the way in which he does it, for everything we read is his unique creation. He does not set himself up as the impartial historian of his world, but rather emphasises the fact that he is in control of both matter and manner.[1] Indeed, this becomes the central concern of his narrative: he constantly draws our attention to the idiosyncratic way of telling his story, to the choices he makes and the paths he leaves unexplored. And it is just this awareness of alternatives, the knowledge that there are many ways of telling a story, and therefore many guises in which he might appear to the reader that make it necessary for Tristram to create an identity for himself (Luhmann, 1979: 322). He constitutes himself not so much through what he does or does not tell, but even more through the act of telling itself and what it reveals about the teller, so that his 'life' and his 'opinions' become not only inseparable but even

[1] Perhaps most glaringly in his use of dashes and asterisks; cf. Schulze, 1980: 394-436.

indistinguishable (Swearingen, 1987: 242). In creating his world, Tristram creates himself (Swearingen, 1977: 70).

Tristram's manner of telling his story is vital for the effect he intends to achieve: he never stays long with one subject, but usually gives us only bits and pieces, cut short either by events in the narrative or by the narrator himself. Emblematic for this procedure is Uncle Toby's constant interrupting of Trim's attempt at telling the story of the King of Bohemia (*TS*: 8.18-19.680-693), but more often than not Tristram interrupts himself. He thus continuously interposes himself between the narrated events and the narrative act: there is an incessant mingling of levels which are all contained in Tristram's metanarrative whose subject is his quest for an identity.

In order to find out about himself, Tristram has first to deconstruct the concept of identity others, especially his father, try to force upon him. He discredits these attempts through exposing the absurd theoretical assumptions on which they rest and then proceeds to disassociate himself from the older generation altogether. Tristram insists that he is fundamentally different from his father and his uncle who are both portrayed as characters with a fixed identity, caught in a self-perpetuating cycle from which they cannot escape, since they lack the awareness - or the means - to step out of it. Walter Shandy is caught within his intellectual preoccupations which effectively prevent him from successfully communicating with anyone, least of all his wife or his son. In this he resembles his brother who defines himself as a soldier - and nothing but a soldier. Neither seems to be able to engage with reality in any meaningful way (Josipovici, 1992: 190). They rather follow their own course irrespective of its consequences. In this way they seem to fulfil the Newtonian law of motion that maintains that a moving body will move with the same speed and in the same direction indefinitely unless other forces come to exert an influence upon it. They are indeed sometimes checked in their course, but only to head off in a new direction. Thus Walter shifts his attention from the importance of the right nose to the importance of the right name and thence to the importance of the right education, which sets him writing the *Tristrapaedia* without paying any attention to the upbringing of his son (New, 1969: 153-154). He changes direction, but the impetus remains the same. He never stops to reflect about himself and what he is doing. Even more, he is not capable of doing it.

The same applies to his brother Toby: he cannot help being a soldier heart and soul and experiencing the world from this perspective (*vide* his Apologetical Oration). He could not even conceive of the possibility of being different. Both brothers are then defined - and define themselves - through what they perceive as being their immutable selves. They certainly possess consciousness, but they lack self-consciousness in the sense of an ability to reflect upon themselves. They are endowed with certain unchangeable and clearly defined attributes and are thus representatives of the idea of the self as substance,[2] whereas Tristram embodies the new idea of the self as consciousness. This entails for him the difficulty of establishing his own identity, and he finds it much easier to assert what he is not, then what he is.

Faced with this dilemma, the only way open to him of defining himself is through stating his difference from others, and this is even perceived by his father who observes with regard to Tristram that he 'should neither think nor act like any other man's child' (*TS*: 1.3.4, cf. also 9.1.737). This insistence on difference as a vital feature in defining identity not only makes Tristram almost a postmodern character (Docherty, 1991: 182-183), but for him it becomes the means of finding out more about himself. His manner of setting about this task is outwardly not different from the usual one: he gives us a self-narrative, that is, a story which should establish his identity for him and for us. This at least is his declared intention:

> I have undertaken [...] to write not only my life, but my opinions also; hoping and expecting that your knowledge of my character, and of what kind of a mortal I am, by the one, would give you a better relish for the other: As you proceed further with me, the slight acquaintance which is now beginning betwixt us, will grow into familiarity; and that, unless one of us is in fault, will terminate in friendship. (*TS*: 1.6.9)

Although there is no reason given for his wishing to become thus acquainted with the reader, the intended goal seems to be clear

[2] Quite likely Toby's being a soldier is an allusion to the joke in Martinus Scriblerus about soldiers being 'the most substantial people in the world' (Pope, 1966: 119).

enough. By what means it is to be achieved, however, is left somewhat vague: '—bear with me,——and let me go on, and tell my story my own way' (*TS*: 1.6.9). The reader is warned not to expect the usual kind of procedure, but this makes it difficult for him to determine what is relevant to an understanding of Tristram and what is not. That is left entirely to Tristram's discretion, which raises the danger of making the story unintelligible to the reader. As if this were not enough, Tristram makes yet another demand on him:

> if I should seem now and then to trifle upon the road,———or should sometimes put on a fool's cap with a bell to it, for a moment or two as we pass along,--don't fly off,——but rather courteously give me credit for a little more wisdom than appears upon my outside (*TS*: 1.6.9-10)

The reader is warned not to expect an orderly tale, that is one in which the narrated events are seen to be connected to one another or even form causal links, but apparently the envisaged goal is only to be achieved in a roundabout way and only when it has been achieved will the narrative take on its conclusive significance:

> ————*O diem praeclarum!*———then nothing which has touched me will be thought trifling in its nature, or tedious in its telling. (*TS*: 1.6.9)

Tristram wants to reach a shared awareness of his identity, but he cannot simply tell the other about himself, since as yet there is no self to tell about - and there never will be in the sense of a 'final product' (Docherty, 1991: 173). Rather, the self will emerge from a process to which the reader is invited to contribute: he has to participate in Tristram's creation of himself and his world, otherwise Tristram's attempt at acquiring an identity fails. This makes him entirely dependent upon the reader and his acquiescence in playing the rôle of an accomplice; in fact, it brings Tristram dangerously near to becoming a postmodern construct (Gergen, 1990: 192). His success in achieving his goal depends on the reader's concurrence, as Tristram is well aware himself:

> As no one, who knows what he is about in good company, would venture to talk all;——so no author, who understands the just boundaries of decorum and good breeding, would presume to think all: The truest respect which you can pay to the reader's understanding, is to halve this

> matter amicably, and leave him something to imagine, in his turn, as well as yourself. (*TS*: 2.11.125)

The reader is thus not only a passive recipient, but becomes an active contributor without whom Tristram's undertaking would fail. The reader's contribution consists in his willingness to let himself be made aware of his own expectations and preconceptions: to set about uncovering hitherto unknown sides of his own identity (Anderson, 1971: 966-973). Even though Tristram can obviously only imagine such a sympathetic reader, this is enough to enable him constantly to reflect upon himself and demonstrate his own 'otherness'. By teasing, surprising and irritating the reader through constantly disappointing his expectations, Tristram creates a pattern which serves to delineate his unique self. At the same time, the reader is made aware of this process and thus comes to share Tristram's experience (Docherty, 1991: 181-182). In this constant confrontation of perspectives the outlines of identity become visible without actually defining and thus delimiting it: it is enough to show the range of possibilities.

Tristram could therefore be thought to be a precursor of postmodern identity, which is also characterised by 'difference' and does not exist on its own, but only in contradistinction to other identities within a web of relationships. The self is defined - and defines itself - only through these external relationships, and since they are continuously changing, so is the self. The same applies to the world in which the self exists, which is also only one of many possible worlds with no particular claim to be considered of any special value. There can be no question of 'gaining an understanding' of this world (or the self, for that matter), since it does not exist apart from the self's particular vision of it. This view of identity in the postmodern world seems also to be a fair description of the subject in the world of the postmodern novel (Brooke-Rose, 1991: 167, 175-178). At first glance, it might appear to fit Tristram quite well, and that is probably why he is so often adduced as an example of postmodernism *avant la lettre* (Imhof, 1986: esp. 36). Yet Tristram is no 'vanishing subject', but on the contrary an emerging one. His aim is to be a distinct and distinctive self of his own making. The way he does that brings to mind the story of Munchausen who has to pull himself (and his horse) out of the mire by his own bootstraps, only that Tristram does not need to do it all by himself, since half the pulling is done by the reader.

Tristram not only takes up the question of identity as posed by Locke and Hume, but he actually goes beyond them in that he is the active maker and shaper of his world which would not exist but for him - and this again bears a close resemblance to the postmodernist stance (Scholes, 1975: 7). But even more remarkable is the fact that Tristram, despite his apparent solipsism, seems to possess certain criteria by which to evaluate himself and his world. This is the more surprising, since he does not accept any authority apart from himself, indeed he goes almost out of his way to discredit all such authority. The interesting question is then: where does he get his ideas from? They seem to arise out of his existential predicament and to be a necessary concomitant to its solution. Since it is foremost his father's mechanical determinism that would preclude him from being himself, its rejection becomes the necessary precondition of his being able to construct his individual identity. He sets against his father's deterministic theories the practice of indeterminacy, that is, the constant demonstration that nothing in his narrative can be shown to follow inevitably from something else. This applies both to the narrated events themselves and to his way of narrating them. He shows up the fortuitous connection of the former through exerting himself to establish bogus causal chains, and he makes an ostentatious display of his own ability to make unexpected and apparently illogical shifts in his narrative. The other (negative) point of departure for him - also inevitably linked to the origin of his existence and therefore to his identity - is the damaged sexuality of the Shandys. Again Tristram's procedure is to ridicule the effects of mechanical inflexibility, for example his father's invariable linking of his marital duties with the winding of the clock and his Uncle Toby's inability to differentiate between love-making and warfare. About his own sexuality, however, Tristram teasingly withholds all information, thereby opening the doors wide to speculation of all kinds (cf. *TS*: 1.18.56-57 and 7.29.624).

This then is the starting point of Tristram's struggle to make himself: the rejection of an imposed identity which would fix him once and for all is the necessary precondition of his freedom. Since it would be self-defeating, if Tristram were to set up against this an equally rigid position of his own, he attempts to arrive at a more flexible one through his use of language. He gradually loosens words from their conventional connotations and eventually also from their conventional meaning - most famously in the disquisition on noses (Josipovici, 1992: 190). Fixed and seemingly unequivocal relationships between words and meanings become unfixed and equivocal, and their significance starts shifting with their context (M. Johnson, 1988: 10). Language thereby becomes a flexible tool for self-reflection, in stark contrast to Walter Shandy's use of language. So nothing Tristram says can be taken as a definite and final statement, but should rather be understood as a provisional position that can be revised at any time. His 'life and opinions' thus must be seen as an indissoluble whole, and together they form his unique identity both in the philosophical sense of difference from others and in the psychological sense of behavioural consistency and self-reflection (Henrich, 1979: 133-186). Despite - or rather because of - his finally indeterminate and indeterminable status, Tristram emerges as a fully developed character whose unknown and unrevealed sides only serve to reinforce this sense of completeness. He leaves the reader speculating about many traits of his personality, and this not only adds more dimensions to it, but is actually the means of making it possible in the first place: personal identity is not a given, nor is it simply the result of one's individual history, rather it evolves during a permanent process of personal intercourse - be it only that between (fictive) writer and (imagined) reader (Swearingen, 1977: 93-94).

Tristram is probably the first character in fiction who thinks of his personal identity as a problem. All his seeming attempts at finding a place in his family's history for himself only serve to show that this is an impossible way of establishing his identity. Nevertheless, the attempt itself is necessary, because only in talking about the historical conditions of his being can Tristram find the means for self-reflection. Through the writing of history - his extended life-narrative - he makes himself in the present, and it is finally not through facts but through his use of words that Tristram constructs his identity.

If epistemology is the sign of the modern, and ontology of the postmodern (McHale, 1987: 10), then Tristram seems to belong to both periods. He attempts to answer not only the question 'Who am I?' but also the question 'What is identity?'. He takes epistemology to and beyond its limits and turns it into ontology (McHale, 1987: 11): Tristram and his world are inextricably one. In thus creating his own identity, Tristram refutes the notion of the self as substance and asserts the freedom of the individual to be himself.

THREE TRAPPED TIGERS IN SHANDY HALL

LOUIS PEGENAUTE

According to Harold Bloom, 'it cannot be accidental that so many of the best contemporary Spanish-American novels are Shandean, whether or not the particular writer actually has read Sterne' (1987:1). We have evidence that Guillermo Cabrera Infante was influenced by his reading of *Tristram Shandy*.[1] The similarities between Sterne, one of the originators of the novel as we now know it, and Infante, writing in another world, in another time, should not be overlooked.

The Cuban-born Cabrera Infante is the author of *Three Trapped Tigers* which, according to D. P. Gallagher (1974: 47), is one of the most original and funniest stories of all South American novels.[2] On its most superficial level, this novel offers a detailed description of nightly life in the times of pre-revolutionary Havana. Although it may seem to be a novel about social injustice, it also deals with the nature of friendship, the possibilities of communication and the inexorable passage of time. Above all, *Three Trapped Tigers* (hereafter: *TTT*) is a novel about the nature of language and literature. In the following

[1] Despite the existence of some parallels between the concept of modernism in the Anglo-Saxon literary tradition and the concept of *modernismo* in the Hispanic one, there are significant differences. Postmodernism moves beyond the methods of the modernists and constitutes a literary movement in itself, while *postmodernismo* is just a chronological label used to describe the generation of artists who come after the *modernistas*. Cf. Davidson (1966). Having said this, I'll remark that, even though Cabrera Infante is a Cuban, he should be described as a postmodernist rather than a *postmodernista*.

[2] *Tres tristes tigres* was published by Seix Barral in Barcelona in 1965. I am using the paperback edition of *Three Trapped Tigers* published by Faber and Faber in 1990. This translation was done by David Gardner and Suzanne Jill Levine with the author, and first published in English in the USA in 1971.

pages I intend to study the similarities between the work of Cabrera Infante and Sterne's *Tristram Shandy*.

A number of critics have tried to establish Cabrera Infante's antecedents in literary history, which coincide with those authors with whom Sterne has frequently been compared. W.T. Little (1970: 635), for example, has considered *TTT* to be the inheritor of the humoristic tradition represented by such works as *Gargantua and Pantagruel*, *Gulliver's Travels* and *Alice in Wonderland*. Those works have been classified by Northrop Frye as representatives of the 'Menippean satire', whose leitmotif is to make fun of the philosophus gloriosus while presenting absurdity as something germane to intellect. According to Frye, 'The Menippean satire deals less with people as such than with mental attitudes' (1957: 309). Writers such as Petronius, Apuleius, Rabelais, Burton, Swift and Voltaire '[rely] on the free play of intellectual fancy and the kind of humorous observation that produces caricature' (309-310). The structure of most of their works is based on intellectual games which bring about significant disjunctions in the traditional narrative order. Some Menippean satires, such as Burton's *Anatomy of Melancholy*, introduce a mass of encyclopaedic erudition, which eventually may constitute the final organizing principle of the whole work.

Cabrera Infante himself has not only admitted his indebtedness to Sterne, but also acknowledged the influence of some of the above mentioned writers.[3] For example, he has testified that long before he had set out to write *TTT*, he had been fascinated by the exuberant descriptions of nightlife in old Rome in the *Satyricon*. The truth is that, in terms of the plot, apart from a similarity between the erotic adventures described by Petronius (and also by Catullus and Sextus Propertius) and those by Infante, there are not many other similarities. Neither are there in *Tristram Shandy*. The notes to The Florida Edition point out the parallelism between Diego's journey to the Promontory of Noses in Sterne and Encolpius' quest for sexual rejuvenation in

[3] The influence of Sterne on Cabrera Infante has been pointed out by, among others, Matas (1974: 184), Monegal (1974: 87-88), Goytisolo (1976: 11), Jiménez (1976: 54-55), Nelson (1980), Toda (1985: 50). Cabrera Infante has often acknowledged his high consideration of Sterne; see the interview conducted by Pereda (1979: 114).

Petronius. Encolpius' insistent efforts to remove the curse of Priapus may also remind us of Tristram's own hints of impotency (as in *TS*: 7.29.624). That is all. However, if we take a closer look at these three works, apart from the characteristics inherent to all Menippean satires, we may appreciate two features of the *Satyricon* which *TTT* and *Tristram Shandy* quite obviously share, namely: the concept of artistic amusement (which brings about a high reliance upon satire and parody) and the stress on the conversational nature of the literary works.

And then there is, of course, Miguel de Cervantes. Both *Tristram Shandy* and *TTT* contain fine examples of intertextual games à la Cervantes. Sterne and Infante remind us that the literary text cannot be judged in isolation, but in relation to the whole system of aesthetic, cultural and historical values which determine its identity - no matter whether that is due to an acceptance or a refusal of them. In the three novels we find fine 'debates' about what literature is or should be like. For a Cervantic reading of *TTT*, see Goytisolo (1976).

Both *Tristram Shandy* and *TTT* can be considered self-conscious novels in the terms formulated by Alter (1975: xi): 'A fully self-conscious novel [...] is one in which from beginning to end, through the style, the handling of narrative viewpoint, the names and words imposed on the characters, the patterning of the narration, the nature of the characters and what befalls them, there is a consistent effort to convey to us a sense of the fictional world as an authorial construct set up against a background of literary tradition and convention'. When talking about self-conscious fiction, especially about novels like these two, where there are recurrent asides to the audience, it is quite convenient to make a subtle distinction between the addressee inside the piece of fiction and the reader in the real world.[4] We may say that the audience to which the narration is addressed is connected with Tristram's biography. We, the readers, find the justification for our existence in Sterne's novel. The former listen, the latter read.

[4] In this sense, Kayser's remarks as cited by Christensen, are helpful: 'The relation of narrator - story - reader is expanded in the [meta]fictional situation to encompass: author - narrator - story- fictional reader (audience) - actual reader. The author and the actual reader [are] external elements in the [meta]fictional world, to which other elements belong as integral parts' (Christensen, 1983: 13).

Critics such as Preston (1979: 206-06) have suggested that we may occasionally make a partial but conscious identification with some of the imaginary readers to whom Tristram makes a few asides. Others, like W. J. Ong (1975), consider the real reader to be 'something like a reader over another reader's shoulders'. When facing a text, our reading is made through that person to whom the narration is addressed in the fictional situation. Dowling (1978) applies this theory to *Tristram Shandy* and states that it 'is a story without an audience - or rather, a work projecting an empty space where an internal or imaginary audience normally exists in literature' (1978: 284). If we accept Dowling's thesis, we may consider the audience to be imaginary in a double sense because, on the one hand, it does not correspond to a group of real readers and, on the other, it is imagined by Tristram the narrator and not by Sterne the author. Be that as it may, the truth is that it is very typical of Sternean prose to make frequent asides to the audience, as reciprocally it is for that very audience to interrupt the narrator with a question or a plea for further explanation. As Wagoner has stated, 'the reader's involvement, on its simplest level, depends on the rhetoric of question' (1966: 337).

The narrator addresses his audience some 350 times throughout the whole novel. It is not a homogeneous audience because Tristram has deliberately divided them and brought them face to face - just as Sterne had done with his public. There are two groups clearly differentiated: those who support his narrative and who are treated in a friendly way, and those who seem to disapprove of his life and opinions. The tone and vocatives used to refer to them are very different.

The question of the identity of the audience is far less complex in *TTT* because it is quite overtly considered to be formed by the group of readers in the real world, that is, 'you who live on the other side of the page' (373). Most of the time the narrator addresses a single reader, who quite obviously happens to be yourself. No references to our gender are made and no particular prejudices or passions seem to rule our relationship. In a few specific instances, Ong's concept of the reader may eventually be personified in one of the characters: '"raven's wing, darling", Livia would say if she was standing behind me and reading this page I'm writing' (148). We are treated with familiarity, but also with a certain degree of respect. The narrators (just like Tristram often does) are quite fond of interrupting their conversation to make an anticipatory reponse to some hypothetical objection of ours:

> It was a case of total recall because in a copula of seconds I had remembered all the afternoons of my life (don't bother, I'm not going to list them for you, dear reader)' (329)

These self-conscious comments on the process of writing are quite commonly exerted through references to the audience, who seem to participate actively in the drafting of the book, in the sense that much of the material presented is intended to suit our desires:

> I will spare the reader any cries of protest, explosions of anger or Damoclean threats from my father; I will not spare you any obscenities: the fact is I never heard him utter any. I will also pass over my mother's weak but very effective arguments, which, goodness knows how, succeeded in neutralizing my father's love for that library which every day became more like the memory of a library.

The narrator (in this particular case, Cué) may even apologise for the temporary lack of inspiration: 'I'm sorry, fellers: I have no other adjective - not at this moment' (138). He behaves as if he had to justify his acts. Of course, all this contributes to the heightening of the effect of 'automatic writing'. In some cases, following *Tristram Shandy*'s policy, we are admonished for having inferred some obscene meaning: 'Feminine fashions tend to homo... Don't get me wrong. To homogenize' (398). Sometimes it is another character who is scolded. Such is the case with the telephone conversation between Beba Longoria and her friend Livia, where we are given only the former's speech: 'Last night the old bugger took me to the Tropicana to celebrate. No, you dumb blonde. Tropic not Toprick' (35).

If it is important to stress the distinction between the reader and the addressee, the same holds for the author and the narrator. Tristram himself calls our attention to his fictional existence when he says, for example: 'as long as I live or write (which in my case means the same thing)' (*TS*: 3.4.191). He is aware that he has no existence outside the covers of the book because he is actually one of the characters in the piece of fiction. What is more, his self-consciousness is underlined by the fact that many of his intruding comments to the addressees concern not only his role as a character but also as a narrator. The distance between the narrator and the author is still widened by the presence of a fictional editor (cf. Christensen 1983: 16), who may eventually point out mistakes in Mr. Shandy's narration (*TS*: 2.19.176; 9.26.791); certify the authenticity of the material presented (*TS*: 3.11.202); apologise for the (unavoidable) deficiencies of Tristram's translation (*TS*: 4.0.303) or make relevant explanations (*TS*: 5.25.457; 8.26.709; 9.24.780).

Cabrera Infante also detaches himself from the narration. Actually, the existence of a 'gallery of voices', makes it difficult to identify the author with any narrator in particular. The narrators may make overt self-conscious reflections about the process of writing: 'It was like a piano roll. That's the word, roll, isn't it?' (68). On the other hand, we also find the presence of an intrusive fictional editor in 'The Tale of a Walking Stick', where we are presented with a chaotic translation plagued with unncessary and absurd footnotes. This is intended to be a satire of the work of so many translators, whose inefficiency brings about a contamination of language with illicit linguistic borrowings.

Both novels introduce a deliberate fragmentation which initiates simultaneous movements on different levels. This should be interpreted as a protest against the usage of hermetic literary structures. *TTT* is presented, in its major part, in the form of monologues or scenes narrated in the first person. The introduction of personal and subjective visions of reality dependent on the intellectual or emotional perspectives of each narrator conveys an impression of ambiguity. Codac's words, similar to the famous ones uttered in *Macbeth*, are quite relevant to the author's intentions: 'this is an island of double and triple entendres told by a drunk idiot signifying everything' (128). At the same time, narration is constantly interrupted by the sudden and somewhat chaotic remembering of the past, digressions, leaps in time, interpolations of texts not bearing any relationship to the main narrative, etc.

We can quite legitimately say that the unity of style becomes the agglutinating narrative feature of both novels. The style of *Tristram Shandy* acquires a great distinctiveness through the incompleteness of predication, the recurrent changes of direction of the sentences, the exuberant and apparently chaotic use of subordination, the great number of punctuation marks (especially the dashes acting as rhetorical pauses), the minute descriptions of gestures, the interruptions and the exploitation of misunderstandings. These distinctive features have repeatedly been cited by the critics from Hazlitt on to underline the conversational nature of Sterne's work.[5] On the other hand, the recurrent usage of the spoken Cuban language provides *TTT* with a definite stylistic cohesion among the different sections and contributes to attenuate the impression of discontinuity (cf. Monegal, 1974: 86). In a number of scenes we are presented with a phonic transcription of oral language and a deliberate disrespect for correct syntax, diction and orthography. Infante himself had warned his readers in the foreword to the Spanish edition of *TTT* that it would not be a bad idea to read his novel aloud, in an attempt to bridge the dichotomy between the literary language of traditional writing and popular oral language.

It is quite paradoxical that, although both authors try to bridge the gap that separates written and oral language, they insist on stressing the tangible and, above all, visual nature of the book as object. Sterne, as it has frequently been pointed out, intended to show how non-linguistic phenomena can communicate or show more than mere words. Much has been said about *Tristram Shandy* as an 'aesthetic object' (De Voogd, 1966 and 1985). This visual aspect of the text is not less visible in *TTT*, where we find an alternation between italics and normal letters (to distinguish the textual segments uttered in English and Spanish); two black pages as mourning for Cué's death (only, alas, in the Spanish edition); texts indented; the word 'elevator' written rising diagonally across the page to convey the impression of Livia's cry ascending with her voice (142); a single sentence standing out in the middle of the page (173); orthographic signs, words and sentences struck through (195-99); words whose letters have been separated by hyphens: 'i-n-t-o-x-i-c-a-t-e-d' (205); a huge capital B occupying one third of page 215; a text in the form of an inverted pyramid conveying the impression that 'the owner got smaller and smaller' (216); a picture representing the position adopted by

[5] Cf. Hilsky (1971), Hnatko (1969 and 1971), Hunter (1980), Milic (1971), Moss (1981), Stedmond (1959), Stewart (1969), Stovel (1984), Wagoner (1966), Warren (1977, 1986), Watt (1967).

Bustrofedon's hands (219); a wordwheel 'which you can begin reading with any of the words and it is the wheel of fortune: David, ávida, vida, avi, vid, ida, dádiva, dad, ad, di, va' (221); a hexagon which a few lines later becomes a cube after it recovers 'its lost third dimension' (226); four blank pages (280-83); a page mirroring the text in the left hand page; a page in which the word 'blen' appears 370 times (in ten columns over 37 lines) representing the lyrics of a song by Chano Pozo (359); words run together in an incoherent speech with no orthographic signs (487), and so on.

Another recurrent feature in both novels is the abundance of interpolations, which, by means of a shift to another kind of language, bring to our attention the discontinuity of the narrative. Some of the interpolations incorporated into the main corpus of the English novel have been excerpted from real sources, some others pretend to quote texts whose existence can only be attributed to Sterne's imagination (see also Rosenblum, 1982). None of the interpolations in *TTT* can be attributed to a real existence outside the frame of the novel. They are far less numerous than the ones in *Tristram Shandy*, but quite relevant to Infante's attempts to disconnect the continuity of the narrative. 'The Death of Trotsky as Described by Various Cuban Writers' pretends to be an anthology of the contributions of seven well known Cuban authors. The topic dealt with is the same in all of them, but it bears no connection with the rest of the events described in the novel. It is just an excuse to satirize the particular stylistic devices of Infante's fellow countrymen. Another interpolation is entitled 'The Story of a Stick, with Some additional Comments by Mrs. Campbell', which is followed by a mock-translation of the text the reader has just been presented with, but pretending to be the English version of a story originally written in Spanish. This is a fine example of the most recurrent mistakes made by translators when transferring a text interlinguistically.

A further characteristic shared by both novels is the recurrent use of bookish references and philosophical maxims providing a large account of erudition. The reader stands in the middle between the narrative to which he is being exposed and all the literature alluded to and, accordingly, his cultural background plays a predominant role in this intertextual game. The use of proverbs constitutes another form of reliance upon external forces: their integration into the narrative brings it closer to common speech while challenging the capacity of the recipients to recognize them as something familiar. Just like the literary references mentioned above, they also have an independent existence outside the realm of the text.[6] If we want the proverbs to perform in an efficient way as envisioned by the author, the reader must be prepared to share with him his same cultural universe. Unfortunately, that is not always possible. While *Tristram Shandy* is dialectically marked by the situational category of temporal provenance, *TTT* presents marks of geographical dialect. The former, as Brady (1971) has pointed out, is spattered with terms which take on slang meanings not current anymore. On the other hand, Cabrera Infante warned his readers about the fact that 'the book is written in Cuban (that is, in the different dialects of the Spanish spoken in Cuba)', a warning not found in the English version. The truth is that, in addition to the particular linguistic features of the Cuban language, the text proves to be deeply culture-linked, and that most of the pages will be meaningless to those readers not brought up in the Caribbean island.[7] *TTT* resembles *Tristram Shandy* in the author's proclivity to manipulate language for specific purposes and, accordingly, it is also quite common to find here both paraproverbs and oblique proverbs:

> He made a muffled sound. What does a sound look like in its muffler? Idiocy of the folk. Muffled noises. Empty vessels make muffled sounds. Sounds to all deaf. Deaf words falling on silk purposes. Till deaf do us part. The early bird catches the first post. You can lead a horse to the water but you can't make him think. (Though you can make him sink.) Too many cocks spoil the brothel. We need a revolution among proverbs, for God's sake. Proverbs a la lanterne. Anyone who says a proverb should be shot. (374)

[6] Rogers (1982) has brought our attention to their stylistic importance in *Tristram Shandy*, where we can find direct proverbial quotations, para-proverbs, (that is, the invention of new proverbial lore bearing a formal resemblance to genuine proverbs) and oblique proverbs (those ones for which we can trace a model which served as inspiration). Among other stylistic characteristics of proverbs, Rogers points out that '[they] can be read both as separate statements, well-known saws which have independent existence outside the text, and as segments of textual discourse, an integral part of the running utterance' (308-9).

[7] Sánchez-Boudy (1971) gives an exhaustive listing and explanation of those word games, set phrases and references that may prove difficult for someone not familiar with Cuban society and its jargon in the 1950s.

A brief survey of Sterne's and Infante's novels will also show the authors' concern for both the metaphysical nature of time and its manipulation for literary purposes. It is quite obvious that in *Tristram Shandy* there are frequent leaps in time and space. According to the narrator, that is nothing to be astonished at : 'When a man is telling a story in the strange way I do mine, he is obliged continually to be going backwards and forwards to keep all tight together' (*TS*: 6.33.557). We appreciate not only sudden temporal and spatial leaps, but also different actions taking place simultaneously:

> I have brought myself into such a situation, as no traveller ever stood before me; for I am this moment walking across the market-place of Auxerre with my father and my uncle Toby, in our way back to dinner ———and I am this moment also entering Lyons with my post-chaise broke into a thousand pieces——and I am moreover this moment in a handsome pavilion built by Pringello (*TS*: 7.28.622)

All the different incidents can be set in a strict chronological order. The novel starts in 1718 and ends in 1714, while some of the events take place as early as 1689 and as late as 1767. Though Sterne's accuracy in dating is remarkable (especially if we consider the intricacy of the machinery of his constant digressions), he was not so much interested in chronological dating as in the discrepancy between duration in terms of clock and psychological time (Mendilow, 1968: 94). His main concern lies in the way the characters experience their actions (that is, their states of mind) rather than the actions themselves. On the other hand, fictional and real time are brought together and contrasted through overt references to how long it takes the narrator to write a certain episode of his life and to how long it takes the readers to read it.

This disparity between fictional and real time is also stressed in Infante's novel. We find that it takes Silvestre longer 'to write what he did than he took doing it' (405). Delia also makes a specific reference to the time devoted to her writing the letter to her old friend Etelvina: 'I just finished doing the dishes and Gilbertos gone back to work, so now I can carry on with this letter I began this morning' (19). We are even asked to perform our reading at a certain speed: the section entitled 'Lot's Steps', which has supposedly been written by Alejo Carpentier is 'to be read in the time it takes to play the Pavane pour une infante defunte', at 33 rpm (255). On the other hand, we see that characters also experience the passage of time according to their own background and the contextual characteristics of each particular incident - and that they consider remembering just another word for living. The protagonists of *TTT* are not less concerned about time than the ones in *Tristram Shandy*: Cué, who 'had this obsession with time' (320), thinks that 'speed turns time into space' while Silvestre thinks that 'the movies turn space into time' (350) and that 'time, like space, also has its laws of gravity' because 'memory induces vertigo' (331).

The metaphysical nature of time constitutes, along with sex, literature and language, one of the favourite topics in the somewhat absurd debates with which the characters amuse themselves. There is quite an important difference between the two novels: the reader finds it very difficult (at least on his first reading) to know which is the chronological order of the incidents described in *TTT*. Actually, in some specific instances, he may not even be sure which character is the narrator. The majority of the debates just mentioned constitutes pure dialectical exercises, whose only purpose is to argue for the sake of arguing. Through them the characters interpret reality according to their particular vision of the world. It does not matter whether they reach a solution to a certain problem: what they are obsessed with is giving a free reign to their witty and somewhat narcissistic impulses.

Occasionally there is a sense of simultaneity (or, in Freedman's words, of 'literary counterpoint'), which can be exemplified with this apparently incongruent temporal perspective: 'It will be a pity Bustrófedon didn't come with us because we were going along El Malecón at forty, fifty, eighty miles an hour [...]. It was a pity Bustrófedon won't come with us to see [...] the motley ocean. [...] It is indeed a pity Bustrófedon isn't coming with us along the Malecón this evening with Aresion Cué and me in his car' (317). Other times, fiction and reality seem to mingle and prove to be quite difficult to disentangle. This is the case, for example, when Silvestre and his brother are caught on their way to the movies in the middle of a shooting just like the one appearing in the film. When they finally reach the door of the cinema they see that there is a black pool of blood under a light and an inquiring crowd surrounding it. Silvestre's comments are as follows: 'I can't for the life of me remember the name of the film we were going to see, which nothing would have stopped us from seeing, which we did see' (33). We never come to know whether they actually saw the shooting or whether it was just the product of his imagination.

Along with time, both novels are deeply concerned with the nature of language. Quite paradoxically, Sterne and Infante prove to be able to expand its possibilities through an awareness of its limits. Sterne was conscious of the imperfections of language: in the novel there are frequent misunderstandings due to the associative power of words and their ability to present more than a univocal meaning. As we all know, Sterne was indebted to Locke, who considered words to stand for nothing but the ideas of the user and to be able to provoke different notions in different individuals.

Cabrera Infante calls our attention to the fact that perfectly built sentences which apparently offer a coherent meaning may prove to be absurd: 'She was sitting in the darkness of the lobby, or rather she was sitting on a sofa in the darkness' (101). He also underlines the fact that words are nothing but the representation of reality, the formal support of our views of the world: 'Excuse me, family, and he really meant it, family, he didn't say the word for the sake of saying it, saying family and really meaning something quite different from family, but family was what he meant, really, and he said: Familia, we have to close' (63).

There is quite an important difference between both novels: while in *Tristram Shandy* words are biased by the hobbyhorses of the characters and associated through an incorrect understanding of their meaning in a particular context, in *TTT* this association is based on the similarity of sound. It is quite typical of Bustrófedon to play with phonic permutations which provoke new lexical categories and ultimately end up by depriving words of any semantic value. He is also quite fond of replacing terms (or parts of those terms) for homonyms or quasi-homonyms in what we might call 'fossilized language' such as coined phrases, titles of songs and books, proper names, and so on. This creativity goes hand in hand with irrationality: Bustrófedon stresses the exuberant ability of language to produce numerous combinations, but at the same time he deprives language of the rudiments necessary to perform its most primordial function: the conveyance of meaningful sequences (cf. Ortega, 1974). From the very title of the book, the phonic aspect of language is emphasized. What Infante is doing is recovering many of the premises postulated by the Dadaists, Futurists, Symbolists and Surrealists, who had tried to break the links between the word and its referent.

There are several other aspects common to *Tristram Shandy* and *TTT*, the study of which would exceed the scope of this paper: death is a significant motif in both novels, sex is pervasive, the question of identity seems to be a constant preoccupation, debating is one of the favourite pastimes, joy for life seems to be the motto of a few of the characters. Some of these are explored by Nelson (1980: 77-81). To recapitulate what has already been said in the previous pages concerning the most distinctive features shared by Sterne and Infante, I would underline the existence of a deliberate fragmentation of the literary work. Neither of them would agree with Archimedes or with cabbage planters in that the best line is the shortest line 'which can be drawn from one given point to another' (*TS*: 6.40.572). While Sterne shows a proclivity for curves, Infante is more inclined to provide a series of brief segments which will eventually constitute a whole. Their disjunction of the traditional narrative order is achieved by means of interpolations, leaps in space and time, digressions, literary parodies, manipulations of the book as object, constant allusions to external entities in the real world, use of different registers, and even different languages, etc. Apart from this disjunction of the formal presentation, we may observe a recurrent presence of conflicting aspects: the comic and the serious, the logical and the irrational, the erudite and the bawdy.

Antithesis might be a nice word to describe the cosmos of these novels. By means of all these disjunctive processes, the authors do away with traditional literary assumptions such as the integrity of the action based on a logical relation of cause-effect, the linear development of the plot (non-existent here) following a chronological order and, in a few words, the conveyance of a coherent message. This strategy brings about a high involvement of the reader in the rewriting of the novel. The novels are not presented as finished products, but as something which would be quite inert without our active participation.

STERNE AND KUNDERA: THE NOVEL OF VARIATIONS AND THE 'NOISY FOOLISHNESS OF HUMAN CERTAINTY'

TIM PARNELL

The consistency with which *Tristram Shandy* is alluded to as a model for much experiment and postmodernist narrative has conferred upon the apparent linkage the status of received wisdom. Consequently, grounds for meaningful comparison have tended to be ignored in favour of an acceptance of unquestioned continuities between Sterne and his twentieth-century admirers. In the case of Milan Kundera's fiction this tendency has been accentuated by his own construction of his literary precursors in which Sterne figures prominently alongside Cervantes, Rabelais and Diderot.

That said, there are enough significant parallels between Sterne and Kundera for a comparison of their work to be illuminating. While Kundera's earlier fiction bears some of the traces of what he has termed the 'depreciated legacy of Cervantes' (Kundera, 1990: 3-20), it is in the postmodernist phase - beginning in 1979 with *The Book of Laughter and Forgetting* - that the relationship with *Tristram Shandy* is most apparent. Indeed, Kundera's brand of metafictional self-consciousness is, in some ways, closer to Sterne's than that of other postmodernists like Barth, Grass or Calvino. Like *Tristram Shandy*, *The Book* and *The Unbearable Lightness of Being* are structured in such a way as to foreground their intergeneric status. Characteristically Kundera's later fiction juxtaposes historical 'fact' with explicitly 'fictional' and fantastic narrative in a way which recalls Sterne's consistent habit of eroding the boundaries between the world and the text.

Kundera also follows Sterne in giving the 'essay' form a key place in the carefully orchestrated polyphony of voices and narratives which are the hallmarks of his novels. The distinctive presence of the discrete essay in Sterne and Kundera serves a dual function: that of reminding the reader of the hybrid and constructed nature of the text and at the same time offering a paradigm of the kind of sceptical rhetoric which in some ways links Kundera with Rabelais, Cervantes and Sterne.[1] While there remain important differences of tone between Kundera's 'essays' on laughter or kitsch and Sterne's on wit and judgement or love, both writers employ the essay because of its essentially speculative nature. Interestingly, the Chambers' *Cyclopaedia*'s entry on the genre, might describe Kundera's practice as well as Sterne's. For Chambers the essay is 'a peculiar kind of composition whose character is to be free, easy, and natural; not tied to strict order, or method, nor worked up and finished, like a formal system' (s.v. 'Essay'). The key factor for both writers is the essay's antithetical relationship to any 'formal system,' or dogmatic discourse.

In Kundera's novels metafictional strategies go beyond intergeneric play to include a problematic confounding of the 'actual' author's identity with that of his characters and narrator. As David Lodge (1990: 163) puts it, in Kundera's fiction, the 'real author has [...] leapfrogged over the implied author, to appear as a trope in his own text'. Similarly, Sterne constantly plays with his relationship to the fictional Tristram and Yorick, as Rabelais does with Alcofribas and Burton with Democritus Junior. Once again the effect of the blending of 'fact' and 'fiction' is to undermine certainty and to allow for the kind of sceptical freeplay which is typical of the narrative tradition with which Kundera aligns his own novelistic practice.

Continuities between Kundera and Sterne are not confined simply to shared narrative strategies. Igor Webb (1990: 357) has recently characterised Kundera negatively as 'a kind of Enlightenment savant' and clearly he shares many thematic preoccupations with Diderot and Sterne. Indeed, it might be argued that it is Diderot's *Jacques the Fatalist*, rather than *Tristram Shandy*, which shares most affinities with postmodernist fiction. In general terms, however, Kundera's scepticism can be seen to be an Enlightenment legacy. His carnivalesque treatment of the erotic, in particular, finds significant parallels in Sterne's refusal to separate love and cuckoldom and

[1] See Wehrs (1988), Parnell (1993). For a discussion of Sterne's debt to some of Montaigne's discursive practices, see Lamb (1980).

Diderot's still more sceptical treatment of love as 'that fragile illusory emotion' (Kundera, 1984: 112). Yet Kundera's cynicism and his preoccupation with how the will to power manifests itself in the sexual arena, finally distinguishes his treatment of sexuality from that of his eighteenth-century models.

Even such a cursory outline of the common ground between Sterne and Kundera would seem to bear out the latter's own view of his literary ancestry and to confirm the commonplace that *Tristram Shandy* is peculiarly prescient in its anticipation of the postmodern condition. But it is worth looking again at the line Kundera traces from Rabelais and Cervantes through Sterne and Diderot to his own practice.

In outlining his literary genealogy Kundera offers both an alternative history of the novel and an explanation of his own narrative practice. Like many critics who take the 'long view' of the novel's history, he equates the emergence of the genre with the publication of *Don Quixote* in 1605. In so doing, he offers a context for his own novels which the predominantly realist nineteenth-century novel is unable to provide. Furthermore, although Kundera makes clear his admiration for such twentieth-century experimenters as Kafka, Broch and Calvino (amongst others) he is keen to stress his true kinship with a narrative tradition which predates the nineteenth century. For Kundera it is the triumvirate of Rabelais, Sterne and Diderot 'who were the greatest experimenters of all time in the form of the novel' (Kundera, 1983: 231) and it is the perception that their legacy has been depreciated which informs his own narrative practice. With regard to *Tristram Shandy* Kundera suggests, in his introduction to *Jacques and his Master*, that the 'history of the novel has exploited to its very limits the example of Samuel Richardson [while] it has paid scant attention to the perspective contained in Sterne's enterprise' (Kundera, 1986: 12). Kundera clearly has a point, but his defence of his narrative tradition leads him to make claims for the novel which recall D.H. Lawrence's similar construction of the genre in quasi-mystical terms. For Kundera, Cervantes' legacy offers the possibility of the novel as the sceptical form *par excellence*:

> The wisdom of the novel comes from having a question for everything [...] the novelist teaches the reader to comprehend the world as a question. There is wisdom and tolerance in that attitude. In a world built

> on sacrosanct certainties the novel is dead. The totalitarian world, whether founded on Marx, Islam, or anything else, is a world of answers rather than questions. There, the novel has no place. (Kundera, 1983: 237)

The appeal of such a 'history' of the novel for a writer, on whose life totalitarianism has impinged in a manner which can only be exotic to a Western audience, is clear. Nevertheless its utopian naivete should not disguise the significance of its blind spots.

In many ways, of course, Kundera's eulogistic view of the sceptical form is endorsed by the tendency of much contemporary criticism to favour the radical possibilities of 'writerly' and 'dialogic' texts over their conservative opposites the 'readerly' and the 'monologic'. But such an approach tends not only to homogenise disparate texts on the grounds of shared formal strategies but also to sever the texts from history. Indeed Kundera's approach to the history of the novel and to his own texts is consistently informed by a desire to deny what Edward Said (1991) has called the 'worldliness' of texts. Nevertheless, Kundera's history of a sceptical narrative tradition is of interest in terms of what it suggests about important differences between eighteenth-century scepticism and its more extreme postmodern equivalent.

It is surely no coincidence that Kundera's reading of the history of the novel should resemble Bakhtin's. That both should characterise the early novel in terms of 'joyful relativity'[2] is less surprising in the light of their common experience of totalitarian oppression. But the problem is that neither Bakhtin nor Kundera is able to distinguish between a scepticism which serves faith - and hence finally religious dogma - and a scepticism which is more or less an end in itself.

Although Kundera is keen to claim Rabelais and Cervantes for a novelistic tradition in which *nothing* is asserted, he is able to do so only by isolating sceptical means from dogmatic ends. Behind the marvellous complexities of *Gargantua and Pantagruel* and *Don Quixote* lies a fideism that is closer to the conservative scepticism of St. Paul than the radical scepticism of postmodernity. It was Erasmus, who in the wake of the Reformation crisis employed in *The Praise of Folly* the rhetoric of Pyrrhonian scepticism in defence of what Terence

[2] The phrase is, of course, Bakhtin's but many of Kundera's ideas on the novel find parallels in the Russian critic's work.

Penelhum (1983: 294) has called a 'middle-of-the-road theology.' After Erasmus the alliance of fideism and the Menippean form became almost exclusively associated with a sceptical interrogation of the human-based search for truth and satire on perceived abuses in religion (Kirk, 1980: ix-xxxiii). Any meaningful treatment of the texts of this sceptical tradition - which includes Cervantes, Rabelais, Burton, Swift and Sterne - has to be aware of the uses to which the sceptical arguments of Sextus Empiricus were put by Catholic and Anglican apologists. The Epistemological crisis of the Reformation made a purely rational defence of religious belief quite untenable, but also produced some extraordinary 'literary' texts in which sceptical discourse comes to serve an artfully disguised negative dogmatism (see Popkin, 1979: 1-87).

If we return to Kundera's reading of Sterne the problem becomes clear. For Kundera, what separates Sterne from dominant tradition of the psychological novel is his conception of 'the novel-as-a-game' (1986: 12) - a conception which leads to the creation of a truly sceptical narrative form:

> [*Tristram Shandy*] is non-serious *throughout*; it doesn't make us believe in anything: neither in the truth of the characters, the truth of the author, nor the truth of the novel as a literary genre: *everything* is put in question, *everything* is put in doubt, *everything* is a game. (Kundera, 1986: 13)

Now, this reading of *Tristram Shandy* finds support in the numerous critical responses which have stressed Sterne's modernity and yet it is hard to defend. In fact, Sterne is keen to affirm all sorts of truths and those truths find their ultimate validation in the Anglican deity. While Sterne exploits the sceptical form as a means of demonstrating the non-linear, labyrinthine nature of the paths to 'truth,' he is also keen, as a satirist and moralist, to demonstrate quite clearly that there *are* some truths. By relentlessly ridiculing the inadequacies of human systems, Sterne is better placed to recommend the haven of Anglican certainty. The notion that *Tristram Shandy* 'doesn't make us believe in anything' is hard to square with Sterne's consistent assaults on false learning and his trenchant attacks on Catholicism and to a lesser extent Methodism. Time and again Sterne leads his readers through the complexities of human-based searches for certainty only to recommend the solution which Toby offers to Walter's tortuous investigations into the mysteries of nose sizes: '——There is no cause but one, replied my uncle *Toby*,——why one man's nose is longer than another's, but because that God pleases to have it so' (*TS*: 3.41.284). The solution is, of course, the one favoured by Rabelais' Grangousier and it is the one which Sterne has Toby, Trim and Yorick espouse at key moments throughout *Tristram Shandy*.[3]

To be sure, *Tristram Shandy* can be read without reference to Sterne's satiric intentions or the value system which underpins them. But such a reading is surely partial if it is unable to comprehend the differences between post-Nietzschean scepticism and post-Reformation attempts to hold on to epistemological certainty. Thus, while Kundera is right in his assessment of the sceptical possibilities of Sterne's narrative strategies he is startlingly blind to the fact that such scepticism is mitigated. Sterne's fideism and the discursive practices which result from it are not peculiarly modern, let alone postmodern, but rather consistent with a conservative tradition of religious apologetics which stretches back to Erasmus and the Reformation crisis. That said, it seems to be the very weakness of the case for the defence which leads Sterne and his forebears to attempt to silence opposition voices with the full range of weapons from the sceptic's arsenal.

Since Harold Bloom's *Anxiety of Influence*, we may be more readily able to accept Kundera's inevitable misreading of his chosen ancestors as a means of validating his own practice. However, the notable silences and omissions in Kundera's construction of an enabling myth of origins can tell us much about important contradictions in his own work and, indeed, in postmodernist narrative practice. For all that the very concept of postmodernism is overdetermined it is a flexible enough category to describe usefully the

[3] While Toby is frequently the butt of Sterne's satire, he also has an important function as a commonsensical foil to Walter's scientific and philosophical excesses. For the theological basis of Toby's 'simplicity' see *TS*: 4.7.332, 6.7.506 and 8.33.718. For Trim's similar function see his preference for 'one home thrust of the bayonet' to the complexities of argumentation indulged in by the 'polemic divines', 5.29.464 and for his *practical* understanding of the Catechism see 5.32.470. For a discussion of Yorick's normative role in *Tristram Shandy* see New, 1969: 75-81.

practice of, say, Barth or Pynchon. But when it comes to the explicitly political fictions of Kundera or Salman Rushdie, postmodern theory and practice become peculiarly suspect. The postmodern insistence on the absence of the centre sits uneasily alongside the specificity of both Rushdie's and Kundera's engagement with history and politics. Both writers seem to have taken their cue from Sterne as they deploy the sceptical form as a foil to what Kundera terms the 'noisy foolishness of human certainty' (Kundera, 1983: 237). And yet the privileging of variation and polyphony over linear and unitary plot never quite offers the hoped for liberation from the tyranny of certainty and affirmation.

By ignoring the fact that Sterne is primarily a satirist and that his scepticism is underpinned by a throughgoing Anglican fideism, Kundera is able to gloss over the *sine qua non* of the eighteenth-century *Tristram Shandy*. However, the ghost of Sterne's paradoxical use of sceptical rhetoric for dogmatic ends remains to haunt Kundera's own fiction. The blind spot that conditions his reading of *Tristram Shandy* also informs a rather desperate desire to disclaim any political context for his own novels. In spite of Kundera's consistent claim that the 'novel does not assert anything' (1983: 237) his novels are inescapably affirmative as they attempt to confront the complex ideology of Cold-War totalitarianism. Furthermore, at a fundamental level Kundera's novels are peculiarly dogmatic in the face of such oppositional, and potentially threatening, discourses as those of sexual politics and 'popular' culture.[4]

The complex manifestations of these contradictions in Kundera's novels can only be touched upon here but they are nonetheless significant. As is well known, Kundera has frequently taken issue with critics of his work who have insisted on reading him as a dissident, or primarily political writer. For Kundera such a reading is typical of 'journalistic non-thought' (Kundera, 1984: 24) in its simplistic narrowing of his work to *one* of its many aspects. Nevertheless, both *The Book of Laughter and Forgetting* and *The Unbearable Lightness of Being* treat explicitly the impact of the Russian invasion of Czechoslovakia in 1968 on his characters and indeed on his own life. Like Rushdie, Kundera takes pains to remind a largely Western

[4] For a discussion of Kundera's problematic representations of women see Smith, 1993: 108-116.

audience of the brute facts of history which it is the business of totalitarian regimes to erase. Although Kundera characteristically stresses the degree to which the public world impinges on the private, he also seeks to prevent collective 'forgetting' on the part of his audience. The dangers inherent in such amnesia are summed up in Part 1 of *The Book*:

> The bloody massacre in Bangladesh quickly covered over the memory of the Russian invasion of Czechoslovakia, the assassination of Allende drowned out the groans of Bangladesh, the war in the Sinai desert made people forget Allende, the Cambodian massacre made people forget Sinai, and so on and so forth until ultimately everyone lets everything to be forgotten. (Kundera, 1983: 7)

The passage is in many ways typical of Kundera and it gains force from the stark contrast with the more conventional narrative which frames it. Yet, for all that the form of *The Book of Laughter and Forgetting* encourages ambiguity and doubt, Kundera is in such instances unequivocally affirmative. Such affirmations are without question justified but their truth-value is surely not undermined by their status as one of a plurality of sometimes conflicting novelistic discourses. And yet Kundera claims - again in the manner of Bakhtin - that the world of single truths is incompatible with the novel form itself. Commenting elsewhere on his habit of offering discrete essays on such personal *bêtes noires* as kitsch, and 'graphomania' Kundera explains that once it becomes part of a novel dogmatic thought turns hypothetical (1990: 79). While such a sleight of hand is one way of distancing the 'actual' author from the 'implied' author of the novel's diegetic utterances, it is not very convincing. Kundera's idealised view of the novel's ability to dialogise and render ambiguous all discourses, cannot so easily explain away the recurrent tendency of his fiction to denigrate both women and popular culture. Nor, in spite of his attacks on the kind of criticism which 'takes revenge on art by forcing it to a purpose beyond the aesthetic' (Kundera, 1990: 140), is it able to address the issue of the status of the political and historical 'truths' which are an insistent presence in the novels.

In one of his essays on *Tristram Shandy*, Melvyn New suggests that Sterne, like Hume, demonstrates that while the suspension of judgement required by classical scepticism may be desirable 'it is not often within the human being's capacity - [since] we cannot refrain from believing in the truth of our own perceptions, our own narratives' (New, 1992: 317). Sterne's acceptance of this fact liberated him to use the rhetoric of scepticism in the service of embattled Anglican orthodoxy. Kundera, on the other hand, remains torn between a desire to embrace the poetics of postmodern relativism as a foil to totalitarian certainty, and a need to offer alternatives which inevitably become reified as dogma. In the end both writers deploy sceptical rhetoric for dogmatic ends, but it is the profound difference between those ends which finally separates Sterne and Kundera.

DELUGE OF FRAGMENTS: RABELAIS'S 'FOURTH BOOK', STERNE'S 'FRAGMENT' AND BECKETT'S 'FIZZLES'

CARLA MARIA LAUDANDO

As Melvyn New (1972) has convincingly argued, the 'Fragment in the Manner of Rabelais', first published in 1775 by Sterne's daughter, Lydia Medalle, was 'Sterne's first attempt at creative writing' after the *Political Romance*. As such, it may offer some intriguing clues as to the artistic *homunculi* which agitated the author's mind at the crucial time of beginning *Tristram Shandy*, providing us with an access, however incomplete and eccentric, to the laboratory of his *écriture*, to the process of Shandean writing/reading. To begin with, the title signals the key-words for a refreshing exploration of the relationship between Rabelais and Sterne: *fragment* and *manner*. Accordingly, my intent here is to propose an inter-textual reading of this literary influence in which Rabelais's manner may work as a model for a rhetoric of discontinuity and fragmentation to stimulate Sterne's beginnings in writing.[1]

It is the *Third Book* of *Gargantua and Pantagruel* which has been mentioned as the main source for Sterne's plagiarisms or exercises in Rabelaisian style, among others by Traugott, who speaks of it as 'an object of Sterne's thieving scholarship' (1954: 45). The 'Fragment' may instead suggest another key of access to try in the inter-textual journey from the Shandean writer to the Pantagruelist in virtue of the 'poor Homenas', who is the homonym of that ludicrous bishop of Papimany in the *Fourth Book*. In spite of the tenuousness of this suggestion, it is an intriguing and rewarding path - indeed a most

[1] My inter-textual analysis was inspired by the reading of Kritzman (1981) In particular see: 'Part 2. Three Rhetorics of Discontinuity: Rabelais, Montaigne, and Diderot', 53-97.

Shandean digression from the common route[2] - since the *Fourth Book* presents a 'splintered journey' from one island fragment to the next which may well have appealed to Sterne's creative imagination. I am referring here to the fine essay by Lawrence D. Kritzman (1981), 'Rabelais's Splintered Voyage', which offers a perspicuous, deconstructive reading of the *Fourth Book* as

> not in search of a final product (story, representation, sense), but rather a response to the author's use of fragments of knowledge as the instrument by which he introduces into literature the plurality and diversity of cultural discourse (54).

The *Fourth Book* is thus a satire in the etymological sense of the word: *satura*, that is a medley, a mixture of heterogeneous elements, a mixing up of fragments. For this activity of literary *bricolage* Kritzman aptly suggests the term of 'fold-in-method', where the use of fragments is evidently of basic relevance: the text is embedded with 'narrative excrescences' (62) and such excrescences do proliferate through the grafting and reframing of the textual fragments which have been pillaged from the learned tradition. Sterne's work delineates a similar scriptural odyssey through the eccentricities of erudition and the very process of writing/reading, where narrative is indeed continuously deferred, interrupted and ultimately not so much embedded as eroded by such grotesque and parodic excrescences and fragments. If in Rabelais's *Fourth Book* conversation substitutes for the actual travel, in the Shandean world travel (more often of a figurative, inner quality) is initiated by conversation. Both authors then celebrate the relentless pleasure of fabulation, exposing the narrative form of the *book* to all sorts of ironic inversions, breaches, parodic redoubling and equivocation which the *fragment* brings forth.

From such a perspective, the episode of the unfrozen words in the Pantagruelist journey may be seen as the delightful epitome for this

[2] New (1972: 1087) suggests that the phrase 'Alass poor Homenas' possibly 'gave Sterne the inspiration for masking himself as the Shakespearean jester in Tristram Shandy'. The name of the bishop of Papimany occurs in the *Fourth Book*, chs. 48-54. At the first occurrence of the name Homenas the translator's note explains: 'This word is a production of that of homme. They use it in Languedoc, when they would say, a great loggerheaded booby, that has neither wit nor breeding' (Rabelais, 1750: 275).

process of splintering and deferring the completion of narrative. The description of these words is a masterpiece of linguistic imagery:

> Here, here, said Pantagruel, here are some that are not yet thaw'd. He then throw'd us on the deck whole handfuls of frozen words, which seemed to us like your sugar plums, of many colours, like those us'd in heraldry; some words gules, [this means also jests and merry sayings] some vert, some azur, some black, some or, [this means fine fair words;] and when we had somewhat warm'd them between our hands, they melted like snow, and we really heard them, but could not understand them, for it was a barbarous gibberish. (Rabelais, 1750: 308)

The fragmentation here reaches the core of language itself, investing not only words but also sounds and noises devoid of significance: instead of the distillation of Platonic/Christian truth or of Orpheus's lyre, as Pantagruel had expected, in the topsy-turvy writing of Rabelais we rather witness the fall of literal splinters from a textual explosion which issues in utter grotesque unintelligibility:

> When they had all melted together, we heard: Hin, hin, hin, hin, his, tick, tock, taack, bradedin, brededack, frr, frr, frr, bou, bou, bou, bou, bou, bou, bou, bou, track, trr, trr, trr, trrr, trrrrrr, on, on, on, on, on, on, ououououon, gog, magog, and I do not know what other barbarous words. (310)

We find a nice example of the physical, mobile dimension of words/ideas in *Tristram Shandy*, where the reader is invited to imagine the dexterous (or rather ambidextrous) narrator half starting out of the chair in search for eventual inspiration from heaven, which is a humorous parody of this classical/christian *topos* in the same spirit of *jouissance*[3] as Rabelais's melting words: 'I believe', says Tristram, 'in my conscience I intercept many a thought which heaven intended for another man' (*TS*: 8.2.657). The physical readiness to intercept an idea directed to someone else coyly adumbrates an act of plagiarism which is thoroughly displayed in the 'Fragment' as an allegorical battle 'poor Homenas' engages with his conscience as well. Apart from the sexual allusions (cf. Howes, 1984, and Myer, 1984b: 47-9) plagiarism is here characterised as a grotesque and ludicrous fall from

[3] I refer, of course, to the concept introduced by Barthes (1973). See also Heath, 1977: 9.

the source copied down, as a kind of caricature, a violation of the *original* work issuing in burlesque breakage and fracture.

It is worth recalling, in this respect, the passage in *Tristram Shandy* where the narrator apologises for tearing out a whole chapter: quite interestingly, in the course of his argumentation, the character of Homenas also makes his entrance as imprudent *exemplum* of writing on the stage of Sterne's major text. He is again 'found out', this time by the Shandean narrator/reader of his unequal notes:

> I'm to preach at court next Sunday, said *Homenas*——run over my notes——so I humm'd over doctor *Homenas*'s notes [...] Your notes, *Homenas*, I should have said, are good notes,——but it was so perpendicular a precipice——so wholly cut off from the rest of the work, that by the first note I humm'd, I found myself flying into the other world, and from thence discovered the vale from whence I came, so deep, so low, and dismal, that I shall never have the heart to descend into it again (*TS*: 4.25.375).

This *exemplum*, where a number of elements are clearly derived from the 'Fragment', serves ultimately to support Tristram's paradoxical conclusion that the consistency of the whole depends upon the fragmentation of its parts: the tearing out of chapters. The apology for a *lacuna* in his text is then exploited by Sterne as a bathetic travesty of literary conventions, while focusing the reader's attention on the significance of the gaps, the interstices, the *betweenness* of the act of writing/reading (McGilchrist, 1982: 41, 63).

A similar bathetic resolution takes place in the very 'Fragment' itself, where a kind of 'allegorical', 'comical', and 'dramatical'[4] battle within Homenas's conscience issues in a parodic purification of his discourse:

> Here, Homenas burst into a Flood of Tears which falling down helter skelter, ding dong, without any kind of intermission for Six Minutes and almost twenty five seconds, had a marvellous Effect upon his Discourse; [...] But moreover, the said tears, by their nitrous Quality did so refrigerate, precipitate, & hurry down to the Bottom of his Soul, all the

[4] So runs the second subtitle of the 'Fragment': 'In which the Reader will begin to form a Judgment, of what an Historical, Dramatical, Anecdotical, Allegorical and Comical Kind of a Work, he has got hold of' (1089). Here Sterne probably alludes to Polonius' mocking praise of the actors in *Hamlet*, II, 2, 392ff.

> unsavoury Particles which lay fermenting (as you saw) in the middle of his Conception, That He went on in the coolest & chastest Stile (for a Soliloquy, I think) that ever mortal Man utter'd [...]. (1090)

The passage already displays that playful, intricate mixture of different registers of discourse which is characteristic of Sterne's linguistic *bricolage*. As Roy Porter opportunely remarks, by the time of the Shandean enterprise a considerable number of technical terms were put into a wider circulation without strict semantic regulation, whereas words belonging up until then to a tangible, concrete field of meaning came eventually to assume abstract or figurative connotations. Sterne's eccentric - in a way, Rabelaisian - linguistic sensibility then capitalised upon the rich and fluid potential of such a cultural phenomenon 'spotlighting how words could be scalpel-probes, revealing the secret ramifications of a man's workings, but uncovering deeper problems all the time' (Porter, 1984: 87). In the 'Fragment', for instance, the clash between concrete and metaphysical meanings is functional to the author's parodic game with the biblical and classical myth of the Flood: the cosmological dimension of the deluge as a divine instrument of punishment and regeneration indeed undergoes a process of bathetic Shandean miniaturisation and fragmentation by being reduced to the haphazard, grotesquely purificatory flood of Homenas's tears over the scriptural battleground of his remorseful conscience.

Intriguingly related to the risk of plagiarism, another critical issue from Sterne's age is already brought into focus and staged in the Rabelaisian farce of the 'Fragment': the obsession with the idea of the *encyclopedia*. In fact, Homenas's plagiarism does interrupt Longinus Rabelaicus's explanation of the *kerukopaedia*, thus working as a mocking counterpoint to the ambitious project of his playful wit. In a way, throughout his work, Sterne comes to mimic a sort of dialectic or polarity between the theory of the encyclopedia/totalisation and the practice of fragmentation/ textuality.

It is inevitable, in this respect, to compare the idea of the *kerukopaedia* with that of the *tristrapaedia* in the novel, since Walter Shandy's writerly plan significantly echoes the main characteristics emphasised by the 'Rabelaic' fellow. The preliminary stage of both enterprises requires the act of collecting the material to unify, and as such it implicitly raises the issue of *copy/original* at stake in the process. The point is indeed illustrated by Tristram with the image of writing as spinning:

> My father spun his [system], every thread of it, out of his own brain,——or reeled and cross-twisted what all other spinners and spinsters had spun before him, that 'twas pretty near the same torture to him. (*TS*: 5.16.445)

The originality of this Shandean collector is then, quite paradoxically, described in terms which adumbrate a substantial analogy with the vicious subjective method of the 'modern' authors dissected by Swift with merciless, unsurpassable acumen in *A Tale of a Tub* and *The Battle of the Books*. Interestingly, a more remote echo of this image is to be found in Bacon, one of the spiritual pillars of the modern, scientific age, who had already warned the learned men not to indulge, like a spider, in the self-entrapping workings of the mind, thus losing the primary and healthy contact with reality (Bacon, 1902: 192).

It is worth stressing that the Baconian issue in defence of experience was then recast by Swift into the form of a 'battel' between books, where 'ancient' and 'modern' are not so much conceived as historical or philological referents as the representative poles (both opposite and complementary) of an ideological conflict. The polemic against the eccentricities and casuistry of 'modern' virtuosi reached its peak in the eighteenth century when the rapid and alarming influence exercised by print in a sense catalysed the fragmentation of national culture 'into innumerable, competing subcultures' that flourished in the wake of the Glorious Revolution, as Daniel Eilon (1991: 123-59) has convincingly argued.

The crisis was perceived and denounced by the Augustans as a deluge of noxious material, which urged a policy of discipline and a realignment of literary and ethical boundaries. The modern mass production and consumption of books seemed thus condemned to a surfeiting play with revision and plagiarism, as Swift's very anxiety testifies in the acute observations of the scholar just mentioned:

> The sheer bulk of extant books, laws, and schemes induces in Swift not so much an anxiety of influence as a fear of drowning. [...] The rubble of disappointed ideals bequeathed by the past leaves the present no genuine (untried) novelty. In the world of Swift's Grub Street Hack all expression

> falls into tautology, because all possible utterance is already extant, simply as a result of the mechanical workings of permutation (Eilon, 1991: 127).

The redundant nature of 'modern' literature/language at stake in the *Tale* also emerges in the encyclopedic plan pursued by the most meticulous of Swift's collectors, Simon Wagstaff in the *Polite Conversation*. Here the sterility of the 'Moderns' is most clearly revealed in the field of oaths. The compiler has in fact not inserted any of such linguistic expressions in his otherwise exhaustive work(!) because of their very transient, permutational paradigm:

> In short, Oaths are the Children of Fashion; they are, in some Sense almost Annuals [...] The old Stock-oaths, I am confident, do not amount to above forty-five, or fifty at most; but, the Way of mingling and compounding them, is almost as various, as that of the Alphabet. (Swift, 1973: 105)

Quite intriguingly, a collection of oaths is, however, interpolated into the book of *Tristram Shandy* as a fragment/sample of Walter Shandy's curious library. This interpolation indeed gives vent to Tristram's mocking disquisition upon the lack of *invention* in a 'modern' world dominated by the cant of criticism. His argument begins with a delightful denial of any originality in the contemporary practice of swearing,[5] and then the focus is briskly shifted to a vexed case of authorial attribution. Sterne's irony here plays with the ambiguity of *original* (cf. Loveridge, 1982: 125-6): Tristram claims that Ernulphus's curse is an original, meaning an aesthetic evaluation of the text; while Walter denies the argument from a philological point of view, suspecting that Ernulphus was the collector rather than the author of the oaths. In a way, this latter hypothesis adumbrates the possibility of an infinite regression - which is one of the main tenets of poststructuralism - in the search for an *originating original* of any text: with Shandean urbanity and agility the source is deferred farther and farther into an irretrievable past, so insinuating the tautological and

[5] See *TS*: 3.12.212: 'Now don't let us give ourselves a parcel of airs, and pretend that the oaths we make free with in this land of liberty of ours are our own; and because we have the spirit to swear them,---imagine that we have had the wit to invent them too'. As Traugott (1954: 119) aptly remarks, Tristram here vindicates the claim that 'true genius has its own copia of invention'.

redundant dimension implied in any act of writing/reading. By the way, it is wholly consistent with the paradoxical strategy of Tristram that Walter, the character expected to be the most *original* thinker, becomes the mouthpiece of the theory which reduces composition to collection, as his very efforts at the *Tristrapaedia* similarly suggest.

From this network of inter-textual threads so far disclosed it appears evident that the *fragment* plays a decisive role in Sterne's work as a self-conscious practice of writing/reading most congenial to his artistic stance: not only does it function as a generative device for the Shandean assemblage of interpolations, but also as a critical tool for asserting his ambiguous status as author at the crucial moment of a proliferation of mixed genres and cultural discourses under the pressure exercised by the new literary market. Instead of assuming the scourging pose of the satirist, like Swift, Sterne rather professed delight in this circulation/promiscuity of books. As John Mullan (1988: 165) remarks, his plagiarisms made a virtue of the fragmentation of that literature which Johnson had defined as 'learning; skill in letters'.

I want to conclude my discourse calling attention to the contemporary fragments of Beckett's *Fizzles*, which force the dimension of (self)-citation and revision to the extreme limit of an '*in*finite' writing (Zaccaria, 1990: 115) exposed to endless permutation and contradiction, as Paola Zaccaria has nicely argued. In a way, *Fizzles* plays with the paradox, exquisitely (post)modern but already anticipated in Swift and Sterne, that permutation is both an escape from and a reinforcement of repetition: indeed, each story/fragment is interchangeable, each enacting the same painful, asymptotic approach to an end never to be achieved, each repeating - from a different narrative perspective - the same predicament of a *text/self* abandoned to an irreversible process of erosion and fragmentation. This aspect has been linked with the compulsion to repeat, that is to say with the death pulse (cf. Zaccaria, 1990: 110 and Connor, 1988: 11). Death serves here to sharpen the focus, as it were, on the (im)possibility to write, to tell, to see 'other people/oneself/*in*-self' (Zaccaria, 1990: 107). The dilemma between self and other, repetition and difference, is expressed through a tense texture of metaphorical polarities, such as light/darkness, sounds/ silence, movement/stillness, blindness/*in*sight, where the opposition is however only illusory, since each pole imperceptibly fades off into its very contrary.

Each fizzle is indeed a sort of liminal journey on the fringe of existence (Harvey, 1970: 247), symbolically focusing on the interchangeability of the two acts to end/to begin. The apparent transition from one moment to the other is always meaningfully signalled by a fall: fall of masses, of memories, of fragments, and ultimately of the subject itself: 'last change of all in the end the expelled falls headlong down and lies back to sky full stretch amidst his ruins' (Beckett, 1984: 181). The story which repeatedly 'fizzles out' in the eight texts thus speaks of this merciless interplay - which Sterne knew all too well - with the beginnings and endings, the maxima and minima, the comings and goings of life and fiction; indeed, it speaks of a *writing/self* probably not so much 'polished' as 'flayed'[6] which bears all the scars of an inextinguishable incompletion. As Paola Zaccaria (1990: 112) says:

> The compact falls and produces fragments and splinters (as far as masses are concerned), death and disintegration (as far as bodies), fragmentation of the discourse (as for narration), dust and rotting (as for the word).

[6] As for this aspect of 'expolition', see Connor (1988: 207); Bernstein's 'An Interview with Jasper Johns', Kritzman (1981: 287). I prefer the term 'flayed' as it suggests the affinity with Swift. For a discussion of Beckett's writing as *écorchée*, see Barker (1990: 199-200).

STERNE, NABOKOV AND THE HAPPY (NON)ENDING OF BIOGRAPHY

MADELEINE DESCARGUES

Should biography be decried in its pretensions to introduce literature and literary writers to the public? Speaking of the 'biographical method' in literary criticism, Proust made some definitive comments in *Contre Sainte Beuve* in 1910: such petty interest in the writers' lives, he wrote, leads one to ignore the essential quality of a book, its deriving from a self other than that of everyday life.[1] When the Victorians' (and particularly Thackeray's) condemnations of Sterne on moral grounds come to mind, one has to agree that not all novelists can be posthumously grateful to the critics who undertook to unravel the intricacies of their works by digging up the secrets of their lives. (Thackeray, 1853).

But the connection between biography and the novel in particular cannot be restricted to the use of biographical elements to study and understand novelists and their works. The borderline between fiction and history is often very hazy and neither of the two genres can be securely categorized, let alone claim 'purity'. Indeed both artistic forms imply an ambiguous relationship to the fictional and historical dimension of the reality that novelists and biographers work with. They even stand akin in literary history, the 'age of the novel' being also 'the age of biography'. A 'striking similarity', in Tracy's words,

[1] Proust thus brilliantly criticized and ridiculed Sainte-Beuve, then reputed to be the outstanding exponent of the French critical school: 'La fameuse méthode [...] qui consiste à ne pas séparer l'homme de l'oeuvre [...] cette méthode méconnaît ce qu'une fréquentation un peu profonde avec nous-mêmes nous apprend: qu'un livre est le produit d'un autre moi que celui que nous manifestons dans nos habitudes, dans la société, dans nos vices' (1954: 126-27). Much later, in the rash seventies, the primacy of the text was often — and wrongly — considered incompatible with the study of writers' lives.

can even be observed 'between developments in the eighteenth-century novel, especially Sterne's, and those in eighteenth-century biography', as regards the choice and treatment of the subject and the growing interest in anecdotes and details, for example (see Tracy, 1971: 99). Further similarities come to mind when one reflects on the aim assigned to many novels later on in the heyday of 'realistic' nineteenth-century schools, giving (the realistic illusion of) a linear retrospective view of the story of a life, seemingly encompassing all the elements within an omniscient narrator's grasp. For these were some of the most often invoked tenets of the dominant literary schools until the beginning of the twentieth century. At that stage modernist novelists called into question the whole set of ideas concerning the novel, including the implied acknowledgement of a relative conformity of the novelist's and the biographer's views - even if the former was granted a freer use of imagination.

So in fact biography as a model form of the novel was or seemed to be discarded or at least to lose its overwhelming influence on novelists of the twentieth century in the context of a general shift of interest in pursuit of new aspects and values of reality. Modernism in literature involved a search for innovative forms, meant to represent an ideal called modernity. Traditional patterns were markedly rejected, since tradition in itself was presumed to jeopardize the necessary freedom from resented constraints. Modernist literature highlighted the transient quality of its very subjects and sources of interest, whether attempting to describe characters, or to account for a switch in the political perspectives of the times, or to express a new quality of self-consciousness. In so doing, novelists emphasized new driving concepts, such as contingency. They stressed the accidental and the ephemeral features of reality, and generally focused on discontinuity as they certainly discontinued writing in conformity with the conventional framework of narrative in prose.

In that context, the biographical description of reality in the form of the coherent interpretation of a succession of events starting from a given beginning to a predictable end was at best a second-rate preoccupation, at worst a deceitful view. But this did not prevent novelists from playing with, that is, often subverting the very themes and structures they were supposed to discard. Biography as a theme of reflection or as the starting point of a narrative has never been totally estranged from the novel and it has even, in the more recent years which have been termed the postmodernist era, seemed to give fresh inspiration to a number of major novelists.

The attitude of postmodernist writers differs from that of their modernist predecessors, firstly because eclectism is once more in favour with novelists and critics alike. Secondly because postmodernism in fact tends to explode the very concept of modernism as the illusion of newness - just another accepted idea - conveyed by the search for modernity. Postmodernist writers give up playing modernity against tradition, and they are led to consider modernist principles in a new light, with a good deal of scepticism. They do not mind flirting with traditions they are supposed to reject, which is another way of using them. Paradoxes or perversities, such as conceiving the narrative of a novel out of one's own hostility to biographers, simply allow them more leeway for creation. Since it is not worth opposing the traditional to the new, because the new is an illusion which does not keep its promises and there is no future behind it, the postmodernist novelist feels free to play with, oppose and parody whatever forms have been inherited from the past.

To avoid rambling investigations, it might be necessary at this stage to narrow the scope of the comparative study of biography and the novel - a subject whose implications would take us too far afield within an essay - to the impact of biography as a form within the novel. More specifically, this paper aims at interpreting the part played by the reference to biography in two passages selected from *The Real Life of Sebastian Knight* and *The Life and Opinions of Tristram Shandy*. In these particular novels, the narrators assert themselves by refusing to become biographers or to behave as such. Nabokov's hostility to the biographical venture is a known fact, whereas Sterne expressed no particular interest, whether positive or negative, in contemporary biographers and biographies. So that it is by turning mainly to Sterne and Nabokov's fiction, not to the story of their lives, that a comparative study may proceed. The handling of the biographical approach in the narrative context might give us a few clues as to its part in the process of narration.

The Real Life of Sebastian Knight (Nabokov, 1960) is in fact quasi-exclusively concerned with the impossibility of writing an honest biography. The narrative opposes a shameless biographer, Mr

Goodman, and a scrupulous would-be biographer, the narrator, whose name is not revealed. The life both men are interested in writing is that of dead author Sebastian Knight, whose real identity remains unknown, despite the fact that his name - his pen name, really - is given in the title. Though he was the narrator's half brother, he seldom met him and is mostly unknown to him, yet familiar in many ways. As for Mr Goodman, who used to be Knight's secretary, he wrongly assumes he knows all about him. And yet, the narrator warns, as early as chapter two:

> It is one thing to be an author's secretary, it is quite another to set down an author's life; and if such a task is prompted by the desire to get one's book into the market while the flowers on a fresh grave may still be watered with profit, it is still another matter to try to combine commercial haste with exhaustive research, fairness and wisdom. (13)

Knight's brother knows better: he is gradually led to realize the inherent difficulty of the task of writing a biography and he eventually gives up the idea of writing one in order to give an account of his failure to do so. His narration is meant to convince the reader of the relevance of his general conclusions as to the dishonesty of most biographies and biographers.

Behind the narrator-narratee relationship involved in the development of the novel, the author's own position can of course be perceived. Nabokov addresses his public for the edification, we presume, of unsuspecting readers of biographies. Perhaps readers of *Tristram Shandy* are not quite as unsuspecting as some. Anyway, at a certain moment in Nabokov's novel, the reader of *Tristram Shandy* may have his attention roused by the faint echo of a well-known comment of Tristram's, and therefore may be tempted to try to understand Nabokov's postmodern distrust of biography in the light of Sterne's particular treatment of biographical time in one episode of his novel.

This occurs during the narrator and Mr Goodman's 'first (and last) interview' (47). Knight's (half-)brother has just introduced himself under his Russian name (that of his and Sebastian's father) to Mr Goodman, who suddenly becomes aware that the name 'Knight', chosen by Sebastian as his nom de plume, was that of his English mother, and that his original name is the Russian name of his half-brother. Mr Goodman's reaction can be guessed from his unfinished comment: 'Too late now to add a ...' (48). Obviously he thinks it safer to rob Sebastian of his real name than to rewrite part of his biography or even to add a correction to it. So here is a biographer, Nabokov implies, who is not even curious ('curious and inquisitive' [*TS*: 1.4.5] in Sterne's words) to know the origin and identity of the man whose life he is writing about.

In stark contrast to that despicable attitude, as the narratee is given to understand, the narrator gives up writing his brother's biography precisely because he seeks to understand him thoroughly. As he gradually identifies with Sebastian to the point of becoming his double in the story, he renounces linear explanations. Refusing to endorse any restrictive interpretation of the few known facts in his brother's life, he testifies to the desire of the writer's self to survive in its initial unruliness, through the text of his novels alone, rather than by means of the reconstituted story of his life. 'Remember that what you are told is really threefold: shaped by the teller, reshaped by the listener, concealed from both by the dead man of the tale. [...] And where is the third party? Rotting peacefully in the cemetery of St Damier. Laughingly alive in five volumes' (44). Clearly the impossibility of writing a biography becomes the subject of the enquiry into reality that a novel constitutes.

There is little need to expatiate upon whose side Nabokov chooses to stand. Mr Goodman prefers lies to truth, and a 'rapid compilation' to 'work' (47); as could be expected, his book is 'slapdash and very misleading' (13). Originally ignorant of a fact concerning Knight, he afterwards chooses to ignore it. By having him assume this, Nabokov brings his moral home to his readers: Mr Goodman is really a very bad man, which would not matter so much if it did not incidentally happen to make him a bad writer, the sort of crime no self-respecting novelist could be expected to condone. Mr Goodman's biography is a lifeless and deceitful text, full of mistakes; it is simply the cynical acceptance of the temporal discrepancy between life and writing about it. Such an approach makes it impossible for him even to dream of recapturing in his text the real texture of life. In Nabokov's view the biographer is guilty of the unforgivable sin of writing without being true to life, true to what he is writing about, and eventually true to himself as he is writing: the biographer shelters the murderer of a writer. And this is two-sided: literally, he feeds on the latter's genius and reputation; but also, and this may even be more significant because it poses the problem of the use and value of literature, he does not behave according to the literary writer's code of ethics, in Nabokov's conception. As to what that is, one of Sebastian's letters gives a few hints:

> But even if there were such a thing as a 'literary career' and I were disqualified merely for riding my own horse [a hobby-horse, most certainly], still I would refuse to change one single word in what I have written. For, believe me, no imminent punishment can be violent enough to make me abandon the pursuit of my pleasure, especially when this pleasure is the firm young bosom of truth. (46-47)

So by betraying the cause of literature, biographers sterilize and kill writers more finally than death may ever do. This is why Sebastian will survive in his brother's memory and perhaps in his future books, rather than in a biography.

Nabokov's 'Too late' is doubtless his own. But it is also, in the realm of intertextual interference, the tragicomic statement heard from Tristram's lips in the first volume of *Tristram Shandy*: 'But, alas, too late!' (*TS*: 1.12.32) is his comment on the eventual execution of the 'plan of the attack' on Yorick, depriving him of the preferment he thought was 'o'ripening' and then of his life since Yorick shortly afterwards dies 'broken hearted' (*TS*: 1.12.33). Tristram's 'too late' prepares Yorick's 'epitaph and elegy' in the same chapter, that is to say the framed 'Alas, poor YORICK!'. And this comes shortly before the real thing, or rather what can serve as the nearest approximation of the reality of death in a novel, that is to say the black page.

Yorick's story, as dealt with by Tristram from Chapter 10 to 12 of the first volume, is a convincing attempt at biography.[2] After telling (in Chapter 10) Yorick's misadventures with horses and humans, Tristram proceeds (in Chapters 11 and 12) to describe Yorick's personality: a piece very much like the character-sketch in

[2] Though Sterne uses numerous autobiographical elements taken from his own life, he has Tristram act as Yorick's biographer. Only Sterne's *Memoirs* can be considered as properly autobiographical, being a written account of his life in his own name (*S-Letters*: 1-5).

the tradition of biography.[3] But this relation of Yorick's life is in a way far too successful. Once completed, it proves lethal to the character. Nothing is left for the narrator to write about. Yorick's story, like most chronological episodes, is bound to conclude with death, as the story of Le Fever also reminds the reader in the sixth volume (*TS*: 6.6-10). No harm in that, except that as a narrator Tristram dreads the possibility of being silenced, once and for all, at the end of a story. So being time-conscious to a fault, he can find no way to parry the danger of silence and death, except in his tour de force: inverting beginning and end (see Warren, 1977).

Both Yorick and Tristram, Sterne's favourite personae, testify to the possibility of refusing to acknowledge the hold of the past over the present, at least in the world of fiction: Yorick does so by dying and entering the novel anew afterwards. Tristram's behaviour is consistently wayward - chronologically speaking - throughout the nine volumes of a 'COCK' and 'BULL' story (*TS*: 9.33.809). At an early stage, parson Yorick was the prisoner of his own story, which determined his confinement in the circle of chronology and ultimately his death: the reconstituting of his life in the form of a linear biography ended in his disappearance in the middle of the first volume of Sterne's novel. Fortunately, opinions being what life is mostly about, Tristram managed to rescue Yorick and all other characters alike, including himself, from oblivion. So by circumscribing the menace of Yorick's finished (historical) past within the narration of Tristram's endless (atemporal) present, Sterne could liberate his fiction from chronology, the unwelcome reminder of transiency and finitude. This certainly implies a measure of suspicion regarding the biographical craft. Indeed, though Tristram calls himself a 'biographical writer' (*TS*: 4.13.341), he seems to dally with biography more than he contributes to the development of the genre.

[3] In 17th and 18th-century biographies, the character-sketch came after a number of selected facts arranged in chronological order. As noted by Tracy (1971: 108): 'The novelists, like the biographers, retained an interest in the formal character-sketch and often used it for the purpose of introducing a new member of their dramatis personae. But in the novel, as in the biography, it declined steadily in importance during the century, falling from its position as a posed full-length portrait to become little more than a stage direction'.

It might also - 'But this by the bye' (*TS*: 1.4.7) - remind the 'curious and inquisitive' (*TS*, 1.4.5) of Sterne's very own story, just to stress that novelists do not get rid of biography so easily. In his case anyway biographical elements do parallel fictional ones. 'Few are the minutes of life, and I do not think that I have any to throw away on any one being'; 'for my own part, I love to run hazards —<th>rather then dye by Inches' (*S-Letters*: 200); this is Sterne. 'Had I not better, Eugenius, fly for my life?' (*TS*: 7.1.577); this is his narrator Tristram.[4]

To Sterne, turning author also meant turning a black page, since his own life, before he became a fashionable author, was darkened by domestic problems and complicated by diverse 'country Entanglements' (*S-Letters*: 66). Sterne the parson farmer could never make a profit: 'Curse on farming (said I) I will try if the pen will not succeed better than the spade' (*S-Letters*: 394).[5] Tristram his narrator clung to his pen as long as he could: 'No———I think, I said, I would write two volumes every year, provided the vile cough which then tormented me, and which to this hour I dread worse than the devil, would but give me leave—and in another place— [...] speaking of my book as a *machine* [...] I swore it should be kept a going at that rate these forty years if it pleased but the fountain of life to bless me so long with health and good spirits' (*TS*: 7.1.575). So one of the problems posed and solved in the expanse of the novel is the achievement of a satisfying perception of time in such conditions of urgency. Tristram needs a swelling of present time to boost his own importance, and his spirits. He adapts space to the requirements of his narration in order to display his prowess and causes it to shrink to its simplest expression. The world is contracted in a first stage: 'by which word *world*, need I in this place inform your worship, that I would be understood to mean no more of it, than a small circle described upon

[4] In the same passage, Tristram remembers the time when 'DEATH himself knocked at [his] door' (7.1.577), upon which Cash comments: 'In writing the passage Sterne was probably recalling his first discovery, at Cambridge, of the disease which would eventually take his life' (Cash, 1992: vol. 1, 61).

[5] Farming was an activity the slow rhythm of which certainly 'mortified' parson Sterne: 'I have 4 Threshers every Day at Work, & they mortify me with declarations, That There is so much Barly they Cannot get thro' that species before X^{mas} Day' (*S-Letters*: 65-66).

the circle of the great world, of four *English* miles diameter, or thereabouts' (*TS*: 1.7.10).[6] But then what is lost in historicity and in geographical scope is gained in the ubiquity of consciousness: the opening up of the pages to Yorick as well as to whoever or whatever crosses Tristram's mind after the black page just proves the worth of his rhetoric, through which present time - his own, the author's and the reader's - can expand in the pages of the novel. The more time flies (and Tristram now and then lets us know he is aware of the fact), the more it can spread in the space of the novel, provided the narrator holds it in place properly:

> I am this month one whole year older than I was this time twelve-month; and having got, as you perceive, almost into the middle of my fourth volume—and no farther than to my first day's life—'tis demonstrative that I have three hundred and sixty-four days more life to write just now, than when I first set out; so that instead of advancing, as a common writer, in my work with what I have been doing at it—on the contrary, I am just thrown so many volumes back—was every day of my life to be as busy a day as this—And why not?—and the transactions and opinions of it to take up as much description—And for what reason should they be cut short? as at this rate I should just live 364 times faster than I should write—It must follow, an' please your worships, that the more I write, the more I shall have to write—and consequently, the more your worships read, the more your worships will have to read. (*TS*: 4.13.341-42)

But this does not mean that Tristram is bound to fail in his narrative or is basically unable to cope with his biographies, as he is wont to complain. It rather suggests that his experience of biography, as in the case of Yorick in the first volume, has too conclusive a result: his attempt is effective to the point of totally absorbing—thus suppressing—the hero whose life he quite successfully summarized and reduced to its simplest expression: a memory in a book, an epitaph. No wonder he should afterwards find it safer to be most content with the present time of his characters's lives in his narration. In his so-

[6] The 'parlour fire-side' (*TS*:2.5.114) at Shandy Hall is one of the cosy places where Tristram is apt to tell the family secrets. But space is even more confined in a few famous instances: 'You shall see the very place, Madam' (*TS*: 9.20.772), Toby promises widow Wadman. This is indeed a mere spot, but of such a revealing intimate nature (whether as understood by Toby or by the widow) that it encapsulates the whole drama of the pair of lovers.

called failure to be a biographer (of others, of himself) Tristram all the same manages to write his (writing) life and to illustrate the author's posture. He rejoices to note and to have his readers note that if no narration can indeed catch up with life, at least, as long as there are pages, there is life. On the part of the writer, this implies stunting the biographical vocation in his narrator by having him postpone the end of his narratives, a strategy in which digressions prove particularly helpful.

Tristram refuses to subject himself to the laws of ordinary biographers. Still he needs to identify and reject their model in order to be able to develop his own rhetoric. He stresses the difficulty of their job, for there is no such thing as Momus's glass: '---But this is an advantage not to be had by the biographer in this planet' (*TS*: 1.23.83). This of course serves to prove the logic of his own choice: 'in a word, I will draw my uncle *Toby*'s character from his HOBBY-HORSE' (*TS*: 1.23.85).

So both novelist and reader should be content with a somewhat evasive text, replacing the full relation of historical events by the unfinished narrative of hobby-horsical stories embedded in one another, throughout a novel striving to fill the blanks in each story with new gossip. As a matter of fact, Tristram's optimism depends, as he well knows, on his readers' willingness to 'jogg on' (*TS*: 1.6.10): '—*O diem proeclarum!*—then nothing which has touched me will be thought trifling in its nature, or tedious in its telling' (*TS*: 1.6.9). If he chooses to behave like an escapist, the novelist also has to pay the price for his light-heartedness, which is that his work cannot claim the serious-faced respectability of historical facts.

In fact neither approach - fictional or historical - can claim total independence. On the contrary, each of the two needs the other to stress its own distinctive features. Though they stand on two different sides of the relation of past to present, the biographer and the novelist grapple with the same elusiveness of time. Biography and the novel can only be hybrid forms between past and present, reality and illusion anyway, the former choosing to acknowledge its link with history, but at the peril of life, at the risk of turning the biographer into a grave-digger, as Nabokov implies; the latter preferring to assume the present time at the peril of memory, at the risk of losing itself in trifles or insignificance, as was more than once said about *Tristram Shandy*.

If they can't be reconciled, the differences are nevertheless stimulating to novelists, as to biographers. In Kendall's words, 'the writer of fiction, out of the mating of his own experience and his imagination, creates a world, to which he attempts to give the illusion of reality. The biographer, out of the mating of an extrinsic experience, imperfectly recorded, and his imagination, recreates a world, to which he attempts to give something of the reality of illusion' (Kendall, 1965: 8). Indeed the best biographies nowadays tend to recognize the part played by fantasy in the biographical craft and to borrow some of the qualities of the novel, by leaving the door open for new questions and interpretations, by shifting the emphasis from clear-cut judgement to sympathetic perception, by acknowledging, as Cash wrote in the preface to his biography of Sterne:

> A biographical fact is nothing concrete: an event evoked in the imagination of the biographer to explain the newspaper story, the letter, the legal document before him — his primary evidence. He may carefully weigh the evidence, refine the facts, work them into what is grandiosely called a 'life', but a biographer can never know that his story is true. [...] A friend once asked me, 'What would you do if by a miracle Laurence Sterne should walk in through that door?' I replied, 'Ask him to forgive me.' (Cash, 1992: xiii)

On the other hand, biography inspires novelists' nostalgia for the completeness a historical vision can provide. They can hardly do without the quest for the past, which gives them a tantalizing subject to pursue. Besides, in its search for origin, biography is emblematic of the very genesis of the novel as a literary form which has never ceased to transform itself. As a floating genre, to refer to Bakhtin's poetics of the novel, the latter is constantly drifting away from its origin in satire, in epic, in romances, in rhapsodies and tends to accept as many influences as possible, old and new (Bakhtin, 1981). So for all that holds them apart, and despite some antagonistic feelings, biography and the novel seem bound to mirror each other, to have their fates linked as two terms in a contradiction. Since Sterne's days, they have shared the same interest for (true) anecdotes or for (invented) details, faced similar questions, borrowed answers from each other and they have thrived and erred together. They have faced the same condescension as 'minor' genres, biography being sometimes regarded as a degenerate form of history, and the novel hastening to call itself an epic when it was in fact a bastard genre, a cross between different genres.[7] As they may encroach on each other's spheres of influence, they also need to live with each other in a state of armed peace.

Sterne and Nabokov both use and abuse biography and biographers. Part of their energy and glee as novelists derives from the very rhetorical contest with their real or imaginary opponents, whether they defame them and their job (Nabokov) or simply nip biographical plans or intentions in the bud (Sterne). One wonders if the connection of their novels with biography is not a precondition for their narrators' lively rhetoric to be as effective as it is. Both Tristram and Sebastian are used by their makers to manifest their unrelenting living presence in their texts, to satisfy the original urge of the writer's self to last and survive in the writing act. In (*The Real Life of*) *Tristram Shandy* and in (*The Life and Opinions of*) *Sebastian Knight* biographical failure means fictional success.

[7] More precisely, of course, 'a comic Epic-Poem in Prose' (Fielding, Preface to *Joseph Andrews*).

HAVE YOU NOT FORGOT TO WIND UP THE CLOCK? TRISTRAM SHANDY AND JACQUES LE FATALISTE ON THE (POST?)MODERN PSYCHOANALYTIC COUCH

LAURENT MILESI

'*Die Gewesenheit entspringt in gewisser Weise der Zukunft*' (Heidegger, *Sein und Zeit*)

In the Beginning was Time

One of the most hotly debated intertextual problems in *Tristram Shandy* is no doubt Sterne's witty novelization of Lockean ideas on time and duration in *An Essay Concerning Human Understanding*, especially II.xiv, "Of Duration, and its simple Modes", which sets off the subjective consciousness of time against the notion of a more mechanical calendar or clock time. Locke is mentioned in early chapters of *Tristram Shandy* (1.4.7 and 2.2.98); Lockean echoes or rephrasings occur in 2.5.107 and 2.8.119, and these anticipate a major discussion in 3.18.222-25. Sterne's incessant blendings of 'the time-structure of the story with the time-infrastructure of the writing' (Mayoux, 1971: 3), a method designed to expose both the inevitability of duration in narration and the inadequacy of the ultimately linear act of writing to inform the constant shiftings of plot time, find expression in an array of now well-documented rhetorical and narrative techniques and devices, such as prolepsis (or anticipation), analepsis (or flashback), aposiopesis (cf. *TS*: 2.6.116), preterition, deferral and especially digression, which directly contribute to stalling the delivery of what is expectedly the main story, the *life* and *opinions* of *Tristram*

Shandy. Sterne's novel arguably tells more about the opinions of Walter Shandy and the life of the family protagonists, especially the irresolution of Uncle Toby's amours, an underplot casually introduced in *TS*: 2.7.117 which builds up to an anticlimax in almost inverse proportion as Tristram's own story recedes into the background. Thus, at the beginning of the lynchpin Chapter 32 of Volume 4, Tristram solemnly declares that 'it is from this point properly, that the story of my LIFE and my OPINIONS sets out', but soon reveals his eagerness to hasten on to Toby's amours, admittedly 'the choicest morsel of my whole story'(*TS*: 4.32.401; recalled in *TS*: 9.24.779). The fact that Sterne manages to write a 'fictional' biography while checking the writing of a character's 'real'autobiography, so that '*Tristram Shandy* is completed; Tristram's "Life and Opinions" is scarcely begun' (Ross, 1983: xix), generates the illusory paradox of a double text at once capable of writing one part of itself while unpicking another half of its project and in which the progressive consecutiveness of the act of writing informs a regressive plot.[1] The essence of this method of composition, which we could therefore more pointedly describe as (counter)productive, is approached by Tristram himself who views its two contrary, though reconciled, motions as both 'digressive' and 'progressive'(*TS*: 1.22.81) and who later argues for the necessity of going forward and backward, owing to the strange way in which he is telling his story (*TS*: 6.33.557-58). It is as if the deliberate frustration of the avowedly 'main' telling and tale eventually tugged the whole narration backward, in spite (or is it because?) of the desire to start the writing '*ab Ovo*' (*TS*: 1.4.5), a metaphor of fictional beginnings which Tristram the perverse autobiographer takes literally by starting with an account of his ominous procreation and then reenacting in writing the protracted event of his deferred 'real' birth. Let us

[1] Shifting constantly between writing time, reading time and plot time, *Tristram Shandy* starts *ab ovo* at the beginning of 1718 and ends in 1713-1714 with the unresolved amours of Uncle Toby with widow Wadman, and, in the interim, goes as far forward as 1766, when the ninth and 'last' volume ever composed was actually written, and backwards to the days of Henry VIII. See for example Baird's excellent (1936) reconstitution of the chronology of events connected to the Shandy family, Fluchère (1965), esp. 104-110, 116-29, and Mendilow, 1972: 188-93, and for a similar attempt to unravel the temporal structure of *Jacques le fataliste*, see especially Chesneau, 1968.

consider how, in the passage leading to the exposition of the digressive-progressive method, the text ironically dons a further layer of digressiveness with its overkill of phatic turns, interpolations and repetitions which buttonhole reader and plot alike:

> For in this long digression which I was accidentally led into, as in all my digressions (one only excepted) there is a masterstroke of digressive skill, the merit of which has all along, I fear, been overlooked by my reader [...] because 'tis an excellence seldom looked for, or expected indeed, in a digression;---and it is this: That tho' my digressions are all fair, as you observe [...] (*TS*: 1.22.80)

Though its manipulations of time schemes are less sophisticated, Diderot's *Jacques le fataliste* equally flaunts its digressiveness to the impatient reader, as, for instance, when Jacques, his master, then the narrator interrupt the story at their respective levels in order to denounce the interruptions of other characters-narrators:

> Jacques - Il est vrai. Les fréquentes interruptions des gens de cette maison m'ont impatienté plus d'une fois.
>
> Le maître - Et moi aussi.
>
> Et vous, Lecteur, parlez sans dissimulation, car vous voyez que nous sommes en beau train de franchise, voulez-vous que nous laissions là cette élégante et prolixe bavarde d'hôtesse, et que nous reprenions les amours de Jacques? Pour moi, je ne tiens à rien. Lorsque cette femme remontera, Jacques le bavard ne demande pas mieux que de reprendre son rôle et que de lui fermer la porte au nez [...] (Diderot, 1981 [hereafter *JF*]: 128)
>
> (Jacques - That is true. The frequent interruptions from the servants of the house have annoyed me several times.
>
> The master - And me too.
>
> And you, Reader, speak without dissimulation, for you can see that we are in a mood for frankness. Would you like us to leave this elegant and prolix gossip of a hostess and come back to the story of Jacques' loves? As for me, I do not mind which. When this woman comes back up, that gossip Jacques would like nothing better than to resume his part and to shut the door in her face [...])

One need not retrace here the numerous narrative and thematic overlappings, the intersecting lines of literary descent from Rabelais and Cervantes, that affiliate *Jacques le fataliste* to *Tristram Shandy* (see Fredman, 1973: *passim*). However, it is worth recalling, for the purpose of this study, how the French text freely adapts, translates, recasts and extends themes, elements of plot and narrative techniques from its predecessor, as for example: the conflicting time schemes, the theme of predestination and the Fates's foreknowledge of the amours between widow Wadman and Uncle Toby (*TS*: 8.14.673) and the discussions on cause-and-effect and fatalism in *Jacques le fataliste*, or the more explicit problematization in Diderot's novel of the relationship between real life story and written (re)enactment on the heavenly scroll as two simultaneous scriptural acts:

> Le maître - Je rêve à une chose, c'est si ton bienfaiteur eût été cocu parce qu'il était écrit là-haut, ou si cela était écrit là-haut parce que tu ferais cocu ton bienfaiteur.
> Jacques - Tous les deux étaient écrits l'un à côté de l'autre. Tout a été écrit à la fois. C'est comme un grand rouleau qui se déploie petit à petit (*JF*: 28)[2]

> (The master - I am wondering about something, that is whether your benefactor would have been cuckolded because it was written up above, or whether it was written up above because you would make your benefactor a cuckold.
> Jacques - The two were written side by side. Everything has been written at the same time. It is like a great scroll that is unfurled little by little)

One of the most judicious comparisons in that respect is William Ray's observation that 'the *temporal* regress of *Tristram Shandy*, which is brought on by Tristram's attempt to account for his account of himself, finds a *structural* counterpart in *Jacques le fataliste*'s hierarchical regress of characters recounting characters recounting

[2] Starobinski's comments in relation to Jacques' hypothesis are worth quoting as they anticipate some of our concerns: 'Que l'écriture du rouleau soit l'annonce ou la trace de l'événement, on en arrive à la même constatation: le rouleau n'est pleinement lisible qu'après coup. [...] La lecture ne s'offre qu'à un regard rétrospectif' (1984: 33), and 'Lorsque vient le tour de la narration [...] la parole inscrit une troisième fois, dans la représentation, ce qui d'abord, selon sa conviction, avait été écriture sur le rouleau, puis événement dans le monde: la lecture du rouleau céleste et de son double réalisé sur terre est un troisième mode de la représentation. [...] L'*a priori* causal se met en place à partir de l'*a posteriori* narratif' (34). Note also Bennington's comment that 'In Diderot's radical practice, "events" in novels both follow and outplay a law which has become undecidably that of chance or necessity, of teleology or of the *après coup*' (1985: 63).

characters' (298). Thus, Sterne writes about Tristram Shandy writing *his* life - the ambiguity of the referent might reflect the not infrequent overlaps between real and fictional lives - in which, he (Tristram), in 1760, relates how Trim in 1723 tells the story of Le Fever's death that took place in 1706. A more straightforward equivalent, involving telling (quoting), writing and (re)enacting, occurs at the beginning of *Jacques le fataliste* and arguably gives the keynote to the whole work:

> Le maître ne disait rien, et Jacques disait que son capitaine disait que tout ce qui nous arrive de bien et de mal ici-bas était écrit là-haut. (*JF*: 23)
>
> (The master was saying nothing, and Jacques was saying that his captain used to say that everything good or bad that befalls us here below was written up above.)

This 'Chinese-box'device[3] is also extended more surreptitiously to the montage of intertextual echoes. The Shandean example *par excellence* occurs at the beginning of the fifth volume, whose title page has quotations from Horace and Erasmus borrowed from Burton's *Anatomy of Melancholy* and soon followed, in the first chapter (*TS*: 5.1.408), by another cribbed passage attacking plagiary in the introduction to the *Anatomy*, followed in the 'original' by the admission that he had 'laboriously collated this Cento out of divine Writers'! A similar strategy could be shown to be at work in *Jacques le fataliste* with regard to Montaigne's *Essais*, also featuring in the intertextual network of *Tristram Shandy*, which likewise undercut both authority and originality (Gearhart, 1984: 223-24).

This overview of the central role played by the aporias of time, originality and beginnings, and the overlaps between the real and the fictional in both novels will serve as ballast for a consideration, not so much of either text as a postmodern work, but rather of their relationship as a postmodern precedent which not only anticipated issues of literary originality, filiation and transmission that will become foregrounded in the contemporary fiction of, say, Nabokov, Pynchon and Gass, but also foresaw their critical articulation, as in

[3] Marian Hobson (1982: esp. 130-31) argues that Diderot's construction does not strictly adhere to this technique as the insertions occasionally overlap, making for instance the Marquis des Arcis both told-about and a teller.

Lyotard's approach to the paradoxes of postmodernity (see the extended **Endnote**, below). As my own 'retrograde' (*TS*: 3.23.243) reading of the postmodernity of *Tristram Shandy* and *Jacques le fataliste* is in a large measure symptomatic of how postmodernism is increasingly taken further back in time, perhaps eventually to designate what will have always started before it had even been aware of its own modernity,[4] I will also resort to the specular notions of foresight and Freud's *Nachträglichkeit* in order to explore how far, in the respective ways in which they thwart the telling of their 'main' story, *Tristram Shandy* and *Jacques le fataliste* stand in mutually implied relationships of anticipation, trauma and reparation-as-originary-repetition.

Sterne's and Diderot's Seductions: Foresight, Oversight and After-Effect

Jacques le fataliste derives its most famous literary filiation from one of those convoluted framing processes recalled above, which feature a *mise en abyme* of tellings, deferrals, digressions and interruptions; indeed, the whole substance of Diderot's novel spends itself within an adaptation of *TS*: 8.19-22. In the source passage, Corporal Trim is constantly interrupted whenever he tries to tell the story of the King of Bohemia and can only narrate 'the manner in which he is prevented from narrating it' (Iser, 1988: 67). The tale is eventually ousted by Trim's own story of the wound to his knee and his subsequent falling in love, after an introductory remark about King William's doctrine of (pre)destination, whose aphoristic 'every ball has it's billet' (*TS*: 8.19.693) will gain notoriety in being passed on to Trim, then to the

[4] Cf. Lyotard (Docherty, 1993: 44): 'A work can become modern only if it is first postmodern. Postmodernism thus understood is not modernism at its end but in the nascent state, and this state is constant'. One is reminded of the motto of the imaginary castle, and of the exposition of its logical incompatibilities, in *JF* (43): '"You were here before you went in, and you will still be here when you have left." - Did they go into this castle? - No, for either the inscription was false, or they were there before they went in. - But, at least, they went out of it? - No, for either the inscription was false, or they were still there after they had left. - And what did they do there? - Jacques said: What is written up above'.

captain and finally to Jacques (cf. *JF*: 23). The wound-love sequence is replayed by Diderot in almost similar terms (see Loy, 1950: 32-39 and Simon, 1985) and spliced at the beginning and end of the novel, the equivocal seduction scene during Trim's nursing by the Beguine being reworked for the end of *Jacques le fataliste*, where its original inconclusiveness acquires a structural function for the novel as a whole.

Thus Diderot's text foregrounds as citational frame and prospective plot an anecdote which, adequately primed by the theme of predestination, first anticipated the *clou* of *Tristram Shandy*, uncle Toby's own amours with widow Wadman, matched by Trim's with Bridget, the master's and servant's campaigns running parallel throughout. Sterne's noble doubling of amours (cf. *TS*: 3.24.246) will itself be relayed in the interwoven tales of Jacques' and his master's loves but more craftily in Diderot's attempts, as it were, to out-Sterne his forerunner and duel with him at his own games of specular doubles (cf. Gearhart, 1984: 216). Not only is the wound to the knee what goads Jacques on to the painstaking telling of his amours, and a similar wound nearly inflicted to his master, but Jacques' flirtation with Denise becomes the 'original' love-story to be narrated and constantly frustrated, atomized in three separate episodes scattered across the entire novel, momentarily superseded by that of his original deflowering, itself turning into a repetition of mock deflowerings by Justine, Suzanne and Marguerite (as if to puncture the myth of original sexual and textual inscription), while countless other intrigues of seduction or debauchery provide thematic back-up, though they equally threaten to short-circuit the promised delivery altogether.... But which? One can no longer talk of digressions or expected plot lines when the text loses sense of what was being (or was to be) narrated and then digressed from, a reversal which opens up the more general question of the relationship between originals and rewritings. Diderot's artistry in his foregrounding of citational framing implicitly suggests that the antecedence on which posterior works can capitalize in order to partially recoup their losses in originality can itself be challenged and turned to new unexpected accounts (see Ray, 1990: 307). There is a sense in which, according to a retrogressive protocol of reading which would take its cue from Tristram's own method of composition, Jacques' recurrent formula '*ce qui est écrit là-haut*' already recycled from his captain, refers to '*ce qui a été écrit avant*' and casts *Tristram Shandy*, from which the formula is actually derived, into the role of the great scroll. Ray's remarks about *Jacques le fataliste* that 'the question boils down to whether *we* write the script of history as we go, or merely act out its pre-existing plot line' (298; cf. *JF*: 28, quoted above) and that 'there is always a larger plot enclosing the minor plots we fabricate' (305) may be brought to bear on the postmodernist preoccupations with the interpretive act and the issue of originality, the implications of the initial 'post' in postmodernism, which will enable us later to envisage an *analytic* reading of the bond between the two texts. Writer and critic John Barth, in his famous 1966 essay on 'The Literature of Exhaustion' where he deals with problems of originality and filiation in fiction in the light of the periodically bemoaned death of the novel as a literary genre, examines how Borges' 'Pierre Menard, Author of the *Quixote*' exemplarily uses the burden of the literary debt in order to transcend the proclaimed impasse of fictional originality into originality itself:[5]

> the important thing to observe is that Borges *doesn't* attribute the *Quixote* to himself, much less recompose it like Pierre Menard; instead, he writes a remarkable and original work of literature, the implicit theme of which is the difficulty, perhaps the unnecessity, of writing original works of literature. His artistic victory, if you like, is that he confronts an intellectual dead end and employs it against itself to accomplish new human work. (8)

It is precisely the insistent claims to originality versus anteriority that underpin the textual drama of the suspended endings of Jacques' amours and make Diderot's dénouement truly original: the writer-narrator, now an editor of memoirs which he regards as spurious and which he confronts with his own unrevealed manuscript (he has therefore been in possession of at least two earlier texts by the time

[5] In 'The Literature of Replenishment' (written in 1979), a companion piece and antidote to the earlier essay, Barth's discussion and tentative examination of what constitutes the essence of postmodernism will trace the lineage of the 'postmodernist literary aesthetic', via modernist and nineteenth-century works, back to such early precursors as *Tristram Shandy* and the *Quixote* (Barth, 1982: 23), while repeatedly stressing his sense of a *déjà vu* in the current debates for or against this 'new' phenomenon (21, 24).

we read the non-manuscript text of *Jacques le fataliste*), introduces the three possible dénouements as follows:

> L'éditeur ajoute: La huitaine est passée. J'ai lu les mémoires en question; des trois paragraphes que j'y trouve de plus que dans le manuscrit dont je suis possesseur, le premier et le dernier me paraissent originaux et celui du milieu évidemment interpolé. (*JF*: 288)

> (Note added by the editor. The week is past. I have read the memoirs in question; of the three paragraphs which I found in addition to the manuscript in my possession, the first and the last seem to me original, but the middle one is obviously an interpolation.)[6]

While taking its ambiguity further, that middle fragment, which, by virtue of its place, can only be an interpolation and this regardless of any status it might have otherwise as an original or spurious document, in essence sums up the episode of Trim's dalliance with his Beguine. It is introduced thus:

> Voici le second paragraphe copié de la vie de *Tristram Shandy*, à moins que l'entretien de Jacques le fataliste et de son maître ne soit antérieur à cet ouvrage et que le ministre Stern ne soit le plagiaire, ce que je ne crois pas, mais par une estime toute particulière de M. Stern que je distingue de la plupart des littérateurs de sa nation dont l'usage assez fréquent est de nous voler et de nous dire des injures. (*JF*: 289)

> (Here is the second paragraph copied from the life of *Tristram Shandy*, unless the conversation of Jacques the Fatalist and his master predates this work and the minister Sterne is himself the plagiarist, which I do not believe, but only out of a very special esteem for Mr. Sterne, whom I distinguish from the majority of his nation's men of letters whose quite frequent custom is to steal from us and insult us.)

In a move that jocularly registers that a citational act inevitably mixes deference with defiance as it repeats the novel's master-slave specular relationship in terms of a larger intertextual plot, the editor entertains the possibility of Sterne having plagiarized the story by positing a

[6] The ambiguous wording of the editor's takeover of the narrative role leaves undecided whether the narrator and the editor are one and the same person or whether one modulates into the other as Diderot, the 'author' who sums up all roles, is about to 'complete' his work. See also Gearhart (1984: 219-220).

temporal lag between oral *telling* by Jacques and copying down and editing by the Englishman, a hypothesis in the light of which one may reread the narrator-writer's wry observation in *Tristram Shandy* that 'Writing, when properly managed (as you may be sure I think mine is), is but a different name for conversation' (*TS*: 2.11.125).[7] This is made even more plausible if one is willing to mix reality with fiction further and remember that Sterne's travels to France are fictionalized in Volume 7 of *Tristram Shandy* and *A Sentimental Journey*, and his friendship with Diderot teasingly alluded to in the latter (135).

One should recall not only Sterne's and Diderot's montage of intertexts around the inescapability of plagiarism to appreciate fully Diderot's token gesture towards a reversal of literary parentage, a cue which he could have taken from Sterne himself who scattered numerous hints at the possible illegitimacy of Tristram in the novel to fit it into his larger design of tricksters and plots of outwitting, but also the various other overlaps in biographies and publication dates which further erase the boundary between reality and fiction. The last book of *Tristram Shandy* was published in 1767 (and not available in French until 1785), some six or seven years before *Jacques le fataliste* was composed by Diderot while travelling - it had started life presumably in 1771 as a short story - and eleven years before the beginning of its prepublication in November 1778. In 1769, one year after Sterne's death and the publication of *A Sentimental Journey*, Frénais' French translation of the latter appeared, as did an alleged continuation of the original work, in a style poorly imitating Sterne's, by one Mlle de Lespinasse, featuring the English novelist himself and one apprentice named Jacques (see Raymond, in Diderot, 1984: 192-95). Besides, Diderot was born on 5 October 1713, a mere fifty days *before* Sterne (24 November 1713) - both being uncannily recalled in the day and month of Tristram's birth (5 November; *TS*: 1.5.8) - at a

[7] See Ray (1990: 296) for the shift from the 'intertextual monologue' of *Tristram Shandy*, chiefly focused on the problematic act of writing, despite the several but more superficial beckonings to the reader, to the dialogic vein of Diderot's novel, which more overtly plays with the reader's frustrations and expectations - Jacques and his master may be seen as further relaying and duplicating the author and the reader in the text. The ensuing paradox is that the reader remains freer to challenge Sterne's text as s/he pleases than with Diderot's, where his/her reactions, expectations, frustrations, are constantly anticipated.

time when Uncle Toby and Corporal Trim were busy reenacting the demolition of Dunkirk (September-November 1713), prior to the nine-month wonder of Uncle Toby's amours with widow Wadman, compressed into six memorable days in *Tristram Shandy*.

A similar mixture of reality and fiction characterizes the reenactment of past campaigns which is a crucial condition of the (telling) cure (cf. *TS*: 1.25.88: 'The history of a soldier's wound beguiles the pain of it', and *TS*: 2.3.101) and, as Ray suggests (277), an analytic process in uncle Toby's case. These strategic reenactments point to the reiterative and duplicitous nature of writing, capable of straddling the two trips to Auxerre (*TS*: 7.28.621-22) and of abolishing the temporal lag between past and future in the ubiquitous present of writing (cf. also *TS*: 3.38.278: 'a cow broke in (to-morrow morning) to my uncle *Toby*'s fortifications' and *JF*, 100: 'j'étais à demain', and see Mayoux, 1971: esp. 7-8, 11-12 for *Tristram Shandy*, and Lecointre, 1972: 229-30 for *Jacques le fataliste*.). In his eagerness to bring about the cathartic understanding of the *ball*istic origin of his 'modesty', Uncle Toby even gets ahead of historical time on one occasion,[8] unlike Shandy *père et fils* who, in failing to reckon with the duration of the act of writing, get so much behind themselves in their respective enterprises that this brings about the failure of both the prospective pedagogical treatise that the *Tristrapaedia* had aimed to be (*TS*: 5.16.448) and the retrospective reenactment of life in writing that Tristram's autobiography ought to be (in *TS*: 3.38.278, Tristram complains that he has 'five minutes less, than no time at all').

Not only does *Tristram Shandy* include Uncle Toby's reenactment, in the minutest detail, of all the military campaigns until he sustained his wound in the groin, as well as feature the reenacting function of (autobiographical) writing, but it can be also argued that Sterne's work has brought about its own possible reenactment(s) in *Jacques le fataliste* in several ways. First, in leaving out the 'real' accounts of the life and opinions of Tristram and shifting the focus to Uncle Toby's amours, Sterne's novel will have been, retrospectively, an anticipation, a foresight of what is to be foregrounded but at best suspended, rather

[8] Thus, Sterne's lapse in computation (Baird, 1936: 819) ironically invalidates Ray's observation (276) that 'totally preoccupied with re-creating that which was, he [Toby] is incapable of structuring the present or preparing the future'.

than ended, in Diderot: the story of Jacques' loves. As Barth writes, borrowing from Borges' essay on Kafka, 'Every writer creates his own precursor' (15).[9] And if *Tristram Shandy* is the foresight or foretelling of *Jacques le fataliste*, then *Jacques* may be envisaged as its traumatic (from Greek *trauma*: wound) reenactment(s). Uncle Toby's sexually crippling wound, answered by the 'shock' (*TS*: 2.7.117; 3.24.245) or trauma of his amours with widow Wadman - which, Forrester would argue, might equally be seen 'as a result of the process of remembering' (197), or, we may add, as the failure of a process of re-membering (cf. *TS*: 2.3.101) - and the wound(s) to the knee in *Jacques le fataliste*, with their power of anamnesis and textual trigger, are comparable strategies of narrative foreplay, titillation and, ultimately, as Irène Simon has shown, frustration, complete with textual/sexual infirmities, maimings, dysfunctionings, sexual beddings and narrative embeddings.

These, however, still leave foreclosed the other scene of writing, that scroll up above (or before) of which *Jacques le fataliste* appears as a fragmentary reorientation, that is Tristram's life and opinions, promised in the title of Sterne's novel (but never delivered), and an undoing of uncle Toby's misadventure with the widow. Diderot's deferred reactivation and redeployment of an event which infantile Uncle Toby, who does not yet know the right end of a woman from the wrong (*TS*: 2.7.117), will not even have interpreted as a (failed) seduction scene may be conceived of as a retroactive post-effect or *Nachträglichkeit*[10] of Sterne's fiction. Freud developed this notion and its built-in logic of repression and trauma in connection with his view of psychical temporality and causality, especially his theory of

[9] In a challenging essay which examines how the intertextual relationships between *JF* and *TS* frustrate theorization, McDonald (1982) implicitly takes the theme of the subversion of literary filiation even further when she observes that Diderot's recycling of the episode of the knee 'suggests [...], with the Borgesian repetition of a pre-existing text in a foreign tongue, that Diderot does not simply want to write another version of *Tristram Shandy*, he wants to write *the Tristram Shandy*' (847).

[10] See Forrester (1990) on the difficulty of rendering Freud's concept and its adjectival form (n. 90, 359-60). 'Retroaction' and 'retroactive', rather than the standard 'deferred action', would partly solve the problem, although the hapax 'post-effect', *ex post facto* and *après coup* have also been resorted to as their configurations fit in more suggestively with our argument.

seduction. According to this theory, a subject reworks memory-traces of an earlier childhood incident, whose sexual significance had then gone unnoticed, in the retrospective light of a later similar scene with which, owing to the advent of puberty which occurred in the meantime, s/he associates sexual feelings with a pathogenic force (see Laplanche, 1988: 111-14, s.v. 'deferred action'). The temporal aporias that characterize Freud's view of the non-linear development of human sexuality are also at work in the analytic view of the processes of imaginary identification which determine much of the fated script that underwrites any subject's life story:

> The neurosis, the patient's symptoms, are an incomprehensible version of the life-history of the person identified with; it is a version of the future based on the premise that the patient is someone other than he or she is. So when the analyst interprets such an identification, he is showing the way in which that identification orients the future through its construction of a past. (Forrester, 1990: 94)[11]

Bearing in mind the possibility that Tristram Shandy may be the scroll of Jacques' fatality, which would write in advance the imaginary part he is to reenact in Diderot's fiction,[12] the following snippet acquires a novel sense:

> Jacques [...] Tout ce qui nous arrive de bien et de mal ici-bas est écrit là-haut. Savez-vous, Monsieur, quelque moyen d'effacer cette écriture? Puis-je n'être pas moi? et étant moi puis-je faire autrement que moi? Puis-je être moi et un autre? (*JF*: 28)

> (Jacques [...] Everything good or bad that befalls us here below is written up above. Do you know of any way, sir, to erase that writing? Can I be anybody else but me? And being me, can I act differently from myself? Can I be both myself and somebody else?)

[11] Cf. Alice Fredman's early comment that Sterne's and Diderot's characters 'are reliving and reacting to what has happened to others, and for the moment it becomes an integral part of their lives. When this occurs [...] the concept of time by the clock breaks down, the barriers between truth and fiction are destroyed, and real and imaginary or vicarious experience are fused into one' (145).

[12] Cf. Hobson (134) who suggests that Jacques' fatality is linked to Diderot's authorial power, 'the obvious bridge being the metaphors which Jacques uses to express his belief: "le grand rouleau" and "tout est écrit là-haut"'. For the slight inconsistency in her position, see Bennington, 1985: 227, n. 166.

The mishap that vitiated Tristram's procreation is imparted to the hero by his uncle (*TS*: 1.3.4), who not only is privy to the family secret but also seems to transmit his 'modesty' to his nephew when, at age five, Tristram falls victim to a similar maiming of his virility (*TS*: 5.17.449-50), an uncanny warping of direct inheritance which unites them in sexual impotence (Tristram's is suggested in *TS*: 7.29.624) and may account, after all, for the shift in focus, from Tristram to Toby, in the projected *auto*biography.[13] We may profitably redirect to (the analysis of) literary genealogy Malcolm Bowie's observation, following his discussion of Freud's notion and Lacanian / Heideggerian overlaps in conceptions of temporality and language, that 'The future in psychoanalysis is always bound to be approachable only by a retrospective and retroactive routc' (39). The successful resolution of the traumatic reenactment of Toby's and Trim's amorous campaigns and of Tristram's abortive autobiographical project that *Jacques le fataliste* tantalizingly offers, hinges on the reader's choice of a happy dénouement or analysis which would unloosen (Greek *analuein*, hence 'analysis') a predestined life of fated identifications (such as the various 'character' shifts in-between reality and fiction seen above) predicated on such Oedipal for(tun)e-telling, which, in Tristram's case, was rightly conceived by his progenitor, the author of an ominously anticipatory dissertation against the name of Tristram in 1716 (*TS*: 1.19.63), in terms of misfortune-telling: '*My Tristram's misfortunes began nine months before ever he came into the world*' (*TS*: 1.3.4; see also 1.4.6).

Thus *Tristram Shandy* holds the position of a primal scene of writing; it is the *pre*-text of a premature child-writer not only frustrating the promised account of the life and opinions of its *post*modern 'title hero' (since, by his own temporal manipulations and reiterations, Tristram is born in[to] writing at once *before* and *after* his 'real' birth) but also standing in a *post*modern relationship to Diderot's novel, if one follows Lyotard's view of postmodernism as a foresight that will have anticipated the oversights of modernism and as an ahistorical process which subverts the temporal linearity of past-

[13] *FW*: 3.4-6 will rightly diagnose Tristram's identificatory symptom and offer an endlessly postponed cure in the coils of its (re)beginnings: 'Sir Tristram [...] had passencore rearrived [...] to wielderfight his penisolate war'.

present-future by attempting to reinscribe modernity *before* it has taken place (just as *post* comes 'first' in 'postmodern') and which, therefore, implies more than a mere 'return backwards':

> *Post modern* would have to be understood according to the paradox of the future [*post*] anterior [*modo*] [...] the 'post-' of 'postmodern' does not signify a movement of *çomeback*, *flashback*, or *feedback* - that is, not a movement of repetition but a procedure in 'ana-': a procedure of analysis, anamnesis, anagogy, and anamorphosis that elaborates an 'initial forgetting'. (in Docherty, 1993: 46, 50)

It is perhaps the possibility of an 'initial forgetting' or oversight implied by Mrs Shandy's fated question '*have you not forgot to wind up the clock?*' (*TS*: 1.1.2) that is responsible not only for the symptomatic propensity in Tristram to stall time in analytic digressions or regressions, and in the narrative to be forever *interrupta* and go anticlockwise, but also for that (un)original filiation of literary works that the reader has to 'analyze'. And it is precisely such a postmodern condition that we have tried to diagnose in and between these two anamorphic works, by setting them up in an analytic rapport, showing how they are bonded by an anamnesic relationship which partially seals up the amnesia of their respective defective tellings - in which, however, the possibility of a traumatic reenactment in *Jacques le fataliste* would jeopardize the reparation of an initial forgetting - the later text anagogically (from Greek *anagein*: to lead up) looking back to the earlier text *Tristram Shandy* as the great scroll up above or before, in order to start again and strike out in a new direction.

Endnote

Compare the problematization of the difficulty to begin in the following sequence from *Tristram Shandy*, 'I begun thus——[END of the SEVENTH VOLUME]' (*TS*: 7.43.651), 'Let us begin it' (*TS*: 8.1.656 [end of the chapter]), 'It is with LOVE as with CUCKOLDOM——But now I am talking of beginning a book [...]'

(*TS*: 8.2.656), and two chapter beginnings (one and three) in Nabokov's *Despair* (whose last chapter junction thematizes the difficulty of ending): 'If I were not perfectly sure of my power to write and of my marvellous ability to express ideas with the utmost grace and vividness [...] So, more or less, I had thought of beginning my tale' (13). And: 'How shall we begin this chapter? I offer several variations to choose from. Number one (readily adopted in novels where the narrative is conducted in the first person by the real or substitute author): [...]' (45). This realization of the impossibility to thematize beginnings which are not already rebeginnings also pervades the tradition of the American epic or long poem and came under close scrutiny in Book 3 of Williams's *Paterson*. As can be seen in the examples above, the failed inscription of a unique origin is indissociable from the realization, turned to creative profit, that the radical gap between enunciation and utterance can never be abolished.

Similarly, the end of *The Crying of Lot 49* turns Pynchon's novelette into a 'pre-text' as it closes on a programmatic repetition of the words of the title: "Oedipa settled back, to await the crying of lot 49" (127). The eminently Pynchonesque theme of entropy, which the aptly named Nefastis defines as a figure of speech or metaphor connecting the world of thermodynamics to the world of information flow (73) and which causes Mucho Maas to modulate his wife's name to Edna Mosh in order to allow for the distortions in radio transmission (96), already plays a crucial role in the circuitous mishandling of information in *Tristram Shandy* (for example, *TS*: 5.26.458), whenever the two brothers are talking at cross hobby-horsical purposes, or when the father's choice name Trismegistus is corrupted to Tristram-gistus, then abbreviated to Tristram (*TS*: 4.16.348). Let us finally mention the centrality of *preterition*, both in its rhetorical and Calvinistic meanings, for *Gravity's Rainbow*, in conjunction with the apocalyptic reversal of cause and effect and temporality brought about by the V2 rockets, whose explosive bang does not come until *after* the destruction and can therefore be heard only by those who have escaped it.

In the second section of *Willie Masters' Lonesome Wife*, William Gass extends to its limits the gadgetty possibilities afforded by *Tristram Shandy*'s parasitical self-editing, especially the decentering effects of asterisks and footnoting (cf. *TS*: 3.14.217) which, together with the stage directions in Gass's text, reverse the text-footnote hierarchy, and recycles Sterne's equation between nose and sex via the intertextual agency of the short story 'The Nose' by Gogol (a promoter of Sterne in Russia), equally distinguished by aposiopesis and withdrawal of information. The opening scene in Gogol's tale, in which one Ivan finds a nose in his bread, is duplicated in Gass's, where a namesake finds his own penis buried in a breakfast bun. The ensuing (and punning) discussion about the bun within the bun works as a metafictional acknowledgement of literary filiation and sets up intertextual Chinese boxes of reference within reference: the bun of Gass's Ivan 'frames' the bread of Gogol's Ivan with both Sterne's and Gogol's noses.

BIBLIOGRAPHY OF WORKS CITED

ALTER, R. (1975) *Partial Magic: The Novel as a Self-Conscious Genre*. U. of California Press.

ANDERSON, H. (1971) 'Tristram Shandy and the Reader's Imagination'. *PMLA* 86: 966-73.

—— (1980) (ed). Laurence Sterne. *Tristram Shandy: The Norton Critical Edition*. Norton.

ATHERTON, J. A. (1959) *The Books at the Wake*. Southern Illinois UP.

BACON, F. (1902) *The Advancement of Learning*. Macmillan.

BAIRD, T. (1936) 'The Time-Scheme in *Tristram Shandy* and a Source'. *PMLA* 51: 803-20.

BAKHTIN, M. (1978) *Esthétique et théorie du roman*. Gallimard.

—— (1981) *The Dialogic Imagination: Four Essays*. M. Holquist (ed); C. Emerson, M. Holquist (trs). U. of Texas Press.

BARKER, S. (1990) 'Conspicuous Absence: *Tracé* & Power in Beckett's Drama'. L. St. John Butler, R. J. Davis (eds). *Rethinking Beckett*. Macmillan: 199-200.

BARTH, J. (1982) *The Literature of Exhaustion and The Literature of Replenishment*. Lord John Press.

BARTHES, R. (1973) *Le plaisir du texte*. Seuil.

BATTESTIN, M. C. and R. R. (1989) *Henry Fielding: A Life*. Routledge.

BECKETT, S. (1984) 'Fizzles'. *Collected Shorter Prose 1945-1980*. Calder.

BELL, M. (1983) *The Sentiment of Reality: Truth of Feeling in the European Novel*. Allen & Unwin.

—— (1990) 'How Primordial is Narrative?'. C. Nash (ed). *Narrative in Culture*. Routledge: 172-98.

BENNINGTON, G. (1985) *Sententiousness and the Novel: Laying Down the Law in Eighteenth-Century French Fiction*. CUP.

BERGSON, H. (1959) *Matière et mémoire*. PUF.

—— (1972) *Durée et simultanéité*. PUF.

BERMAN, M. (1983) *All That is Solid Melts into Air: The Experience of Modernity*. Verso Books.

BLASI, A. (1988) 'Identity and the Development of the Self'. D. K. Lapsley, F. C. Power (eds). *Self, Ego, and Identity: Integrative Approaches*. Springer: 226-42.

BLOOM, H. (1979) (ed). *Deconstruction and Criticism*. Routledge.

—— (1987) *Laurence Sterne's Tristram Shandy*. Chelsea House Publishers.

BORGES, J. (1970) 'Partial Magic in the *Quixote*'. D. A. Yates, J. E. Irby (eds). *Labyrinths*. Penguin.

BOWIE, M. (1993) *Psychoanalysis and the Fututre of Theory*. Blackwell.

BRADLEY, A. C. (1981) *Shakespearean Tragedy: Lectures on 'Hamlet', 'Othello', 'King Lear', 'Macbeth'*. Macmillan.

BRADY, F. (1971) 'Tristram Shandy: Sexuality, Morality, and Sensibility'. *Eighteenth-Century Studies* 4: 41-56.

BREYTENBACH, B. (1985) *A Season in Paradise*. Faber & Faber.

BRISSENDEN, R. F. (1974) *Virtue in Distress: Studies in the Novel of Sentiment from Richardson to Sade*. Macmillan.

BROOKE-ROSE, C. (1991) *Stories, Theories and Things*. CUP.

BROWN, R. (1992) *James Joyce: A Post-Culturalist Perspective*. Macmillan.

BUDGEN, F. (1989) *James Joyce and the Making of 'Ulysses'*. OUP.

BYRD, M. (1985) *Tristram Shandy*. Allen & Unwin.

CABRERA INFANTE, G. (1965) *Tres Tristes Tigres*. Seix Barral.

—— (1990) *Three Trapped Tigers*. D. Gardner, S. Levine (trs). Faber & Faber.

CASANOVA, G. (1988) *Das Duell oder Versuch über das Leben des Venezianers G.C.* H. Scheible (tr). Piper Verlag.

CASH, A. H. (1971) (ed., with J. M. Stedmond) *The Winged Skull: Papers from the Laurence Sterne Bicentenary Conference*. Methuen.

—— (1992) *Laurence Sterne: The Early and Middle Years; The Later Years*. 2 vols. Routledge.

CERVANTES, M. DE CERVANTES SAAVEDRA (1981) *The Adventures of Don Quixote*. J. M. Cohen (tr). Penguin.

CHAMBERS, E. (1741, 1743) *Cyclopaedia: or, an Universal Dictionary of Arts and Sciences*.

CHESNEAU, A. (1968) 'La structure temporelle de *Jacques le Fataliste*: Jacques et son maître à la recherche du temps perdu'. *Revue des sciences humaines* 33: 401-13.

CHRISTENSEN, I. (1983) *The Meaning of Metafiction: A Critical Study of Selected Novels by Sterne, Nabokov, Barth and Beckett*. Bergen Universitetsforlaget.

CONNOR, S. (1988) *Samuel Beckett: Repetition, Theory and Text*. Blackwell.

CONRAD, P. (1978) *Shandyism: The Character of Romantic Irony*. Blackwell.

CRIMP, D. (1983) 'On the Museum's Ruins'. H. Foster (ed). *The Anti-Aesthetic: Essays on Postmodern Culture*. Bay Press.

DAVIDSON, N. J. (1966) *The Concept of Modernism in Hispanic Criticism*. Pruett Press.

DAVIS, L. J. (1983) *Factual Fictions: The Origin of the English Novel*. Columbia UP.

DELEUZE, G. (1983) *L'image-mouvement*. Minuit.

—— (1985) *L'image-temps*. Minuit.

DEMING, R. (1970) *James Joyce: The Critical Heritage*. Routledge.

DERRIDA, J. (1984) *Signeponge/Signsponge*. R. Rand (tr). Columbia UP.

DIDEROT, D. (1965) 'Eloge de Richardson'. P. Verniere (ed). *Oeuvres esthétiques*. Garnier: 30-31.

—— (1981) *Jacques le fataliste*. J. Proust (ed). *Oeuvres complètes*. Hermann: vol. 23: 1-291.

—— (1984) *Jack the Fatalist and His Master: A New Translation from the French of Denis Diderot*. W. D. Camp, A. G. Raymond (trs). Peter Lang.

DOCHERTY, T. (1991) 'Postmodern Characterization: The Ethics of Alterity', E. J. Smythe (ed). *Postmodernism and Contemporary Fiction*. Batsford: 169-88.

—— (1993) (ed). *Postmodernism: A Reader*. Columbia UP.

DOWLING, W. C. (1978) 'Tristram Shandy's Phantom Audience'. *Novel* 13: 284-95.

EILON, D. (1991) *Factions' Fictions: Ideological Closure in Swift's Satire*. U. of Delaware Press.

ELLMANN, R. (1972) *Ulysses on the Liffey*. OUP.

—— (1982) *James Joyce*. OUP.

FERRIAR, J. (1798) *Illustrations of Sterne*. Cadell & Davies.

FIELDING, H. (1966) *Tom Jones*. R. P. C. Mutter (ed). Penguin.

FLUCHÈRE, H. (1965) *Laurence Sterne: From Tristram to Yorick; An Interpretation of Tristram Shandy*. B. Bray (tr). OUP.

FORRESTER, J. (1990) *The Seductions of Psychoanalysis: Freud, Lacan and Derrida*. CUP.

FOUCAULT, M. (1984) 'What is Enlightenment?'. P. Rabinow (ed). *The Foucault Reader*. Penguin.

FOWLER, A. (1982) *Kinds of Literature: An Introduction to the Theory of Genres and Modes*. Harvard UP.

FOX, C. (1988) *Locke and the Scriblerians: Identity and Consciousness in Early Eighteenth-Century Britain*. U. of California Press.

FREDMAN, A. G. (1973) *Diderot and Sterne*. Columbia UP.

FRYE, N. (1957) *Anatomy of Criticism*. Princeton UP.

FUENTES, C. (1987) 'Carlos Fuentes: an Interview'. J. King (ed). *Modern Latin American Fiction: A Survey*. Faber & Faber.

GALLAGHER, D. P. (1974) 'Guillermo Cabrera Infante (Cuba, 1929-)'. Ortega, 1974: 47-78.

GASS, W. (1989) *Willie Masters' Lonesome Wife*. Dalkey Archive.

GEARHART, S. (1984) *The Open Boundary of History and Fiction: A Critical Approach to the French Enlightenment*. Princeton UP.

GENETTE, G. (1991) *Fiction et diction*. Seuil.

GERGEN, K. J. AND M. M. (1988) 'Narrative and the Self as Relationship'. L. Berkowitz (ed). *Advances in Experimental Social Psychology*. Academic Press: 17-56.

GERGEN, K. J. (1990) 'Die Konstruktion des Selbst im Zeitalter der Postmoderne'. *Psychologische Rundschau* 40: 191-99.

GIFFORD, D., AND R. J. SEIDMAN (1988) *Ulysses Annotated: Notes for James Joyce's 'Ulysses'*. U. of California Press.

GLEICK, J. (1988) *Chaos: Making a New Science*. Sphere Books.

GOYTISOLO, J. (1976) 'Lectura cervantina de Tres Tristes Tigres'. *Revista Iberoamericana* 42: 1-18.

HABERMAS, J. (1985) 'Modernity - An Incomplete Project'. H. Foster (ed). *Postmodern Culture*. Pluto Press.

—— (1987) *The Philosophical Discourse of Modernity*. F. Lawrence (tr). Columbia UP.

HARDING, D. W. (1939) 'Regulated Hatred: an Aspect of the Work of Jane Austen'. *Scrutiny* 8: 346-62.

HARTER, S. (1988) 'The Construction and Conservation of the Self: James and Cooley Revisited'. D. K. Lapsley and F. C. Power (eds). *Self, Ego, and Identity. Integrative Approaches*. Springer: 43-70.

HARTLEY, L. (1970) '"Swiftly-Sterneward": The Question of Sterne's Influence on Joyce'. *Studies in the Literary Imagination* 3: 37-47.

HARVEY, L. E. (1970) *Samuel Beckett, Poet & Critic*. Princeton UP.

HEATH, S. (1977) (tr). R. Barthes, *Image, Music, Text*. Fontana Press.

HENRICH, D. (1979) '"Identität" - Begriffe, Probleme, Grenzen'. *Identität, Poetik und Hermeneutik*, vol. 8, O. Marquard, K. Stierle (eds). Fink Verlag: 133-86.

HILSKY, M. (1971) 'A Note on the Style of Tristram Shandy'. *Prague Studies in English* 14: 41-55.

HNATKO, E. (1969) 'Sterne's Whimsical Syntax: The Pseudo-Archaic Style'. *Style* 3: 68-81.

—— (1971) 'Sterne's Conversational Style'. Cash, 1971: 229-36.

HOBSON, M. (1982) *The Object of Art: The Theory of Illusion in Eighteenth-Century France*. CUP.

HOWES, A. B. (1974) (ed). *Sterne: The Critical Heritage*. Routledge.

—— (1984) 'Laurence Sterne, Rabelais and Cervantes: The Two Kinds of Laughter in *Tristram Shandy*'. Myer, 1984b: 39-56.

HUME, D. (1962) *A Treatise of Human Nature*. D. G. C. Macnabb (ed). William Collins.

—— (1978) *A Treatise of Human Nature*. L. A. Selby-Bigge (ed), P. H. Nidditch (rev.). Clarendon.

HUNTER, J. P. (1980) 'Response as Affirmation: Tristram Shandy and the Art of Interruption'. Anderson, 1980: 623-40.

HUTCHEON, L. (1984) *Narcissistic Narrative: The Metafictional Paradox*. Methuen.

—— (1985) *A Theory of Parody*. Methuen.

—— (1988) *A Poetics of Postmodernism: History, Theory, Fiction*. Routledge.

IMHOF, R. (1986) *Contemporary Metafiction: A Poetological Study of Metafiction in English since 1939*. Carl Winter.

ISER, W. (1988) *Tristram Shandy*. D. H. Wilson (tr). CUP.

—— (1991) *Das Fiktive und das Imaginäre: Perspektiven literarischer Anthropologie*. Suhrkamp.

JACK, I. (1984) (ed). L. Sterne. *A Sentimental Journey*. OUP.

JEFFERSON, D. W. (1968) '*Tristram Shandy* and the Tradition of Learned Wit'. Traugott, 1968:148-67.

JIMÉNEZ, R. J. (1976) *Tristes Tigres*. Universal.

JOHNSON, M. L. (1988) *Mind, Language, Machine: Artificial Intelligence in the Poststructuralist Age*. Macmillan.

JOHNSON, S. (1755) *A Dictionary Of the English Language*. Strahan, et al.

JOHNSON, S. (1963) *Poetry and Prose*. M. Wilson (ed). Rupert Hart-Davis.

JOLAS, E. (1948) 'My Friend James Joyce'. S. Givens (ed). *James Joyce: Two Decades of Criticism*. Vanguard Press: 3-18.

JOSIPOVICI, G. (1992) *Text and Voice: Essays 1981-1991*. Carcanet Press.

KANT, I. (1984) 'An Answer to the Question: What is Enlightenment?'. D. Simpson (ed). *German Aesthetic and Literary Criticism : Kant, Fichte, Schelling, Schopenhauer, Hegel*. CUP.

KENDALL, P. M. (1965) *The Art of Biography*. Norton.

KIRK, E. (1980) *Menippean Satire: An Annotated Catalogue*. Garland.

KLEIN, H. G. (1992) 'Wer ist Tristrams Vater? - Paternität und Identität in Laurence Sternes *Tristram Shandy*'. *Germanisch-Romanische Monatsschrift (Neue Folge)* 42/4: 415-27.

KOCH, S. (1991) *Dichtung als Archäologie: Die Lyrik Seamus Heaneys*. LIT Verlag.

KRITZMAN, L. D. (1981) (ed). *Fragments: Incompletion and Discontinuity*. Literary Forum.

KUNDERA, M. (1983) 'Afterword: A Talk with the Author by Philip Roth'. *The Book of Laughter and Forgetting*. M. H. Heim (tr). Penguin.

—— (1984) 'An Interview with Milan Kundera'. *Granta* 11.

—— (1986) *Jacques and his Master*. S. Callow (tr). Faber & Faber.

—— (1990) *The Art of the Novel*. Faber & Faber.

LAMB, J. (1980) 'Sterne's Use of Montaigne'. *Comparative Literature* 32/1: 1-41.

LAMPKIN, L. (1984) '*Tristram Shandy* and *A Portrait of the Artist*: The Gestation of Identical Twins'. *James Joyce Quarterly* 21/2: 137-45.

LANHAM, R. A. (1973) *'Tristram Shandy' and The Games of Pleasure*. U. of California Press.

LAPLANCHE, J., and J. B. PONTALIS. (1988) *The Language of Psycho-Analysis*. D. Nicholson-Smith (tr). Karnac Books.
LECOINTRE, S. AND J. LE GALLIOT. (1972) 'L'appareil formel de l'énonciation dans *Jacques le Fataliste*'. *Le français moderne* 40: 222-31.
LEVIN, H. (1941) *James Joyce: A Critical Introduction*. New Directions.
LITTLE, W. T. (1970) 'Notas acerca de *Tres Tristes Tigres*'. *Revista Iberoamericana* 36: 635-42.
LOCKE, J. (1964) *An Essay Concerning Human Understanding*. A. D. Woozley (ed). William Collins.
—— (1975) *An Essay Concerning Human Understanding*. P. H. Nidditch (ed). Clarendon.
LODGE, D. (1990) 'Milan Kundera, and the Idea of the Author in Modern Criticism'. *After Bakhtin: Essays on Fiction and Criticism*. Routledge.
LOLL, U. (1992) *James Joyce - Genie im Patriarchat*. Metzler Verlag.
LOVERIDGE, M. (1982) *Laurence Sterne and the Argument about Design*. Macmillan.
LOY, J. R. (1950) *Diderot's Determined Fatalist: A Critical Appreciation of* 'Jacques le Fataliste'. King's Crown Press.
LUHMANN, N. (1979) 'Identitätsgebrauch in selbstsubstitutiven Ordnungen, besonders Gesellschaften'. O. Marquard, K. Stierle (eds). *Identität, Poetik und Hermeneutik*, 8. Fink Verlag: 315-45.
LYOTARD, J-F. (1984) *The Postmodern Condition: A Report on Knowledge*. G. Bennington, B. Massumi. Manchester UP.
—— (1988) 'A propos du Différend, Entretien avec Jean-François Lyotard: discussion publique au cours d'une séance du Cabinet de Lecture au C.N.A.C Georges Pompidou, le 9 Mai 1984'. *Les Cahiers de Philosophie* 5.
MCCAFFERY, L. (1986) (ed). *Postmodern Fiction: A Bio-Bibliographical Guide*. Greenwood Press.
MCDONALD, C. V. (1982) 'Fractured Readers'. *Modern Language Notes* 97: 840-48.
MCGILCHRIST, I. (1982) *Against Criticism*. Faber & Faber.
MCHALE, B. (1987) *Postmodernist Fiction*. Methuen.
MCKEON, M. (1987) *The Origins of the English Novel, 1600 - 1740*. Johns Hopkins UP.
MANN, T. (1947) 'Voyage with Don Quixote'. *Essays of Three Decades*. H. T. Lowe-Porter (tr). Secker & Warburg.
MARKOVA, I. (1987) 'Knowledge of the Self through Interaction'. *Self and Identity: Psychosocial Perspectives*. K. Yardley, T. Honess (eds). John Wiley & Sons: 65-80.
MÁRQUEZ, G. G. (1970) 'Partial Magic in the *Quixote*'. D. A. Yates, J. E. Irby (eds). *Labyrinths*. Penguin.
—— (1982) *Obra Periodistica*. J. Gilard (ed). Vol. 4: *de Europa y America*. Bruguera.

—— (1985) *The Labyrinth of Solitude*. L. Kemp (tr). Penguin.
—— (1987) *Cien años de soledad*. J. Joset (ed). Cátedra.
MATAS, J. 'CABRERA INFANTE'. ORTEGA, 1974: 187-207.
MAYOUX, J. J. (1971) 'Variations on the Time-sense in *Tristram Shandy*'. Cash, 1971: 3-18.
MENDILOW, A. A. (1968) 'The Revolt of Sterne'. Traugott, 1968: 90-107.
—— (1972) *Time and the Novel*. Humanities Press.
MILIC, L. T. (1971) 'Information Theory and the Style of *Tristram Shandy*'. Cash, 1971: 239-46.
MONEGAL, E. R. (1974) 'Estructura y significación de *Tres Tristes Tigres*'. Ortega, 1974: 81-127.
MORETTI, F. (1987) *The Way of the World: The Bildungsroman in European Culture*. Verso Books.
MOSS, R. B. (1981) 'Sterne's Punctuation'. *Eighteenth-Century Studies* 15: 179-200.
MUDFORD, W. (1811) 'Critical Observations upon *Tristram Shandy* and the *Sentimental Journey*'. *The British Novelists*. Clarke, et al.
MÜLLER, H. (1992) *Krieg ohne Schlachten: Leben in zwei Diktaturen*. Kiepenheuer & Witsch.
MULLAN, J. (1988) *Sentiment and Sociability: The Language of Feeling in the Eighteenth Century*. Clarendon.
MYER, V. G. (1984a) 'Tristram and the Animal Spirits'. Myer, 1984b: 99-112.
MYER, V. G. (1984b) *Laurence Sterne: Riddles & Mysteries*. Vision Press.
NABOKOV, V. (1960) *The Real Life of Sebastian Knight*. Weidenfeld & Nicolson.
—— (1965) *Despair*. Penguin.
NASHE, T. (1987) *The Unfortunate Traveller. An Anthology of Elizabethan Prose Fiction*. OUP: 205-311.
NELSON, A. L. (1980) 'Characterization and Menipean Satire in the Major Works of Guillermo Cabrera Infante.' Unpublished diss. Indiana University.
NEW, M. (1969) *Laurence Sterne as Satirist: A Reading of* 'Tristram Shandy'. U. of Florida Press.
—— (1972) 'Sterne's Rabelaisian Fragment: A Text from the Holograph Manuscript.' *PMLA* 87: 1083-92.
—— (1988) 'Proust's Influence on Sterne: Remembrance of Things to Come.' *Modern Language Notes* 103/5: 1031-55.
—— (1992) 'Sterne and Narrative Determinateness'. *Eighteenth-Century Fiction* 4/4: 315-29.
ONG, W. J. (1975) 'The Writer's Audience is Always a Fiction.' *PMLA* 90: 9-21.
ORTEGA, J. (1974) (ed) *Guillermo Cabrera Infante*. Fundamentos.
PARNELL, J. T. (1993) 'Swift, Sterne and the Skeptical Tradition'. *Studies in Eighteenth-Century Culture* 23: 221-42.

PATTANAYAK, C. (1983) 'Interview with Salman Rushdie'. *The Literary Criterion* 18/3: 19-22.

PAZ, O. (1985) *The Labyrinth of Solitude*. L. Kemp (tr). Penguin.

PENELHUM, T. (1983) 'Skepticism and Fideism'. M. Burnyeat (ed). *The Skeptical Tradition*. U. of California Press.

PEREDA, R. M. (1979) *Cabrera Infante*. Edaf.

PIERCE, D. (1992) *James Joyce's Ireland*. Yale UP.

POPE, A. (1966) *The Memoirs of the Extraordinary Life, Works, and Discoveries of Martinus Scriblerus*. C. Kerby-Miller (ed). Russell & Russell.

POPKIN, R. H. (1979) *The History of Skepticism from Erasmus to Spinoza*. U. of California Press.

PORTER, R. (1984) 'Against the Spleen'. Myer, 1984b: 84-98.

PRESTON, J. (1970) *The Created Self: The Reader's Role in Eighteenth-Century Fiction*. Barnes & Noble.

PROUST, M. (1954) *Contre Sainte-Beuve*. B. de Fallois (ed). Gallimard.

—— (1988) *Sodome et Gomorrhe*. A. Compagnon (ed). Gallimard.

PYNCHON, T. (1965) *The Crying of Lot 49*. Picador.

RABELAIS, F. (1750) *The Works of Francis Rabelais*. M. Motteux (tr). John Hart, et al.

—— (1927) *The Complete Works of Doctor François Rabelais*, T. Urquhart (tr). John Lane.

RAY, W. (1990) *Story and History: Narrative Authority and Social Identity in the Eighteenth-Century French and English Novel*. Blackwell.

ROGERS, P. (1982) 'Tristram Shandy's Polite Conversation'. *Essays in Criticism* 32: 305-20.

ROSENBLUM, M. (1982) 'The Art of Interpolation in *Tristram Shandy*'. *Studies in Philology* 15: 472-91.

ROSS, I. C. (1983) 'Introduction'. L. Sterne. *The Life and Opinions of Tristram Shandy, Gentleman*. OUP.

RUSHDIE, S. (1982) *Midnight's Children*. Picador.

—— (1988) The Satanic Verses. Viking.

—— (1992) *Imaginary Homelands: Essays and Criticism 1981-1991*. Penguin.

SAID, E. W. (1991) 'The World, The Text, and the Critic'. *The World, The Text, and the Critic*. Vintage: 31-53.

SÁNCHEZ-BOUDY, J. (1971) *La nueva novela hispanoamericana y Tres Tristes Tigres*. Universal.

SAVAGE, R. (1984) 'The Bastard'. R. Lonsdale (ed). *The New Oxford Book of Eighteenth-Century Verse*. OUP.

SCHOLES, R. (1975) *Structural Fabulation: An Essay on Fiction of the Future*. U. of Notre Dame Press.

SCHULTE-SASSE, J. (1984) 'Foreword: Theory of Modernism Versus Theory of the Avant-Garde'. P. Bürger. *Theory of the Avant-Garde*. Manchester UP.

SCHULZE, M. (1980) 'Do You Know the Meaning of *****? - Die markierte Aussparung als Indiz für die planvolle Komposition des "Tristram Shandy"'. G. Rohmann (ed). *Laurence Sterne*. Wissenschaftliche Buchgesellschaft: 394-436.

SEDGWICK, E. K. (1985) *Between Men: English Literature and Male Homosocial Desire*. Columbia UP.

SHAKESPEARE, W. (1988) *The Complete Works*. S. Wells (ed). OUP.

SHKLOVSKY, V. (1965) 'Sterne's *Tristram Shandy*: A Stylistic Commentary'. L. T. Lemon, M. J. Reis (eds). *Russian Formalist Criticism*. U. of Nebraska Press.

SIMON, I. (1985) 'Frustration as Theme and as Narrative Device in *Tristram Shandy*, *Jacques le Fataliste* , and *La Disparition*'. *Revue belge de philologie et d'histoire* 63/3: 504-12.

SLOTERDIJK, P. (1988) *Critique of Cynical Reason*. M. Eldred (ed). Verso Books.

SMITH, A. (1976) *The Theory of Moral Sentiments*. D. D. Raphael, A. L. Macfie (eds). Clarendon.

SMITH, J. (1993) 'Czeck Mate'. *Misogynies: Reflections on Myths and Malice*. Faber & Faber.

STAROBINSKI, J. (1984) '"Chaque balle a son billet": Destin et répétition dans *Jacques le Fataliste'*. *Nouvelle Revue de Psychanalyse* 30: 17-38.

STEDMOND, J. M. (1959) 'Style and Tristram Shandy'. *Modern Language Quarterly* 20: 243-51.

STEVENSON, J. A. (1990) *The British Novel, Defoe to Austen: A Critical History*. Twayne.

STEWART, J. F. (1969) 'Some Critical Metaphors for Shandean Style'. *College Language Association* 12: 183-87.

STONEHILL, B. (1988) *The Self-Conscious Novel*. U. of Pennsylvania Press.

STOVEL, B. (1984) 'Tristram Shandy and the Art of Gossip'. Myer, 1984b: 115-25.

SWEARINGEN, J. E. (1977) *Reflexivity in Tristram Shandy: An Essay in Phenomenological Criticism*. Yale UP.

—— (1987) 'Reflexivity and the Decentered Self in *Tristram Shandy*'. S. J. Bartlett, P. Sube (eds). *Self-Reference: Reflections on Reflexivity*. Martinus Nijhoff: 239-56.

SWIFT, J. (1973) *Polite Conversation*. H. Davis, L. Landa (eds). Blackwell.

TAYLOR, C. (1989) *The Sources of the Self: The Making of Modern Identity*. CUP.

THACKERAY, W. M. (1853) 'Sterne and Goldsmith'. *The English Humourists of the Eighteenth Century*. Smith, Elder & Co.

TODA, F. (1985) (ed). L. Sterne. *Vida y opiniones del caballero Tristram Shandy*. Cátedra.

TRACY, C. (1971) 'As Many Chapters as Steps'. Cash, 1971: 97-111.

TRAUGOTT, J. (1954) *Tristram Shandy's World: Sterne's Philosophical Rhetoric*. U. of California Press.

TRAUGOTT, J. (1968) (ed). *Laurence Sterne: A Collection of Critical Essays*. Prentice-Hall.

DE VOOGD, P. J. (1985) 'Laurence Sterne: the Marbled Page and "the Use of Accidents"'. *Word and Image* 1: 279-87.

—— (1988) '*Tristram Shandy* as Aesthetic Object'. *Word and Image* 5: 383-92.

—— (1991) *De invloed van Joyce op Sterne*. Athenaeum - Polak & Van Gennep.

WAGONER, M. S. (1966) 'Satire of the Reader in *Tristram Shandy*'. *Texas Studies in Literature and Language* 3: 337-44.

WARNER, J. M. (1993) *Joyce's Grandfathers: Myth and History in Defoe, Smollett, Sterne & Joyce*. U. of Georgia Press.

WARNING, R. (1965) *Illusion und Wirklichkeit in 'Tristram Shandy' und 'Jacques le Fataliste'*. Fink Verlag.

WARREN, L. E. (1977) 'The Constant Speaker: Aspects of Conversation in *Tristram Shandy*', *University of Texas Quarterly* 46: 51-67.

WARREN, L. E. (1986) 'Getting into the Talk: Tristram Shandy through Conversation'. M. New (ed). *Approches to Teaching Sterne's Tristram Shandy*. MLA: 61-66.

WATT, I. (1967) 'The Comic Syntax of *Tristram Shandy*'. H. Anderson, J. Shea (eds). *Studies in Criticism and Aesthetics, 1660-1800: Essays in Honor of Samuel Holt Monk*. U. of Minnesota Press: 315-31.

WEBB, I. (1990) 'Milan Kundera and the Limits of Skepticism'. *The Massachusetts Review* 31:3.

WEHRS, D. (1988) 'Sterne, Cervantes, Montaigne: Fideistic Skepticism and the Rhetoric of Desire'. *Comparative Literature Studies* 25: 127-51.

WOOLF, V. (1932) *The Common Reader: Second Series*. Hogarth Press.

ZACCARIA, P. (1990) '*Fizzles* by Samuel Beckett: the Failure of the Dream of a Never-ending Verticality'. L. St. J. Butler, R. J. Davis (eds). *Rethinking Beckett*. Macmillan.

INDEX

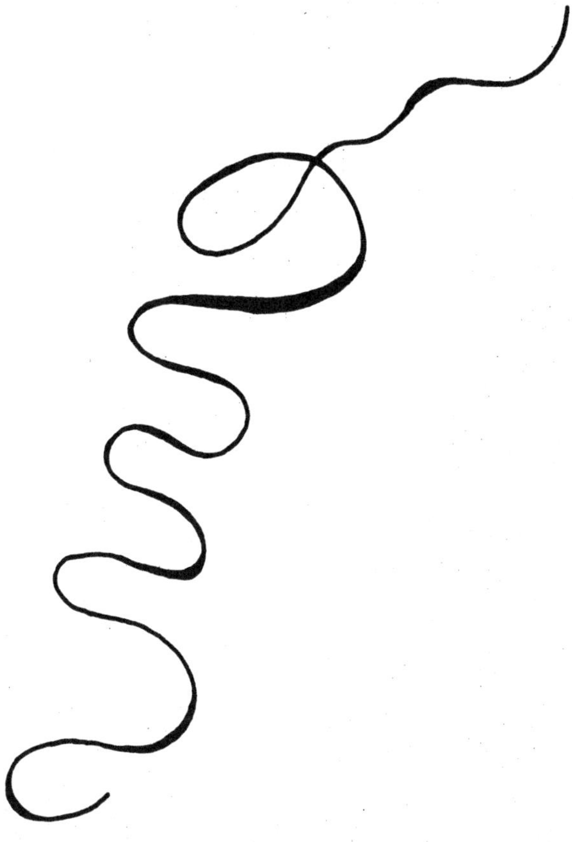

A TALENT(ED) DIGGER

Creations, Cameos, and Essays in honour of Anna Rutherford

Ed. by Hena Maes-Jelinek, Gordon Collier
Geoffrey V. Davis

Amsterdam/Atlanta, GA 1996. XIX,519 pp.
(Cross/Cultures 20)
ISBN: 90-5183-964-2 Bound Hfl. 250,-/US-$ 165.-
ISBN: 90-5183-953-7 Paper Hfl. 55,-/US-$ 36.50

Anna Rutherford has been the most dynamic ambassador of Australian culture in Europe. More than any other single person, she has been instrumental in spreading interest in Commonwealth and post-colonial studies. Wherever she has been in the world, she has brought people together in friendship and intellectual endeavour. This volume ranges widely over the areas Anna has promoted as teacher, editor and publisher.

USA/Canada: Editions Rodopi B.V., 2015 South Park Place, Atlanta, GA 30339, Tel. (770) 933-0027, *Call toll-free* (U.S. only) 1-800-225- 3998, Fax (770) 933-9644, *E-mail:* F.van.der.Zee@rodopi.nl

All Other Countries: Editions Rodopi B.V., Keizersgracht 302-304, 1016 EX Amsterdam, The Netherlands. Tel. + + 31 (0)20-622-75-07, Fax + + 31 (0)20-638-09-48, *E-mail:* F.van.der.Zee@rodopi.nl